AMERICA VISIT & STAY

JN090708

日英対訳

# アメリカ暮らし完全ガイド

ダニエル・ヴァン・ノストランド
Daniel Van Nostrand＝著

八町晶子＝日本語訳

IBCパブリッシング

カバーデザイン　岩目地英樹（コムデザイン）

# まえがき

　この本を手にとってくださった方の中にはアメリカに興味がある、行こうかなと迷っている、もしくは滞在することが決まってさてどうしよう?! と焦っている方もいらっしゃるかもしれません。

　ご存知の通り、アメリカは日本といろいろな意味でまったく異なる国です。その違いは心から楽しめるものもあれば、イライラし不安になるようなこともあると思います。時には露骨に嫌だ、耐えられない! と感じることもあるかもしれません。そうした不安を抱えつつもアメリカに行こうと思ってくださる皆様に、少しでもアメリカという国と向き合うための情報を提供できればと思い、本書を執筆しました。

　本書では、アメリカという国と接することになれば間違いなく直面するだろうさまざまな事項について、私の知る限りのことをお伝えしようと心がけました。もちろん全てをカバーすることはできません。ですから、この本で納得できないこと、理解できないことがあれば、どんどんアメリカ人に質問してください! アメリカ人は、うまくいっていることを自慢したり、逆にそうでないことには文句を言ったり、どちらにせよとにかく自分の国について知らない人とおしゃべりするのが大好きなのです。どんな質問であっても、アメリカ人は自国について興味を持ってくれているあなた方のことが好きで、話をするのが楽しくてしかたないのです。

　本書ではアメリカ生活に必要な事項を説明するとともにに、注意した方がいい点についても言及しています。例えば政治に関する話です。アメリカでは民主党と共和党が対立しています。民主党支持者は都会に住み、共和党支持者は田舎に多いと一般的に言われますが、実際は必ずしもそうではありません。ですから簡単にアメリカ人の政治信条を推測するのは危険です。アメリカ社会で政治的に議論されている話題は、本書でも言及しましたので参考にしてみてください。

　ほとんどのアメリカ人は日本人に対してとても好意的な感情を持っています。自己紹介で「日本から来ました」といえば、第一印象はバッチリです!

　アメリカにようこそ! リラックスして滞在を楽しんでください。

Daniel Van Nostrand

# Dear Readers

As a young American, I had the good fortune to travel to 48 states, with brief visits to the Bahamas and Canada. Before graduating from college, I was given an opportunity to visit five European countries. As an adult, I have added dozens of foreign countries to my list, including Japan, where I have resided for decades.

Reflecting back on these experiences, I realize that I was very fortunate to travel widely around the huge country in which I was born. Meeting people with different jobs, political views, and religious beliefs, in addition to enjoying different geographical features and delicious foods was something I could not have experienced in any classroom or through books. Despite being lucky enough to travel so widely, however, I was still "traveling."

When I first came to Japan a half-century ago, I continued traveling, as far north as Rebun Island and as far south as Kagoshima. But living in Japan was a different experience. It required a broader, deeper knowledge of Japanese people and how to interact with them. The people I met, at work and in casual encounters, were generally kind enough to overlook my inadequate understanding of how things should be done, how to communicate appropriately in Japanese, and, to some degree, how to "think" in Japanese.

Early on, I discovered that thinking in English and trying to express myself in Japanese was a major hurdle. I began studying Japanese as seriously as I could, but that road was long and filled with obstacles. Fortunately, thanks to the people I met, I managed to continue my study of the language.

I quickly realized that I needed to read about Japan—literature, society, history, and religion—in English, before I could do that in Japanese. My generation did not begin with manga, anime, and cosplay. We began with Zen Buddhism, Shogun, the Meiji Restoration, Lafcadio Hearn, and Kawabata Yasunari.

## 読者の皆さんへ

　若い頃、私は幸運にもアメリカの48州を旅して回ることができました。短い滞在でしたが、バハマとカナダにも足を延ばしました。大学卒業の前には、ヨーロッパの5カ国を旅する機会にも恵まれました。その後、大人になり私の旅行先リストには、さらに何十カ国も追加されたのです。そこには何十年も暮らすことになった日本も含まれています。

　こうした経験を振り返ってみると、自分の生まれたこの広大な国を旅して回れたことがどんなに貴重なことだったか思い知ります。単に地域ごとの特徴や美味しい食べ物を楽しんだだけではなく、様々な職業の人、異なる政治的スタンスを持つ人、宗教が異なる人にも会うことができました。それは教室や本からでは経験できなかったことです。幸運にもこれだけ広範な旅ができたのですが、それでも私の「旅」は続きました。

　半世紀前のことです。最初に日本にやってきた私は、北は礼文島から南は鹿児島まで旅をしました。しかし、日本に「住む」ということは全く予想もできない経験でした。住むためにはもっと広く深く日本の人たちのことを知り、どのように接するかを知る必要がありました。職場で出会った人も何気なく出会った人も、日本人は大抵、物事の進め方や日本語でのコミュニケーション、そして、日本語でどう「考えるか」について、ある程度私の理解不足を大目に見てくれました。

　比較的早い時期に、英語で考え、それを日本語で表現することの難しさに気づいた私は、できる限り真剣に日本語学習に取り組みましたが、その道は長く、障害だらけでした。出会った人たちにも恵まれ、私はどうにか日本語の勉強を続けることができましたが。

　私が真っ先に気づいたのは、日本の文学、社会、歴史、宗教について日本語で読む前に英語で読む必要があるということでした。私の世代は、漫画やアニメ、コスプレなどではなく、禅、『将軍』、明治維新、ラフカディオ・ハーン、そして川端康成から始めました。

Most of all, we learned from watching and listening to everything around us. It was all new. And it was fascinating—and it still is, a half century later.

I have dwelt on my own experience for one simple reason: to encourage the reader to do something similar in reverse, to not just travel in America, but to actually go and live in America for a significant period of time. It could be for one month or one year for a start. It could be a study abroad program, an employment opportunity, or a transfer to an office somewhere in States.

The benefits to be gained from living in America are considerable.

First, needing to use English on an everyday basis will improve your language skills. When items in a grocery, transportation maps, and directions for taking medicine are in English, you dig in and learn things one at a time. It is, of course, a lifetime project and sometime frustrating. But there is rapid progress when you live in an all-English environment. And Americans basically assume that if you live in America, you naturally speak English.

A second benefit is slowly learning how different Americans think. Not everyone you meet and converse with will share the same views. Getting into a deep discussion of ideas and experiences can be enormously rewarding. There is little doubt that your view of the world will expand significantly through these encounters, some with complete strangers and some with friends you become close to.

Finally, a third benefit is you will begin to see yourself and your native culture from a different perspective. You will be able to look at your personal world objectively and wonder why you do certain things in a particular way.

This book is an excellent way to get started, whether you are still thinking about living in America or are already in the planning stage. Read it carefully and look forward to a rewarding experience.

James M. Vardaman

何より、私たちは周りのすべてのことを見たり聞いたりして学びます。すべてが新鮮で、興味は尽きません。それは半世紀経った今でも同じことなのです。

長々と私の経験を書いたのは単純な理由からです。それは、読者の皆さんに逆のことをやってもらいたいからです。ただアメリカに行くのではなく、本当に飛び込んで長期にわたってアメリカに住んでみてください。まずは1カ月でも1年でもいいのです。留学でも就労のチャンスでも、アメリカのどこかへの転勤でも構いません。

アメリカに住むことから得られるメリットは大きいはずです。

当然、日常ベースで英語を使いますから、語学力アップが期待できます。食料品店の品物、交通機関の地図、薬の飲み方、あらゆるものが英語です。それをその都度、掘り下げ、学ぶことになるのですから、これはいつ終わるともしれない、挫折しないとも限らないプロジェクトなのです。しかし、周りが全て英語の環境に飛び込めば、上達も速いはずです。それに、アメリカ人は基本的に、アメリカに住んでいる以上は、あなたは当然英語を話すのだろうと思い込んでいるのです。

時間は多少かかるかもしれませんが、アメリカ人の考え方もわかってきます。これが2番目のメリットです。アメリカで出会い、話すようになった人が皆同じ意見とは限りません。ですから、それぞれ異なる考え方や経験を深く知ることは非常に実りあるものになるはずです。全く知らない人との出会いであれ、友人として親しくなった人との出会いであれ、こうした出会いを通し、あなたの世界観が驚くほど広がるのは間違いありません。

最後のメリットは、自分自身や母国の文化を異なる視点から見られるようになるということです。自分のことを客観的に見て、自分はどうしてこの事をこうやるのだろう、と考えるのです。

本書はアメリカでの生活を迷っている人にも、すでに計画進行中の人にとっても、まずはスタートするのに最適な一冊と言えます。じっくり読んで、実り多き経験ができることを楽しみにしてください。

ジェームス・M・バーダマン

**Dear Readers** James M. Vardaman ·································· 4


## Part 1 Let's Get to Know America ··············· 19
General Knowledge and Culture


### 1 Geography of the United States ························ 20
Five regions of the USA ······20
Climate characteristics by region ······24
Industry by region ······28


### 2 American Background and People ·················· 32
Origins of the United States ······32
History of Immigration ······36
Languages spoken in the US ······40
Religion in America ······44


### 3 Politics in the US ································· 52
Federal and State ······52
President and Congress ······54
Two-party system (Democrats and Republicans) ······60
Judicial system (composition of courts and jury system) ······62
Local Politics (Laws by Region) ······64


## Part 2 Let's Go to America ··························· 73
Preparing for a Visit


### 1 VISA or Permanent Residence/Citizenship? ······· 74
To enter the country ······74

読者の皆さんへ　ジェームス・M・バーダマン‥‥‥‥‥‥‥‥‥‥‥‥‥‥‥5


## Part 1　アメリカを知ろう‥‥‥‥‥‥‥‥‥19
### 一般的知識と文化

### 1 アメリカの地理‥‥‥‥‥‥‥‥‥‥‥‥‥‥‥21
アメリカの5つの地域‥‥‥‥21
地域別の気候の特徴‥‥‥‥25
地域別の産業‥‥‥‥29

### 2 アメリカの背景と人々‥‥‥‥‥‥‥‥‥33
アメリカの成り立ち‥‥‥‥33
移民の歴史‥‥‥‥37
アメリカで使われている言語‥‥‥‥41
アメリカの宗教‥‥‥‥45

### 3 アメリカの政治‥‥‥‥‥‥‥‥‥‥‥‥‥53
連邦と州‥‥‥‥53
大統領と議会‥‥‥‥55
二大政党制（民主党と共和党）‥‥‥‥61
司法制度（裁判所の構成と陪審制度）‥‥‥‥63
地方政治（地域ごとの法律）‥‥‥‥65


## Part 2　アメリカへ行こう‥‥‥‥‥‥‥73
### 出発前の準備

### 1 ビザか永住権/市民権か？‥‥‥‥‥‥‥75
入国するには‥‥‥‥75

Visa Waiver Program······78
Student Visa (Visa Requirements)······80
Work Visa Types and Conditions······84
Route to Permanent Residence······86
Eligibility and testing for citizenship······88

## 2 Transportation ······ 92

Airplane······92
Railroads ······96
Buses and subways······100
Cabs/ Rideshares······102
Automobile······104
Bicycles (shared bikes)······110

## 3 Communication ······ 112

Phones······112
Email······114
SNS······118
Postal and courier······120

## 4 Lodging ······ 122

Hotels and Airbnb······122
Vacation rentals (long-term stay option)······124

## 5 Restaurants ······ 128

Fine dining······128
Casual restaurants······132
Fast food, food court······136
Food Trucks······136
Take-out······138

## 6 Shopping ······ 144

Online shopping······144

ビザ免除プログラム……79
学生ビザの要件……81
就労ビザの種類と条件……85
永住権への道……87
市民権取得のための資格と試験……89

2 **交通機関** ……………………………………………………… 93
飛行機……93
鉄道……97
バスと地下鉄……101
タクシー/ライドシェア……103
自動車……105
自転車(シェアサイクル)……111

3 **コミュニケーション** ………………………………………… 113
電話……113
Eメール……115
SNS……119
郵便と宅配便……121

4 **宿泊** …………………………………………………………… 123
ホテルとAirbnb……123
バケーションレンタル(長期滞在向け)……125

5 **レストラン** …………………………………………………… 129
高級レストラン……129
カジュアルなレストラン……133
ファストフード/フードコート……137
フードトラック……137
テイクアウト……139

6 **ショッピング** ………………………………………………… 145
オンラインショッピング……145

Cashless······148
Sale times······150

# 7 Activities ······ 154

Exercise······154
Sports······158
Films······164
Performing arts······168
Museums······170

# Part 3  Let's Live in America ······ 177
## Living in the USA

# 1 Housing ······ 178

Where to live?······178
Single-family and multi-family (condo and co-op)······180
Roommate······188
Purchase ······190
Sell the property······196

# 2 Financials ······ 200

Banking······200
Social Security ······206
Taxes ······208
Investments······212

# 3 Cars ······ 216

Driver's license ······216
Purchase or lease a vehicle······218
Maintenance······220

キャッシュレス……149
セール時期……151

## 7 アクティビティ ……………………………………… 155

エクササイズ……155
スポーツ……159
映画……165
舞台芸術……169
博物館……171

# Part 3　アメリカに住もう ……………177
## 暮らしの常識

## 1 住宅 ………………………………………………… 179

どこに住むか？……179
戸建住宅と集合住宅……181
ルームメイト……189
購入……191
売却する……197

## 2 ファイナンス ……………………………………… 201

銀行……201
社会保障番号……207
税金……209
投資……213

## 3 車…………………………………………………… 217

運転免許証……217
車の購入とリース……219
メンテナンス……221

## 4 Health ......................................................... 224

Health insurance ······224
Medical care system ······226
Medical checkups and vaccinations······228
Emergency ······230

## 5 Food ............................................................ 234

Breakfast ······234
Lunch······236
Dinner ······240
Health conscious eating······244

## 6 Family .......................................................... 248

Diverse family structures······248
Marriage ······252
Raising Children······256
Divorce······260
Remarriage and Step-families ······262
Pets······264

## 7 Education ...................................................... 270

Early childhood education ······270
Required education ······272
Universities······278

## 8 Weddings and Funerals .................................... 284

Weddings ······284
Funeral······288
Birthdays······290

## 4 健康 ·················· 225

健康保険······225
医療制度······227
健康診断と予防注射······229
緊急事態······231

## 5 食事 ·················· 235

朝食······235
昼食······237
夕食······241
健康重視の食事······245

## 6 家族 ·················· 249

多様な家族構成······249
結婚······253
子育て······257
離婚······261
再婚とステップファミリー······263
ペット······265

## 7 教育 ·················· 271

幼児教育······271
義務教育······273
大学······279

## 8 冠婚葬祭 ·················· 285

結婚······285
葬儀······289
誕生日······291

アメリカ合衆国地域別地図 ·················· 16
［コラム］アメリカの移民の歴史と現在 ·················· 70
［コラム］アメリカの国立公園を楽しむ ·················· 174

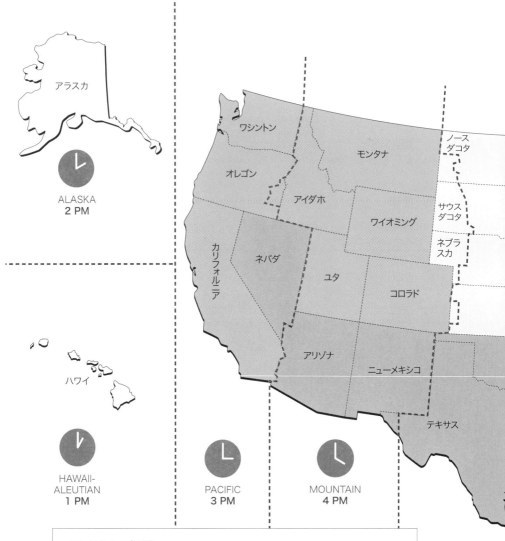

アラスカ

ALASKA
2 PM

ハワイ

HAWAII-
ALEUTIAN
1 PM

ワシントン

オレゴン

モンタナ

ノース
ダコタ

アイダホ

サウス
ダコタ

ワイオミング

ネブラ
スカ

カリフォルニア

ネバダ

ユタ

コロラド

アリゾナ

ニューメキシコ

テキサス

PACIFIC
3 PM

MOUNTAIN
4 PM

## アメリカの概要

正式名称：アメリカ合衆国　United States of America

面　　積：9,833,517平方キロメートル（日本の約26倍）

人　　口：約3億3,500万人

首　　都：ワシントンD.C.

言　　語：法律上の定めはないが主に英語

宗　　教：主にキリスト教

政　　体：大統領制、連邦制

議　　会：上院・下院の二院制

通　　貨：米ドル

# アメリカ合衆国地域別地図

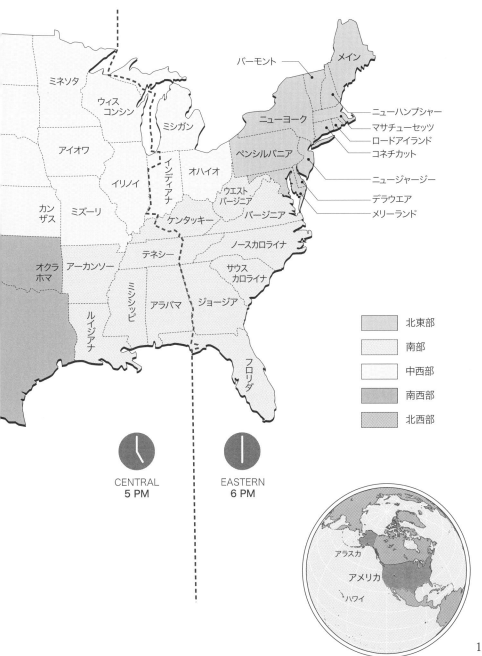

バーモント

メイン

ニューハンプシャー
マサチューセッツ
ロードアイランド
コネチカット

ニュージャージー

デラウエア

メリーランド

ミネソタ

ウィスコンシン

ミシガン

ニューヨーク

ペンシルバニア

アイオワ

イリノイ

インディアナ

オハイオ

ウエストバージニア

バージニア

カンザス

ミズーリ

ケンタッキー

ノースカロライナ

オクラホマ

アーカンソー

テネシー

サウスカロライナ

ミシシッピ

アラバマ

ジョージア

ルイジアナ

フロリダ

| | 北東部 |
| | 南部 |
| | 中西部 |
| | 南西部 |
| | 北西部 |

CENTRAL
5 PM

EASTERN
6 PM

アラスカ

アメリカ

ハワイ

17

# Part 1

# Let's Get to Know America

*General Knowledge and Culture*

# アメリカを知ろう

一般的知識と文化

# 1 Geography of the United States

........................................................................

(**Key Words**) Heartland, Time Zones, Daylight Saving Time, Arid, Mediterranean, Marine, Drought, Wildfire, Manufacturing

## Five regions of the USA

The United States is a large country with many different regions. Think of it this way: the entire European Union could fit inside the United States, with plenty of room to spare! Let's start with a bird's eye view of the major **geographic regions** of the United States:

Northeast: This region includes states such as Maine, Vermont, New Hampshire, Massachusetts, Rhode Island, Connecticut, New York, New Jersey, Pennsylvania, Maryland, Delaware, and Washington, D.C. It is known for its rich history, **immigrant traditions**, and **city centers** like Boston and New York City.

Midwest: The Midwest includes states like Ohio, Indiana, Illinois, Michigan, Wisconsin, Minnesota, Iowa, Missouri, North Dakota, South Dakota, Kansas, and Nebraska. This region is often referred to as the "heartland" of the country, and is known for **vast farmlands**, **factory cities** like Chicago and Detroit, and a **strong sense of community**.

South: The Southern region of the United States includes states like Virginia, West Virginia, Kentucky, Tennessee, North

# アメリカの地理

**キーワード** ハートランド、タイムゾーン、サマータイム、乾燥、地中海、海洋、干ばつ、山火事、製造業

## アメリカの5つの地域

アメリカは国土が広く、さまざまな地域があります。このように考えてみてください。欧州連合全体がアメリカにすっぽり収まっても、まだ十分に余裕があるのです！まずアメリカの主な**地域区分**の概観を見ていきます。

**北東部**：この地域には、メイン州、バーモント州、ニューハンプシャー州、マサチューセッツ州、ロードアイランド州、コネチカット州、ニューヨーク州、ニュージャージー州、ペンシルベニア州、メリーランド州、デラウェア州、それにワシントンD.C.が含まれます。古い歴史や**移民の伝統**、ボストンやニューヨーク市といった**都心**で知られています。

**中西部**：中西部にはオハイオ州、インディアナ州、イリノイ州、ミシガン州、ウィスコンシン州、ミネソタ州、アイオワ州、ミズーリ州、ノースダコタ州、サウスダコタ州、カンザス州、ネブラスカ州があります。この地域はよく、「ハートランド」と呼ばれ、**広大な農地**と、シカゴやデトロイトといった**工業都市**、そして**地域の強い連帯感**で知られています。

**南部**：アメリカの南部にはバージニア州、ウェストバージニア州、ケンタッキー州、テネシー州、ノースカロ

メリーランド、デラウェア、ワシントンD.C.を南部とする分け方もある。

ハートランド
かつては炭鉱や製鉄業などの重工業のイメージが強いハートランド地域だが、近年は安価な電力と広大な土地を利用したデータセンター、大学や研究機関との連携によるバイオテクノロジー関連企業、3Dプリンティング関連企業の進出が盛んになってきている。

21

Carolina, South Carolina, Georgia, Alabama, Mississippi, Arkansas, Louisiana, and Florida. This region is known for its warm weather and unique culture, including **distinctive music**, food, and architecture.

Southwest: The Southwest includes states like Texas, Oklahoma, New Mexico, Arizona, and Nevada. This region is known for its hot and dry weather, mountains, and its mix of Native American, Hispanic, and Anglo cultures. Major cities in this region include Houston, Dallas, Phoenix, and Las Vegas.

Northwest: The Northwestern region of the United States includes states like California, Oregon, Washington, Idaho, Montana, Wyoming, Utah, Colorado, and Alaska. This region is known for its **natural beauty**, including mountains, forests, deserts, and beaches. Major cities in this region include Los Angeles, San Francisco, Seattle, and Denver.

## Time Zones and Daylight Saving Time

Unlike smaller countries, the United States is large enough that it is split into four different time zones. People in the Eastern time zone start their days the earliest. Moving west, there is the Central time zone, Mountain time zone, and finally the Pacific time zone. Each one of these zones is **one hour behind** the other. It might not seem like much, but it becomes more noticeable when people in New York are finishing their days while those in Los Angeles are still in the middle of the afternoon.

You may have heard of something called Daylight Saving Time, a tradition in which everyone in America either sets their **clocks forward or backwards** one hour depending on the season. If this seems confusing or strange, most Americans agree with you! There have been laws proposed that would end Daylight Saving Time, but for now, the practice will continue.

ライナ州、サウスカロライナ州、ジョージア州、アラバマ州、ミシシッピ州、アーカンソー州、ルイジアナ州、フロリダ州があります。この地域は温暖な気候や**特有の音楽、食べ物、建築**といったユニークな文化で知られています。

　**南西部**：南西部にはテキサス州、オクラホマ州、ニューメキシコ州、アリゾナ州、ネバダ州があります。この地域は暑く乾燥した気候と、山々やネイティブ・アメリカン、ヒスパニック、アングロ文化が混在していることで知られています。この地域の主な都市はヒューストン、ダラス、フェニックス、ラスベガスなどです。

　**北西部**：アメリカの西部にはカリフォルニア州、オレゴン州、ワシントン州、アイダホ州、モンタナ州、ワイオミング州、ユタ州、コロラド州、アラスカ州があります。この地域は山や森、砂漠やビーチなど**自然の美しさ**で知られています。この地域の主な都市はロサンゼルスやサンフランシスコ、シアトル、デンバーなどです。

**ユニークな文化**
ルイジアナ州近辺ではクリオール文化がアイデンティティーの一つになっている。これはアフリカ、フランス、スペイン、そしてネイティブ・アメリカンの文化が融合した独特なもの。17世紀にフランスがルイジアナを植民地化した際に、アフリカから奴隷が連れてこられた結果、入植者、ネイティブ・アメリカンとの交流を通じて独自の文化を形成した。

**アングロ文化**
アングロサクソン系またはイギリス系の人々の文化、伝統、慣習。

### 覚えておきたいタイムゾーンとサマータイム

　小さな国と違って、アメリカは国土が広いため4つの異なるタイムゾーンが設けられています。東部標準時の人が最も早く1日をスタートさせ、西へ行くにつれて中部標準時、山岳部標準時、最後に太平洋標準時となります。これらのタイムゾーンにはそれぞれ**1時間ずつの遅れ**があります。大したことではなさそうですが、ニューヨークの人々が1日を終えようとしている頃、ロサンゼルスの人々はまだ午後の真っ最中であることを考えるとより分かりやすくなります。

　アメリカでは季節によって**時計を1時間早めたり遅らせたりする**、サマータイムという習慣があることを聞いたことがあるでしょう。ややこしいとか、おかしいとか思われたなら、ほとんどのアメリカ人はその意見に賛成です！　サマータイムを廃止する法律も提案されているのですが、今のところ、この習慣は継続されることになっています。

廃止論も出る中、サマータイムの賛成意見には、日照時間が長くなり夜間の活動時間が増え、経済活性化につながる、エネルギー消費量が削減できるなどがある。反対意見としては、朝が暗くなるので子供の登校が危険、農業や漁業など一部の産業に支障が出るなどがある。

## Climate characteristics by region

If you're going to spend time in America, you need to be prepared for the weather. Here is a quick look at the main climate zones of the United States:

Tropical climate: This climate zone is found in Hawaii and southern Florida. It is characterized by hot and humid weather **year-round**, with very little **temperature variation** between seasons. Rain is common but is often light and passes quickly.

Arid and semi-arid climate: This climate zone covers much of the southwestern United States, including parts of California, Nevada, Utah, Arizona, and New Mexico. You can think of it as close to a **desert climate**, with hot, dry summers and mild winters. Remember, this climate zone gets much colder at night than it is during the day.

Mediterranean climate: This climate zone is found in parts of California, Oregon, and Washington. It is characterized by mild, wet winters and hot, dry summers. It is generally considered to be one of the **most comfortable climates**, although it can get a little cold.

Humid subtropical climate: This climate zone covers much of the southeastern United States, including parts of Florida, Georgia, Alabama, Mississippi, Louisiana, Tennessee, North Carolina, and South Carolina. Prepare for **hot, humid summers** and mild winters, although the moisture in the air can make winters feel colder than they are.

Marine west coast climate: This climate zone is found in the Pacific Northwest, including parts of Washington, Oregon, and northern California. With mild, wet winters and cool, dry summers, it is a lot like the Mediterranean climate, but colder.

## 地域別の気候の特徴

　アメリカで過ごすなら、天候への備えが必要です。ここでは、アメリカの主な気候帯について簡単に紹介します。

　**熱帯気候**：この気候帯はハワイと南フロリダで見られます。**年間を通して高温多湿で季節による気温差**が少ないのが特徴です。雨はよく降りますが、たいていは小雨ですぐに止みます。

ハワイの熱帯気候は、さまざまな動植物の生息地となっている。

　**乾燥・半乾燥帯気候**：この気候帯はカリフォルニア州、ネバダ州、ユタ州、アリゾナ州、そしてニューメキシコ州の各所を含むアメリカ南西部の大部分で見られます。夏は暑く乾燥し、冬は温暖で**砂漠気候**に似ています。この気候帯は、日中よりも夜間の方がずっと寒くなることを覚えておきましょう。

水不足、土壌の塩分化、砂漠化などがこの気候帯下の問題として挙げられる。

　**地中海性気候**：この気候帯はカリフォルニア州、オレゴン州、ワシントン州の各所で見られます。温暖で雨の多い冬と暑く乾燥する夏が特徴です。一般的に**最も過ごしやすい気候**のひとつとされていますが、冬は少し寒くなります。

常緑樹林や草原が広がる自然豊かな地域。果樹栽培やワイン生産も盛ん。

　**湿潤亜熱帯気候**：この気候帯はフロリダ州、ジョージア州、アラバマ州、ミシシッピ州、ルイジアナ州、テネシー州、ノースカロライナ州、そしてサウスカロライナ州の各所を含むアメリカ南東部の大部分で見られます。冬は湿った空気のため実際より寒く感じられることがあるものの、**夏は高温多湿で冬は穏やかだ**と覚えておきましょう。

土壌は肥沃で、綿花、大豆、タバコなどの栽培が盛ん。

　**西岸海洋性気候**：この気候帯はワシントン州、オレゴン州、カリフォルニア州北部の各所を含む太平洋岸北西部で見られます。冬は穏やかで雨が多く、夏は涼しく乾燥するため、地中海性気候とよく似ていますが、より寒冷です。

針葉樹林や常緑樹林が広がる豊かな自然が魅力。果樹栽培や酪農が盛ん。

Continental climate: This climate zone covers much of the northern United States, including parts of Montana, North Dakota, South Dakota, Minnesota, Wisconsin, Michigan, and New York. It is characterized by cold winters and warm summers. In the **Great Lakes region**, certain weather effects can cause extremely cold winters, so bring a heavy coat!

Alpine and highland climate: This climate zone is found in **mountainous areas** throughout the United States, including parts of the Rocky Mountains, the Sierra Nevada, and the Appalachian Mountains. It is characterized by cool to cold temperatures year-round, with increasing rain and snow up in the mountains.

## Climate Change Concerns and Extreme Weather in Various Regions

**Climate change** is a global issue that affects every region of the world, and the United States is no different. Here are some of the major climate change concerns across the United States:

Northeast: **Rising sea levels** and increased frequency and strength of storms are the major climate change concerns in the Northeast. Since the major cities of New York, Boston, and Philadelphia are all on the coast, they are at risk of flooding due to rising sea levels. The region is also experiencing dangerous heat waves during the summer, which are a risk to **low-income people** living in apartments without air-conditioning.

Southeast: The Southeast experiences hurricanes, and climate change is making these storms more frequent and intense. Rising sea levels and **increased rainfall** are also major concerns in the region, as they can lead to severe **flooding**.

Midwest: The Midwest is suffering from rising temperatures, which can lead to **heat-related illnesses** and deaths. The region is also experiencing more rain and snow, which can lead to flooding, damaging farm land and buildings.

　**大陸性気候**：この気候帯はモンタナ州、ノースダコタ州、サウスダコタ州、ミネソタ州、ウィスコンシン州、ミシガン州、そしてニューヨーク州の各所を含むアメリカ北部の大部分で見られます。寒い冬と暑い夏が特徴です。**五大湖周辺の地域**では、天候の影響で冬が特に寒くなることがあるため、厚手のコートを持っていきましょう！

　**高山および高地気候**：この気候帯はロッキー山脈、シエラネバダ山脈、アパラチア山脈の各所を含むアメリカ全土の山岳地帯に見られます。年間を通して涼しく低温で、山の上の方では雨や雪が多いのが特徴です。

土壌は乾燥しており、農業は灌漑によって行われている。

これらの山脈には、多くの国立公園や州立公園があり、登山・ハイキングなどアウトドアのアクティビティが楽しめる。

## 気候変動の懸念と各地の異常気象

　気候変動は世界各地に影響を及ぼすグローバルな課題で、それはアメリカにおいても同様です。ここでは、アメリカ全土で懸念されている主な気候変動を紹介します。

　**北東部**：**海面の上昇**や、激しさを増す暴風雨の頻発が、北東部における気候変動の主な懸念事項です。ニューヨークやボストン、フィラデルフィアなどの主要都市はすべて海岸沿いに位置するため、海面上昇による洪水のリスクにさらされています。また、夏場は危険な熱波に見舞われ、エアコンのないアパートで暮らす**低所得者**たちにとっての脅威となっています。

　**南東部**：南東部にはハリケーンが発生しますが、気候変動によってさらに強い暴風雨が頻発しています。深刻な**洪水**を引き起こす可能性のある海面の上昇や、**降水量の増加**もまた懸念されています。

　**中西部**：中西部は**熱中症**や死者を出す可能性のある、気温の上昇に悩まされています。雨や雪の量も増え、それが洪水を引き起こし農地や建物の被害につながるのです。

2020年、ハリケーン「ローラ」、2021年にはハリケーン「アイダ」がルイジアナ州に上陸し、停電、洪水など甚大な被害をもたらした。

Southwest: The Southwest is experiencing more **droughts**, which can lead to **water shortages**, farming problems, and increased risk of wildfires. Rising temperatures are also a major concern in the region, as they can make droughts worse and lead to health problems.

West Coast: The West Coast's main problem is wildfires, which can lead to **property damage**, loss of life, and long-term health effects from breathing smoke. Rising sea levels and increased storm activity are also concerns, as they can lead to flooding and ecosystem damage along the coast.

Overall, the impacts of climate change are widespread and affect every region of the United States in different ways. In response to these problems, many students are trying to help the environment at the local and government levels. Among younger Americans, it is considered important to take action in order to protect communities and ensure a **sustainable world** for future generations.

## Industry by region

The economics of the different United States regions are largely a result of geography and history, but factors like immigration play a role as well:

Northeast Region: The Northeast region of the United States is home to several major industries and is the wealthiest region of the country. Some of the significant industries here include finance, technology, healthcare, education, and manufacturing. The region is also known for its tourism industry, which is centered around the **historical landmarks** and **cultural attractions** in cities like Boston, New York, and Philadelphia.

Midwest Region: The Midwest region of the United States is known for its manufacturing industry, particularly in the automotive, steel, and machinery sectors. During the second

　**南西部**：南西部では**干ばつ**が増加し、**水不足**や農業への被害、山火事の危険性が高まっています。気温の上昇も大きな懸念事項で、干ばつがより深刻になり健康被害につながる可能性があります。

　**西海岸**：西海岸の主な問題は山火事で、**家や財産の損失**、人命の損失、煙を吸い込むことによる長期的な健康被害につながる可能性があります。海面の上昇と暴風雨の頻発も深刻で、沿岸部では洪水や生態系へのダメージが懸念されています。

　このように、気候変動の影響はアメリカの広い範囲におよび、各地域に様々な形で影響しています。これらの問題に対処するため、多くの学生が地域や政府レベルで環境保護に取り組んでいます。アメリカの若者たちは、地域社会を守り、未来の世代に**持続可能な世界**を残せるよう行動を起こすことが大切だと考えています。

## 地域別の産業

　アメリカの地域ごとの経済は、地理や歴史に関係するところが大きいものの、移民などの要因も関係しています。

　**北東部**：いくつかの主要産業が生まれたアメリカの北東部は、国内で最も裕福な地域です。この地域の主要産業には金融業、テクノロジー、医療、教育、製造業などがあります。また、ボストンやニューヨーク、フィラデルフィアなどの都市は、**歴史的建造物**や**文化的な名所**を中心とした観光産業でも知られています。

　**中西部**：アメリカの中西部は、主に自動車や鉄鋼、機械などの製造業で知られています。この地域の産業は20世紀後半、**工場での仕事**が海外流出したことで衰退をし

**山火事**
2020年、カリフォルニア州で史上最大規模の山火事が発生し、400万ヘクタール（東京都の約4.5倍）以上の森林が消失。21年にもオレゴン州、ワシントン州で山火事が発生し、多くの住民が避難を余儀なくされた。

**ボストン**
1630年に町の基礎が作られ始めた独立革命の中心地。ハーバード大学をはじめ、多くの有名大学がある学術都市でもある。

**ニューヨーク**
1626年にオランダ人の入植者がネイティブ・アメリカン（レナペ族）からマンハッタン島を安値で購入してから、町が始まる。1664年にイギリス人が征服してからニューヨークと呼ばれるようになった。

**フィラデルフィア**
1682年、クエーカー教徒が住みはじめた。18世紀になるとイギリス領土内でもロンドンの次に大きな都市となった。1776年に独立宣言がこの地で採決されたことで、アメリカ誕生の場所として知られている。

**自動車**
ホンダ（オハイオ州）、トヨタ（ケンタッキー州、インディアナ州）、日産（テネシー州、ミシシッピ州）とそのほかスバル、マツダ等の多くの日本の自動車メーカーがこの地域に進出し、多くの雇用を生み出している。

half of the twentieth century, this region experienced decline as **factory jobs** spread to other countries. However, the region is also a **significant agricultural producer** like corn, wheat, and soybean, which has helped with a slow economic recovery over the last 20 years.

South Region: The South region of the United States is a **major producer** of oil, natural gas, and coal. As climate change causes the government to move away from those resources, though, the economy of the south appears to be threatened. Currently, southern states are making an effort to find an advantage in the **manufacturing industry**, where they have companies based in the aerospace, automotive, and defense industries. Other industries in the South include healthcare, tourism, and agriculture, but those are limited to specific areas.

West Region: The West region of the United States is filled with a range of industries, and is the second wealthiest part of the country. The region is a center for technology development, with Silicon Valley in California and the Seattle area in Washington state serving as centers for growth. The West is also a significant producer of farm products, with California being the largest such **producer** in the country. The region is also known for its entertainment industry, with Hollywood in California and Las Vegas in Nevada serving as destinations for film, music, and gaming.

It's important to note that these industries are not exclusive to these regions, and there are many other smaller industries and markets that contribute to the overall **economic output** of the United States. It is not uncommon to find towns that rely on tourism, **factory production**, and education all within a few miles of one another.

ましたが、ここ20年はトウモロコシや小麦、大豆などの**農産物の主要産地**として、ゆるやかに回復しつつあります。

　**南部**：アメリカの南部は石油や天然ガス、石炭の**主要な産地**です。気候変動により政府がこれらの資源を敬遠するようになり、南部の経済は打撃を受けているようです。現在は航空宇宙や自動車、防衛産業を基盤とする企業がある**製造業**に強みを見出そうとしています。他の産業では、医療や観光、農業などがありますが、これらは特定の地域に限られています。

　**西部**：アメリカの西部はあらゆる産業が集まる、国内でも2番目に裕福な地域です。この地域は技術開発の中核地で、カリフォルニア州のシリコンバレーやワシントン州のシアトルが成長の中心になっています。また農産物の生産も盛んで、カリフォルニア州は国内最大の**農産地**です。カリフォルニア州のハリウッドやネバダ州のラスベガスなど、エンターテインメント産業でも知られるこの地域は、映画や音楽、ゲームの中心地でもあります。

19世紀後半から多くの日本人が経済的な理由や新たな生活を求めて、この地に移住してきた。その数は1890年代には約20万人に達した。日系人は差別や偏見に耐えながらも生活を築き、排日運動や戦後の収容所生活を乗り越え、現在に至る。日系人は今では、政治、経済、文化などの様々な分野で活躍している。

　これらの産業は限られた地域だけにあるのではなく、アメリカ全体の**経済生産高**に貢献している小規模な産業や市場がたくさんあることを知っておいてください。観光業や**工場生産業**、教育などに頼っている町が、数マイル以内のところにあることも珍しくないのです。

アメリカの名目GDPは約25兆ドル、世界全体の約25%を占める世界最大の経済規模を誇る。

# 2 American Background and People

**Key Words** Ethnicity, Indigenous, Diversity, Individuality, Discrimination, Segregation, Dialects, Protestant, Catholic, Mindfulness

## Origins of the United States

To better understand American culture, it might be useful to consider the big picture of American history. Before the arrival of European explorers, the land that is now the United States was inhabited by various native peoples who had developed their own cultures and societies.

In 1492, Christopher Columbus arrived in the Caribbean. For the next few hundred years, diseases and violence caused **indigenous populations** to decline or disappear entirely. In the 17th century, European countries started **colonies** in what is now the United States. Even from the beginning, American culture was diverse. The British created a **religious colony** in Massachusetts and an **economic settlement** in Virginia, while the Spanish had small towns across the southern United States. Even the French and Dutch had cities scattered around, contributing to the United States' development as a **multi-cultural society**.

In 1783 America successfully broke away from British rule, resulting in the official formation of the United States of America in 1783. Over the next hundred years, the United States wrote the **Constitution** that is the foundation for its government, expanded west across the continent, and developed the **two-party political system** that is still in place today. In 1861-1865, the **American**

# アメリカの背景と人々

**キーワード** 民族性、先住の、多様性、個性、差別、分離、訛り、プロテスタント、カトリック、マインドフルネス

## アメリカの成り立ち

　アメリカの文化をより理解するために、その歴史の全体像について考えてみましょう。ヨーロッパの探検家たちがやって来る前、現在のアメリカの地には様々な先住民が暮らし、独自の文化や社会を育んでいました。

　クリストファー・コロンブスがカリブ海に到達したのが1492年。それから数百年、**先住民の人口は病気や暴力によって減少し、あるいは全く姿を消してしまいました**。17世紀になると、ヨーロッパ諸国は現在のアメリカに**植民地**を作りました。アメリカの文化は最初から多様でした。イギリスはマサチューセッツに**宗教的な植民地**を、バージニアに**経済的な入植地**を作り、一方でスペインはアメリカの南部一帯に小さな町を作りました。フランスやオランダも各地に点々と町を作り、**多文化社会であるア**メリカの発展に貢献しました。

　1783年、アメリカはイギリスの支配からようやく脱却し、同年、正式にアメリカ合衆国が誕生します。その後100年以上にわたって、政府の基盤となる**憲法**を制定し、国土を大陸の西へと拡大、今日に至る**二大政党制**を確立させました。1861年から1865年にかけては、奴隷制と州の権利をかけた**南北戦争**が続き、その結果南東部の州は

アメリカ大陸にヨーロッパ人が到達した15世紀末頃、大陸には様々な先住民族が住んでおり、その数は数百と言われる。異なる言語、文化、社会を持っており、代表的な部族として北東部のアルゴンキン族、イロコイ族、南東部のムスコギー族、チョクトー族、中央のスー族、ラコタ族、南西部のプエブロ族、ナバホ族、西海岸はカリフォルニア・インディアンなどがある。

アメリカの独立まで、フレンチ・インディアン戦争 (1754-1763)、印紙法 (1765)、ボストン茶会事件 (1773)、レキシントン・コンコードの戦い (1775) などを経て、1776年に独立を宣言。1777年のサラトガの戦いの後、1783年にイギリスがアメリカを独立国として承認した。

**Civil War** was fought over the issue of slavery and states' rights, resulting in the defeat of the southeastern states at the hands of the northeast. To this day there is still some tension left over from the war, with southerners seeing the north as **wealthy bullies** and northerners seeing the south as **poorly educated** and often racist. Despite attempts to erase these stereotypes, they have persisted for 150 years and **political rivalries** mostly make the problem worse.

By the late 19th and early 20th centuries the US became a global economic power, with rapid economic growth and the emergence of new technologies such as the telephone, electricity, and the automobile. After World War II, the US became a world superpower while still facing **domestic struggles** such as the **Civil Rights Movement** and the Vietnam War.

There was a brief time after the fall of the Soviet Union in 1991 that the US emerged as the world's only true superpower. However, the country faced new challenges in the form of terrorism and a changing global economy, and these would only increase in the 21st century. Since then, the US has continued to face political, economic, and social problems including the September 11 attacks in 2001, the **Great Recession** of 2008, and the COVID-19 pandemic. It has also become increasingly split politically, with deep divisions between political parties and regions of the country.

This history has had a noticeable effect on US culture. **Values differ**, of course, between individuals, families, and communities, but there are some clear trends. Perhaps because of America's beginnings as a **rebel country**, Americans tend to question those in positions of authority and come up with their own solutions to issues. Similarly, there is a strong sense of being an individual that most likely comes from the expansion west, when many families were encouraged to go out and form their own communities in the wilderness. Finally, due to the multiple economic "booms"

北東部の州に敗北しました。この戦争による緊張は今なお残っており、南部の人は北部の人を**裕福で意地悪**、北部の人は南部の人を**教育水準が低く**、人種差別的だと見ています。こうしたステレオタイプを払拭しようとする試みも虚しく、この状況は150年間も続いており、**政治的対立**が事態を悪化させています。

19世紀後半から20世紀初頭にかけて、電話、電気、自動車などの新技術が登場すると、アメリカは急速な経済成長を遂げ、世界の経済大国になりました。第二次世界大戦を経て、アメリカは**公民権運動**やベトナム戦争といった**国内問題**に直面しながらも、世界の超大国となります。

1991年のソ連崩壊以降、アメリカは世界で唯一の超大国として台頭していた時期もありました。しかし、その後テロリズムやグローバル経済の変化という新しい課題に直面し、21世紀になると、それらはさらに深刻化します。2001年9月11日に起きた同時多発テロ、2008年の**大不況**、コロナウイルスによるパンデミックなど、その後のアメリカは政治的、経済的、社会的問題に苦しみ続けています。また、政治的な分裂も顕著で、国内での政党間、また地域間の溝は深まるばかりです。

こうした歴史はアメリカの文化にも大きな影響を与えました。個人や家族、地域によって**価値観の違い**があることはもちろんですが、そこには明らかな傾向がいくつか見られます。おそらく、アメリカが**反逆国家**として始まったことに起因するのでしょうが、アメリカ人は権威をもつ人々に疑問を持ち、自分たちで問題の解決策を見つけようとする傾向があります。同時に、彼らが持つ強い個人主義の意識は、多くの家族が荒野に出て自分たちのコミュニティーを形成することを奨励された西部開拓

南北戦争はアメリカ史上最も激しい戦争の一つ。南軍が敗北し北軍に主導権が移ったとされるゲティスバーグの戦い（1863年）、リンカーン大統領が奴隷解放宣言を発表するきっかけとなったアンティータムの戦い（1862年）、戦争終結を早める結果となったシャーマンの海への進軍（1864年）、最後の戦いであるアパラチコーラ川の戦い（1865年）などがある。戦いの結果、奴隷制は廃止され、より平等な社会へと歩み出すことになった。

**公民権運動**
1950年代から60年代にかけて起こった黒人差別撤廃と法の下の平等を求める運動。指導したマーティン・ルーサー・キング・ジュニア牧師の非暴力主義を語った「I have a dream」の演説（1963年）はあまりにも有名。1964年に公民権法は成立した。

**ベトナム戦争**
1954年から75年までベトナムが戦場となる。フランスからの独立後、ベトナムが南北に分裂したことで、北ベトナムの共産主義化を恐れたアメリカが反発して起きた。ベトナム側、アメリカ側双方に大きな死傷者を出し、国際社会に大きな影響を与えた。

in American history, there is a strong belief that hard work will lead to wealth, although that viewpoint is less common among younger generations since the **economic struggles** after 2008.

## History of Immigration

The other side to American culture is its long history of immigration. During the 19th and early 20th centuries, the United States experienced waves of immigration from Europe and Asia. Many of these immigrants faced **discrimination and abuse** from white Americans, who viewed them as a threat to their jobs and culture. The Chinese Exclusion Act of 1882 and the Immigration Act of 1924, which established **immigration limits** based on nationality, were two examples of the racist policies passed into law during this time period.

African-Americans, who were brought to the United States as slaves, faced **racism** and discrimination throughout American history. Even after slavery was ended, African-Americans were forced to live separately from white people in a system known as **segregation**. African-Americans were excluded from many aspects of American society, including housing, education, and voting.

 **Important note**

The terms used to describe the peoples who lived in America before Europeans arrived have been controversial throughout US history. Terms like "Indian" are no longer considered appropriate, and "Indigenous" is now most commonly used by academic sources. Most people still say "Native American", and you can usually do so as well without offending anyone.

時代から引き継がれたものでしょう。アメリカの歴史の中で何度も「好景気」を経験したことで、勤勉な労働が富につながるという強い信念があるものの、2008年以降の**経済苦境**を経て、それは若い世代では消えつつあります。

## 移民の歴史

　アメリカ文化のもうひとつの側面として、長い移民の歴史があります。19世紀から20世紀初頭にかけて、アメリカにはヨーロッパやアジアから移民が押し寄せました。これらの移民の多くは、自分たちの仕事や文化が脅かされると考えた白人アメリカ人からの**差別**や**虐待**に直面しました。国籍に基づく**移民制限**を定めた1882年の中国人排斥法と1924年の移民法は、この時代に成立した人種差別政策の2つの例です。

　奴隷としてアメリカに連れてこられたアフリカ系アメリカ人は、歴史を通して**人種的偏見**や差別に苦しみました。奴隷制度の廃止以降も、「**隔離**」と呼ばれる制度で白人から切り離された生活を余儀なくされました。アフリカ系アメリカ人は、住む場所や教育、投票など、アメリカ社会の多くの側面から除外されたのです。このことが

17世紀〜18世紀は主に宗教的な自由を求めたイギリス、ドイツ、フランスなど、ヨーロッパからの移民が中心。

19世紀は、さらにアイルランドで大飢饉があったことでアイルランド移民が急増。そのほか、イタリア、東欧からの移民がやって来た。

20世紀前半は、第二次世界大戦の影響で移民数は減少したものの、後半になるとアジア、ラテンアメリカ、特にメキシコ、中米、南米からの移民が急増。21世紀になると中国、インド、フィリピンなど中には高スキル労働者もいる。

---

 **大切な点**

　ヨーロッパ人が到来する以前から、アメリカに定住していた人々をどう呼ぶかについては、アメリカの歴史を通じて議論されてきました。「インディアン」という呼び方はもはや適切とは見なされず、現在の学識資料では「インディジナス」が最も頻繁に使用されています。「ネイティブ・アメリカン」という呼び名も未だによく使われ、たいていの場合は誰の気分も害さずに使用できるでしょう。

This led to poverty and violence in African-American communities that has **continued for decades**.

In the mid-20th century, the Civil Rights Movement led to major advances in **racial equality** and **immigration policy**. The Immigration and Nationality Act of 1965 prevented discrimination based on nationality, and other new laws provided paths toward citizenship for those who entered and lived in the country illegally.

However, immigration and race remain incredibly serious issues in American politics. The 2016 presidential election and resulting policy changes have brought new attention to issues such as **border security**, housing for refugees, and the status of illegal immigrants. The United States continues to deal with questions about how to create a society that values **diversity** while also addressing the economic and security concerns that can come from welcoming people from around the world.

## Occupations and Immigrant Groups

Across America, there are many different ideas about the role that immigrants have in the economy.

In general, immigrants tend to work most frequently in the agriculture, construction, and service industries. This is partly because these industries tend to have **low-skilled**, **low-paying** jobs that are often difficult to fill with **native-born workers**. However, the specific immigrant groups that are represented in these industries can vary. For example, immigrants from Central and South America are often found working in agriculture and construction, while immigrants from South and East Asia are more likely to work in high-tech industries.

As immigrants spend more time in the United States, gaining education and work experience, they may move into different occupations and industries. For example, **second-generation immigrants** are more likely to work in professional and management positions than their parents.

アフリカ系アメリカ人のコミュニティーの貧困と暴力を
引き起こし、それは**何十年も続い**ています。

　20世紀半ば、公民権運動によって**人種平等**や**移民政策**
は大きく進展しました。1965年には国籍による差別を
防止する移民国籍法が制定され、続く新しい法律では不
法入国者や不法居住者への市民権取得の道が開かれまし
た。

　とはいえ、移民と人種問題は、アメリカの政治において
今なお極めて深刻です。2016年の大統領選挙と、それに
伴う政策変更では、**国境の警備**や難民の住居、不法移民の
地位といった問題が新たな焦点となりました。アメリカ
は**多様性**を重視する社会づくりに取り組みながらも、一
方で世界中から人々を受け入れることで起こりうる経済
的、安全保障的な課題に対処し続けています。

2016年、トランプ氏は特に移民制度改革に重点を置き、不法移民を防ぐためにメキシコとの国境に壁を建設することを公約に掲げた。移民政策を厳格にし、イスラム教徒の米国入国を一時的に禁止することもあった。対するヒラリー・クリントンは彼の案を非人間的だと批判するが、結局、トランプ氏が勝利し、第45代のアメリカ合衆国大統領に就任。

## 職業と移民グループ

　経済における移民の役割については、アメリカ全土で
様々な考え方があります。

　一般的に、移民は農業や建設業、サービス業で働く傾向
があります。これらの産業は**低技能**、**低賃金**の仕事である
ことが多く、**アメリカ生まれの労働者**で充足することが難
しいためです。ですが、こうした産業においても、業種に
より移民のグループはある程度分かれます。例えば、中南
米からの移民は農業や建設業で働くことが多い一方、南ア
ジアや東アジアからの移民はハイテク産業で働くことが
よくあります。

　移民は、アメリカでの滞在期間が長くなると、教育や仕
事の経験を積むことで、別の職業や産業に移ることがあり
ます。例えば、**2世移民**は親と比べ、より専門的な職や管
理職に就く傾向があります。

**Useful Note**

"African American" and "Black" are used more or less equally in America. African American has a more formal, academic tone, while Black has a more casual tone. Therefore, if you are in a situation where you are particularly concerned about not offending anyone, "African American" is the safer choice.

## Languages spoken in the US

As you probably already know, the many different cultural groups in America speak a wide variety of languages and dialects.

**English** is the most commonly spoken language in the United States, and it is the official language of the country. However, there are many different **dialects** of English spoken throughout the country, including Southern, New England, Midwestern, and Western dialects. Most of these dialects can be understood by everyone, although some people find the Southern accent a little hard to comprehend.

**Spanish** is the second most common language in the United States, and it is spoken by more than 40 million people. You will definitely hear it in the Southwestern and Western states, but it is spoken all over the country.

**Chinese** is spoken by more than 3 million people in the United States, primarily in large groups of Chinese immigrants called "Chinatowns" and other urban areas. Mandarin and Cantonese are the most common Chinese dialects spoken in the United States.

**Tagalog** is spoken by more than 1.5 million people in the United States, mainly by Filipino Americans. It is most commonly

**役立ちメモ**

　アメリカでは「アフリカ系アメリカ人」や「黒人」は、ほとんど同じように使われています。「アフリカ系アメリカ人」はより形式的でアカデミックな響きがあり、「黒人」はどちらかというとカジュアルな響きがあります。そのため、人の気分を害さないよう特に気を遣う場面では「アフリカ系アメリカ人」を使うのが無難です。

## アメリカで使われている言語

　すでにご存知のように、アメリカには多くの異なる文化的集団があり、多種多様な言語や方言が話されています。

　**英語**はアメリカで最も一般的に話されている言語であり、公用語です。とはいえ、アメリカ全土で話されている英語には、南部方言やニューイングランド方言、中西部方言、西部方言など様々な**方言**があります。これらの方言の多くは誰もが理解できますが、南部訛りは少し難しいと感じる人もいます。

　**スペイン語**はアメリカで二番目に多く話されている言語で、4千万人以上の人々が話しています。南西部や西部の州では必ず耳にし、全米で話されています。

　**中国語**はアメリカで3千万人以上の人々に話されており、主に「チャイナタウン」と呼ばれる大きな中華系移民の地区や、その他の都市部で話されています。北京語と広東語がアメリカにおける最も一般的な中国語の方言です。

　**タガログ語**は主にフィリピン系アメリカ人の人々によって話されており、150万人以上の人々が話しています。

実は憲法では公用語についての規定はなく、英語が公用語と法的に認められているわけではない。しかし、最も広く話されている言語であり、かつ29の州では正式な公用語と定めている。

spoken in California and Hawaii, which are the areas with the largest **Filipino populations**.

**European languages** are not spoken in America as much as you might think, given the country's European cultural background. French is spoken by more than 1 million people in the United States, mostly in the state of Louisiana, German is spoken by more than 1 million people in the Great Lakes region, and Italian is spoken by more than 700,000 people, mainly in the Northeast.

**Arabic** is spoken by more than 600,000 people in the United States, generally by immigrants from the Middle East and North Africa, who live in **urban areas** all over the country.

**Korean** is spoken by more than 400,000 people in the United States, mainly in urban areas with large Korean populations, such as Los Angeles and New York City.

If you want to find **Japanese** speakers, your best bet is San Francisco, although smaller groups can be found in Washington state, Hawaii, and New York City.

Additionally, many people in the United States speak **multiple languages** or dialects, and switching between languages and dialects is common.

## English Dialects

English dialects in the United States can mostly be mapped out to cultural regions, each with their own unique features and variations. Here are some of the most famous ones:

**Northeastern Dialects** include the New England and Mid-Atlantic regions. The most distinct feature of this dialect is not saying the "r" that would normally be pronounced after a **vowel**. For example, speakers of this dialect might pronounce "car" as "cah".

フィリピン系の人々が最も多いカリフォルニア州とハワイ州でよく耳にします。

**ヨーロッパの言語**はアメリカがヨーロッパの文化的背景を持つ国であるにもかかわらず、思ったほどは話されていません。フランス語はルイジアナ州を中心に100万人以上、ドイツ語は五大湖の周辺地域で100万人以上、イタリア語は北東部を中心に70万人以上の人々が話しています。

**アラビア語**はアメリカで60万人以上の人々に話されており、主に**都市部**で暮らす中東や北アフリカの移民の人々によって話されています。

**韓国語**は主にロサンゼルスやニューヨークなど、韓国系住民の多い都市部で40万人以上の人々に話されています。

**日本語**を話す人を探すならワシントン州、ハワイ州、ニューヨーク州にも小さなグループはありますが、サンフランシスコが最も多いでしょう。

また、アメリカでは多くの人が**複数の言語や方言**を話し、それらを切り替えることも一般的です。

## 英語の訛りについて

アメリカにおける英語の方言は、そのほとんどが文化的な地域と合致しており、それぞれに独自の特徴やバリエーションがあります。ここでは、最もよく知られているものを紹介します。

**北東部の方言**は、ニューイングランド地方と中部大西洋地方で聞かれます。この方言の最も顕著な特徴は、通常は**母音**の後に発音される「r」を発音しないことです。例えば、この方言を持つ人は「car」のことを「cah」と発音したりします。

The **Southern dialects** are spoken in the southeastern states, including Virginia, North and South Carolina, Georgia, Alabama, Mississippi, Louisiana, and Texas. The accent is characterized by stretched out pronunciation of vowels, and the "r" sound being emphasized in words, unlike in the Northeastern dialects.

The **Midwestern dialects** are mainly spoken in the Great Lakes region. They are known for having a **flat tone** used for vowels and consonants, as well as a soft pronunciation of vowels. For example, speakers of this dialect might pronounce "yeah" as "yah".

The **Western dialects** are spoken in the western region of the United States, including California, Oregon, Washington, and Nevada. This dialect is characterized by **rapid speech**, not pronouncing some consonants, and heavy use of slang. In other words, paying attention to **context** is key when speaking to someone who uses a western dialect!

**African-American Vernacular English** is a dialect spoken by many African-Americans, particularly in the Southern United States. It is characterized by its use of **double negatives** such as "I don't want none of that", the **omission** of the final "s" in plural nouns and verbs, and the use of certain slang words and phrases. Like the western dialect, an inexperienced listener should pay attention to context when speaking to someone using African-American Vernacular.

## Religion in America

Religion played a significant role in shaping American history and culture for hundreds of years. The United States has a **diverse religious** landscape, with Christianity being the dominant religion, followed by other faiths such as Judaism, Islam, Buddhism, Hinduism, and others.

**Christianity** is the largest religion in the United States, with over 70% of Americans identifying as Christians. The majority of Christians in the US are Protestant, with the largest **denominations**

　南部の方言は、バージニア州、ノースカロライナ州、サウスカロライナ州、ジョージア州、アラバマ州、ミシシッピ州、ルイジアナ州、テキサス州などの南東部で話されています。母音の音が引き伸ばされるのが特徴で、北東部の方言とは異なり、単語の中の「r」の音が強調されます。

　中西部の方言は主に五大湖地方で聞かれます。母音や子音の調子が平坦で、母音を柔らかく発音することで知られています。例えば、この方言を使う人は「yeah」を「yah」と発音したりします。

　西部の方言は、カリフォルニア州やオレゴン州、ワシントン州、ネバダ州などのアメリカ西部で聞かれます。この方言の特徴は、早口であること、いくつかの子音を発音しないこと、スラングをよく使うことです。つまり、西部方言を使う人と話す時は、文脈に注意を払うことが鍵なのです！

　アフリカ系アメリカ人固有の英語は、アフリカ系アメリカ人の方言で、とりわけアメリカ南部で話されています。「I don't want none of that」のような二重否定、名詞の複数形や動詞の最後にくる「s」の省略、特定のスラングや言い回しを使うことが特徴です。西部の方言と同様に、聞き慣れていない人がこうした方言を使う人と話すときは、文脈に注意すると良いでしょう。

## アメリカの宗教

　宗教は何百年にもわたり、アメリカの歴史と文化の形成に重要な役割を果たしてきました。アメリカには、多様な宗教があり、大多数の人々が信仰しているキリスト教をはじめ、ユダヤ教、イスラム教、仏教、ヒンドゥー教など信仰がそれに続きます。

　キリスト教はアメリカ最大の宗教で70％以上の人が「クリスチャン」と自認しています。その大半はプロテスタントで、最大の宗派はバプテスト、メソジスト、長老

俗にプロテスタントと呼ばれる人は、ドイツ、イギリス、オランダから、カトリックは特にアイルランド、イタリア、ポーランドからの移民の子孫が多くを占めている。

45

being Baptist, Methodist, and Presbyterian. Roman Catholics make up the second-largest religious group in the country. However, there is a vast difference in **practices and beliefs** among Christians. For instance, only around 20% of Americans attend Church every week, and of that number, many do so for social or family reasons. Over the last century, the percentages of American Christians who identify **as religious** has dropped steadily, with the most enthusiastic Christian communities generally existing in rural areas.

**Judaism** is the second-largest non-Christian religion in the United States, with about 2% of Americans identifying as **Jewish**. Islam is the third-largest non-Christian religion, with about 1% of Americans identifying as **Muslim**. Buddhism, Hinduism, and other Eastern religions make up a small but growing percentage of the religious landscape in the United States.

**Religious freedom** is written into the U.S. Constitution, and the country has a tradition of respecting and protecting religious diversity. However, there have been ongoing debates and controversies over the role of religion in public life, including issues such as **prayer in schools**, the teaching of **evolution** in science classes, and the display of religious symbols in public spaces.

## Buddhism is Cool

Among younger Americans, Buddhism has been gaining **followers** for decades. There are a number of things that tend to make this religion popular.

First, Buddhism emphasizes the practice of mindfulness, which has become a major topic in Western culture. Mindfulness involves being present in the moment, focusing on your thoughts, feelings, and sensations without judgment. This practice can help **reduce**

派です。ローマ・カトリックが国内で2番目に大きな宗教グループです。ただ、キリスト教徒の間でも、その**慣例や信仰**には大きな違いがあります。例えば、アメリカ人のうち、毎週教会へ行く人は全体の20％に過ぎず、それらの人の中には社交上の付き合いや家族の事情で行く人が多くいます。この100年間で、**宗教的である**と自認するキリスト教徒の割合は減少し続け、熱心な信者のコミュニティーは、一般的には地方に見られます。

　**ユダヤ教**は、キリスト教以外ではアメリカで2番目に大きな宗教で、国民の約2％が**ユダヤ教徒**です。3番目に大きな宗教はイスラム教で、アメリカ人の約1％が**イスラム教徒**です。仏教やヒンドゥー教、その他東洋の宗教はアメリカの宗教分布においてはわずかですが、その割合は増えつつあります。

　**宗教の自由**はアメリカ合衆国憲法にも明記されており、アメリカには宗教の多様性を尊重し、保護しようとする伝統があります。しかし、**学校でのお祈り**や、科学の授業での**進化論**の位置づけ、公の場での宗教的シンボルの展示など、公共生活における宗教の役割をめぐっては、議論や論争が続いています。

ユダヤ教徒の中には特に正統派と呼ばれる厳格な信者がいる（英語でOrthodox Jews）。ニューヨークのブルックリン地区には、生活様式、服装、宗教施設など、正統派ユダヤの暮らしを続けるコミュニティーがある。

アメリカでは科学的根拠に基づいた進化論を授業で教えるべきという主張と、聖書に基づき神の存在を信じる（創造論）を支持し、学校では教えるべきではないという主張が今でも対立している。州によっても教育現場での扱いは異なっている。

## 仏教はカッコいい

　ここ数十年、アメリカの若者の間で仏教の**信者**が増えています。仏教に人気が集まる背景はいくつかあります。

　ひとつには、西洋文化でよく話題になるマインドフルネスの実践が、仏教で重視されていることがあります。マインドフルネスとは、自分の思考や、感情、感覚に集中し、様々なことを判断せず、今この瞬間に目を向けることを言

**stress**, improve concentration, and increase overall well-being. With the world becoming fast-paced and challenging, especially for young people who are struggling to find a place in the work force, this mindfulness can be quite helpful.

Buddhism also teaches **non-violence** and **compassion** towards all living beings. This philosophy has led to the development of vegetarianism and veganism as a lifestyle choice for many Buddhists, which can help with physical health and fitness. Buddhism is known for its philosophical and spiritual teachings on **wisdom**, **enlightenment**, and the nature of reality. These teachings are often seen as insightful and thought-provoking, attracting many people to study and learn from them.

Similar to mindfulness, Buddhism emphasizes the **practice of meditation**, which has been scientifically proven to have many physical and mental health benefits. Meditation can help reduce anxiety and depression, improve focus and concentration, and increase feelings of calm and relaxation. Since these techniques are possible to practice in one's own home, they are attractive to people who might not be interested in making a weekly commitment to travel to church.

Finally, Buddhism is often seen as a welcoming and inclusive community, where people from all walks of life can come together to practice and learn. Although it originated in India, Buddhism developed all over Asia, and is now seen as a truly **global religion**. Compared to other religions that might be seen as unwelcoming to those who are different, this sense of community can be particularly appealing to those who are looking for a spiritual or philosophical home.

います。そうすることで**ストレスを軽減**し、集中力を高め、全体的な幸福感を得ることができるのです。世の中が目まぐるしく変化し困難な時代にある今、特に仕事での居場所を見つけるのに苦労している若者にとって、このマインドフルネスはとても有効です。

　仏教はまた、すべての生き物への**非暴力**と**慈悲**を説いています。この哲学は、多くの仏教徒がライフスタイルの選択肢として菜食主義や（厳格な菜食主義である）ヴィーガニズムを選ぶきっかけになるとともに、健康やフィットネスにも役立っています。仏教は、**知恵**、**悟り**、現実の本質に関する哲学的、そして精神的な教えでもあります。その教えはしばしば洞察力に満ち、示唆に富んでいるとされ、多くの人々が学び、それを体得しようとしています。

　マインドフルネスと同様に、仏教では**瞑想の実践**にも力を入れており、それには多くの身体的、精神的な健康効果があることが科学的に証明されています。瞑想は不安や憂鬱を軽減し、やる気や集中力を高め、穏やかでリラックスした感覚を高めます。これらのテクニックは自宅でもできるため、毎週教会に通うことに興味がない人にとっては魅力的です。

　最後に、仏教は、来る者を拒まない包含的なコミュニティーと見なされ、あらゆる背景を持つ人が集まり、修行し学ぶことができる宗教と考えられています。インドで発祥して以降アジア全域に広がった仏教は、今では真に**グローバルな宗教**となりました。異質な人々を歓迎しないように映る他の宗教と比べて、仏教の共同体意識は、精神的、哲学的なより所を探している人々にとって特に魅力的なのです。

## National Holidays

The United States has **ten official federal holidays** each year. These holidays are established by Congress and apply to federal workers and many private company employees as well. Here's a brief explanation of each of the ten national holidays in the United States.

| | |
|---|---|
| **New Year's Day** (January 1st) | Marks the start of the new year and is celebrated with parades, parties, and fireworks displays. |
| **Martin Luther King Jr. Day** (Third Monday in January) | Honors the life and achievements of civil rights leader Martin Luther King Jr. |
| **Presidents' Day** (Third Monday in February) | Celebrates the birthdays of George Washington and Abraham Lincoln, two of the most famous and important presidents in US history. |
| **Memorial Day** (Last Monday in May) | Remembers the men and women who died while serving in the US military. |
| **Independence Day** (July 4th) | Celebrates the signing of the Declaration of Independence on July 4, 1776, which was when the United States officially broke away from the British Empire. |
| **Labor Day** (First Monday in September) | Appreciates the contributions of workers in the American economy. |
| **Columbus Day*** (Second Monday in October) | This holiday celebrates the arrival of Christopher Columbus in the Americas in 1492. |
| **Veterans Day** (November 11th) | This holiday honors all veterans who have served in the US military. It is different from Memorial day in that it applies to all veterans, not just those who were killed while fighting. |
| **Thanksgiving Day** (Fourth Thursday in November) | This is an old-fashioned and traditional holiday celebrating the harvest, and is seen as a time for families to come together and give thanks for what they have in life. There are also some connections to the early American settlers and the Native Americans, but that is ignored by most adults. |
| **Christmas Day** (December 25th) | This holiday celebrates the birth of Jesus Christ and is a time for gift-giving, family gatherings, and religious observances. Most Americans, though, celebrate Christmas as a general winter holiday, with a focus on decorations, food, and family. There is some tension between more traditional Christians and those who celebrate Christmas as a basically non-religious time. |

## 国民の祝日

　アメリカには毎年10日の**公式な連邦祝祭日**があります。これらの祝日は議会で定められ、連邦政府職員や民間企業の職員にも適用されます。ここではアメリカの10の祝祭日について説明します。

| | |
|---|---|
| **元旦**<br>（1月1日） | 新年をスタートする日としてパレードやパーティー、花火大会が行われます。 |
| **キング牧師記念日**<br>（1月第3月曜日） | 公民権運動の指導者マーティン・ルーサー・キング・ジュニアの生涯と功績を称える日です。 |
| **大統領の日**<br>（2月第3月曜日） | アメリカ史上最も有名で重要な2人の大統領であるジョージ・ワシントンとエイブラハム・リンカーンの誕生日を祝う日です。 |
| **戦没将兵追悼記念日**<br>（5月最終月曜日） | アメリカ軍として戦死した男女を追悼する日です。 |
| **独立記念日**<br>（7月4日） | アメリカ合衆国が正式に大英帝国から脱退した1776年7月4日の独立宣言調印を祝う日です。 |
| **勤労感謝の日**<br>（9月第1月曜日） | アメリカ経済における労働者の貢献を称える日です。 |
| **コロンブス記念日***<br>（10月第2月曜日） | 1492年のクリストファー・コロンブスによるアメリカ大陸到着を祝う日です。 |
| **退役軍人の日**<br>（11月11日） | アメリカ軍に従事した全ての退役軍人を称える日です。戦死した退役軍人だけでなく、全ての退役軍人を称えるという点で戦没将兵追悼記念日とは異なります。 |
| **感謝祭**<br>（11月第4木曜日） | 収穫を祝うための歴史ある伝統的な祝日で、家族が集まり日々の生活に感謝する日とされています。初期のアメリカ入植者やネイティブ・アメリカンとも関連がありますが、それらを意識している人はほとんどいません。 |
| **クリスマス**<br>（12月25日） | イエス・キリストの誕生を祝ってプレゼントを交換し、家族で集まり、宗教的な行事を行う日です。ただ、ほとんどのアメリカ人はクリスマスを飾り付けや食事をし、家族と過ごす一般的な冬の休日として捉えています。伝統的なキリスト教徒と、基本的に無宗教でクリスマスを祝う人々との間には、多少緊張関係があります。 |

***Useful Note**  Columbus Day has become controversial in recent years, given Columbus's violent treatment of indigenous peoples. For that reason, many Americans will refer to Columbus Day as Indigenous People's Day.

***役立ちメモ**　コロンブス記念日は近年、コロンブスが先住民を虐殺していた史実があることから、物議を醸しています。そのため、多くのアメリカ人はこの日を「先住民の日」と呼びます。

# 3 Politics in the US

**Key Words** Federal, Executive, Legislative, Judicial, Veto, Electoral College, Ordinance

## Federal and State

The **federal and state government system** of the United States is one in which power is divided between a central government (the federal government) and individual state governments. This system is also known as **federalism**.

The United States Constitution first described the framework for this system, with the federal government being responsible for matters that affect the country as a whole, while the state governments handle more **local matters**.

The federal government is composed of three branches: the **executive branch**, the **legislative branch**, and the **judicial branch**. The President is the head of the executive branch, with the Department of State (handling foreign policy), the Department of Defense, and the Department of Justice. The legislative branch is composed of the **Senate and the House of Representatives**, and is responsible for creating laws. The judicial branch is responsible for interpreting the law and deciding if certain laws follow the Constitution. It is composed of the Supreme Court and lower federal courts.

Each state has its own government, which is also divided into the three branches mentioned above. The **governor** is the head of the executive branch, which includes the departments of education,

# 3 アメリカの政治

................................................................

**キーワード** 連邦、行政、立法、司法、拒否権、選挙人団、条例

## 連邦と州

　アメリカの**連邦・州政府体制**においては、中央政府（連邦政府）と各州政府の間で権力が分割されています。この体制はまた、**連邦制**とも呼ばれます。

　アメリカ合衆国憲法では、最初にこの制度の枠組みが説明されており、連邦政府は国全体に影響する事柄に責任を持ち、州政府はより**地方的な事柄**を扱うと明記されています。

　連邦政府は**行政府、立法府、司法府**の3つから成ります。大統領は国務省（外交政策を扱う）、国防総省、司法省がある行政の長です。立法府は**上院**と**下院**から成り、法律を制定する役割があります。司法府は法律の解釈、また特定の法律が憲法に準じているかを決定する役割があり、最高裁判所と下級連邦裁判所で構成されています。

国章

1776年に創設のアメリカ合衆国連邦政府は、首都ワシントンD.C.（コロンビア特別区）にある。ワシントンには、ホワイトハウス、連邦議会議事堂、最高裁判所など主要な政府機関が集まっている。

　各州には独自の政府があり、その政府も前述のような3つの部門に分かれています。**州知事**は教育、交通、保健部門を有する行政の長です。それ以外の立法や司法部門

transportation, and health. Outside of that, the state legislative and judicial branches function much how they do at the federal level.

The federal and state governments have overlapping powers, but there are also areas in which one government has **full control**. For example, the federal government has the power to regulate economic activities among states, while the states have the power to **regulate commerce** within their borders.

Overall, the federal and state government system of the United States is designed to balance the power of the central government with the rights and responsibilities of individual states. This system allows for a certain level of power for individual states while still maintaining a strong central government to oversee matters that affect the entire country. There have been a number of conflicts between state and federal government over the years, the most significant being the Civil War. In recent years, debates over topics such as **abortion** and **gun ownership** have also centered on the rights that states do or do not have to make laws affecting their citizens.

## President and Congress

The relationship between the President of the United States and **Congress** is complicated. Congress has the power to make laws, but the President has the power to put those laws into action. Without a good relationship between the two, it is hard for the country to operate effectively.

The President also has the power to "**veto**" bills passed by Congress. In other words, even if Congress votes to make a new law, the President has the power to cancel it. However, if 2/3 of Congress agrees, they can move pass the President's veto. The President can also propose new laws to Congress and use their own powers to take action. Exactly how much action the President should be allowed to take **without the approval of Congress** has

も、連邦の基準と同じように機能します。

　連邦政府と州政府の権限は重複していますが、一方の政府が**権限の全て**を握っている分野もあります。例えば、連邦政府は州の間での経済活動を規制する権限を有していますが、州政府は州内の**商取引を規制**する権限を有しています。

　概して、アメリカの連邦政府と州政府の制度は、中央政府の権力と各州の権利や責任のバランスがとれるように配慮されています。この制度は、各州に一定の権限を与えながらも、一方では国全体に関わる事項を監督する強力な中央政府を維持しています。州と連邦政府との間には長年にわたり多くの衝突がありましたが、最も重大だったのは南北戦争です。近年では**人口妊娠中絶や銃の所持**といった問題をめぐり、市民に影響を与える法律の制定に州が権限を持つか否かが争点となっています。

## 大統領と議会

　アメリカ合衆国大統領と**議会**の関係は複雑です。議会には法律を制定する権限がありますが、大統領にはその法律を実行に移す権限があります。両者の関係が良好でなければ、国を円滑に運営することが難しいのです。

　大統領はまた、議会が可決した法案に対し「**拒否権**」を発動する権限も持っています。つまり、たとえ議会が新しい法律の制定を決議しても、大統領にはそれを取り消す権限があるのです。とはいえ、議会の3分の2が賛成すれば、大統領の拒否権を覆すことができます。大統領はまた、新しい法律を議会に提案し、自らの権限のもとで実行することも可能です。大統領が**議会の承認なしに**、実

連邦と州（地方）と言えば、FBI（連邦捜査局）と地元警察（例えばNYPD＝ニューヨーク警察）にも対立があることがある。FBIは基本的に国内の治安維持を担うが、時に複数の州にわたる広域事件も担当する。そうした場合、地元警察と捜査法、法の解釈などで対立するのだ。

led to arguments many times over throughout the history of the United States.

Congress is limited by the fact that it is not a single group. New laws must pass both the Senate and House before they can be sent to the President for signature, so if the two chambers are controlled by different political parties (for example, a Democratic Senate and a Republican House of Representatives) there will be difficulty agreeing on **what laws to pass**.

There are often disagreements and tensions between the President and Congress, as well as within congress itself, but ultimately they must find ways to work together to govern the country.

## What is the Electoral College?

The **Electoral College** is the system used in the United States to elect its President and Vice President. When the **presidential election** happens, the candidate who receives the most **total votes** does not necessarily become president. Instead, "**electors**" from each state get to vote for the presidential candidate that receives the most votes in their state. Who electors actually are and how they are chosen is complicated, but you can think of it as a system where each state is worth a certain number of points. The candidate who receives a majority of the **electoral votes** (points from states) becomes the President.

While the Electoral College system has been in place since the adoption of the U.S. Constitution in 1787, it has been criticized throughout history. One of the most common criticisms of the Electoral College is that it gives too much influence to smaller states. In theory, each state gets a certain number of electors based on their population, but smaller states are given more electoral votes per person than larger states. As a result, a candidate can become president by winning the electoral vote even if they lose the popular vote, which seems unfair to many Americans.

質どの程度の権限が許されるかは、アメリカの歴史の中で幾度となく議論されてきました。

　議会は単一のグループであってはならないとされています。署名のために大統領へ提出される新しい法律は、上院と下院の両方を通過していなければならず、両院が異なる政党（例えば、上院が民主党で下院が共和党）に支配されている場合は、**法律を通過させる**ための合意が難しくなります。

　大統領と議会の間、また議会内でも意見の相違や緊張は度々見られますが、最終的には国を統治するための方法を協力して見つけることが重要です。

## 選挙人団とは？

　選挙人団とは、大統領と副大統領を選出するためにアメリカで用いられている制度です。**大統領選挙**では、**総得票数**が最も多い候補者が大統領になるわけではありません。実際は、各州の「選挙人」が、その州で最も多くの票を獲得した候補者に投票をします。誰がどのように選挙人に選ばれるかは複雑なため、各州に一定数のポイントが与えられていると考えれば良いでしょう。**選挙人による投票**（州からのポイント）の過半数を獲得した候補者が大統領になります。

　選挙人団制度は、1787年にアメリカ合衆国憲法が採択されて以来、変わらず実施されてきましたが、その歴史を通じて批判もされてきました。選挙人団制度に対して最もよく聞かれる批判のひとつは、小さな州に影響力を与えすぎるということです。というのも、各州はその人口に応じて一定数の選挙人を獲得しますが、理論上、小さな州は大きな州に比べ一人当たりの選挙人の数が多くなります。その結果、一般投票で敗けた候補者が、選挙人投票で勝利すれば大統領になれることから、多くのアメリカ人はこれを不公平だと感じています。

副大統領は、大統領候補によって指名され、その後党の全国大会で正式に承認される。選挙人団による選挙では本人に直接投票するのではなく、各政党が出す選挙人名簿に投票することになるので、間接的に副大統領候補も大統領と共に選出されることになる。

In most states, the candidate who gets the most votes in that state gets all of its electoral votes. This means that a candidate can win a state by a tiny amount and receive all of its electoral votes, even if a large percentage of the state's voters supported the other candidate. This has led to criticism that the system **does not accurately represent the will of the people**.

Furthermore, most states are either strongly Democratic or Republican, which means that the Electoral College has been criticized for creating a system where candidates focus their campaigns and resources on the handful of "**swing states**" that are likely to determine the outcome of the election. This means that the concerns and issues of voters in other states are often overlooked or ignored. After all, if it doesn't matter whether a candidate wins a state with 60 or 80% of the vote, why bother?

Although rare, there have even been situations where electors have voted against their state's **popular vote**. This has led to questions about the **legitimacy of the Electoral College** in general and whether it should be reformed or eliminated, since such abuses in the future could threaten the outcome of an entire election.

These controversies have led to ongoing debates about the need to change or even remove the Electoral College system. While some argue that it is an important part of US politics, others believe that it is **outdated and unfair**. Ultimately, any changes to the Electoral College system would require changing the Constitution, which is an extremely difficult process.

---

 **Useful Note**

Sometimes Americans will use "veto" as a slang term, meaning they are refusing to agree with a suggestion. For example, a wife might "veto" her husband's plan to get pizza for dinner.

　ほとんどの州では、その州で一番多くの票を獲得した候補者が、すべての選挙人の票を獲得します。これでは、州の有権者の大多数が他の候補者を支持していたとしても、わずかな票差で勝利した候補者が、その州全ての選挙人の票を獲得できるのです。そのため、この制度は**民意を正確に反映していない**という批判があります。

　さらに、ほとんどの州では民主党か共和党のどちらかが強いため、候補者によって選挙結果が左右されやすい一握りの「**スイング・ステート（激戦州）**」に選挙キャンペーンや資金が集中されるシステムができあがっており、それを選挙人団が創り出しているという批判もあります。つまり、その他の州の有権者の関心事や問題点は、往々にして見過ごされたり無視されたりするのです。結局のところ、候補者が60%の投票数で勝利しても、80%の投票数で勝利しても、結果が同じなのであればそんなに悩むこともないのでは？

　ごくまれに、選挙人団が自州の**一般投票**に対し反対投票をすることがあります。このような権利の乱用は、将来の選挙結果全体をも脅かしかねないことから、**選挙人団の正当性**や、改革または廃止についても議論されています。

　このような論争により、選挙人団制度の変更、あるいは撤廃さえも視野に入れた議論が続けられています。アメリカ政治において選挙人団制度は重要な役割を果たすと言う人もいれば、**時代遅れで不平等**だと言う人もいます。ただ、選挙人団制度に手を加えるには憲法の改正が必要なため、非常に困難なプロセスとなることは確かです。

選挙結果を左右する可能性のあるスイング・ステートは、一般的にフロリダ州、オハイオ州、ペンシルベニア州、ミシガン州、ウィスコンシン州、ノースカロライナ州、アリゾナ州、ジョージア州、アイオワ州、ネバダ州などが挙げられる。これらの州には多大な資源と関心を集中し、選挙キャンペーンが行われる。

---

★ **役立ちメモ**

　アメリカ人は何かの提案に同意しないときに、「拒否権（veto）」をスラングとして使うことがあります。例えば、夕食にピザを食べようと言う夫の提案に、妻が「veto」と言ったりします。

## Two-party system (Democrats and Republicans)

The United States has **two major political parties**, the Democrats and the Republicans. In this system, the two parties typically hold most of the political power and influence, and other political parties struggle to make their voices heard.

The two parties have changed greatly since their origins in the American Civil War. Today, the Democratic Party generally supports "**progressive** (focused on positive change)" policies, such as increased government control over the economy, growth of social programs, and support for minority groups. The Republican Party generally supports "**conservative** (traditional)" policies, such as limited government control of the economy, lower taxes, and a strong national defense.

The other political parties in the United States typically struggle to gain significant political influence due to a variety of factors, including the structure of the electoral system, the dominance of the two major parties in media, and the belief that candidates from other parties are not worth voting for.

### Red or Blue?

The terms "red state" and "blue state" gained popularity during the 2000 United States presidential election, when the American media began using them to describe the **electoral map**. Red states typically vote for Republican candidates, while blue states typically vote for Democratic candidates.

It is worth noting that the terms "red state" and "blue state" are not **official designations**, and there is some flexibility in how they are used. Additionally, while some states are often referred to as "solidly" red or blue, there is often considerable **political diversity** within each state. For instance, urban areas tend to be more blue and rural areas tend to be more red. Finally, the **political leanings** of a given state can shift over time, with some states becoming more reliably red or blue

## 二大政党制（民主党と共和党）

　アメリカには民主党と共和党という**二大政党**があります。この制度では、主にこの二政党が政治権力と影響力の大半を握っており、他の政党は自分たちの声を届けることに苦戦しています。

　この二つの政党は、南北戦争に端を発して以来、大きく変化してきました。今日、民主党は主に「**進歩的**（前向きな変化に焦点を当てた）」な政策を支持し、経済に対する政府関与の強化や社会制度の拡大、マイノリティー・グループへの支援などを掲げています。共和党は政府による経済への介入の制限、税金の引き下げ、国防の強化をはじめとした、主に「**保守的**（伝統的）」な政策を支持しています。

　その他の政党は一般的に、選挙制度の構造や二大政党によるメディアの独占、また他の政党の候補者は投票に値しないという思い込みなど、様々な理由によって政治的に十分な影響力を持てないでいます。

第三極の政党として出てきた党としては、ホイッグ党、自由土壌党、ポピュリスト党、進歩党、リバタリアン党、緑の党などがある。

### 赤か青か？

　「レッドステート（赤い州）」と「ブルーステート（青い州）」という表現は、2000年のアメリカ大統領選挙でアメリカのメディアが**選挙地図**を表すために使い始めたことで広まりました。赤い州は共和党に、青い州は民主党に投票することを表しています。

　「赤い州」と「青い州」は**公式な用語**というわけではなく、その使い方は柔軟です。さらに、「絶対に」赤か青と言われている州であっても、その州内ではかなりの**政治的揺らぎ**があることがあります。また、都市部では青が多く、田舎に行くほど赤が多い傾向もあります。結局のところ、州の**政治的傾向**はその時々で変化するので、赤または青が確実な州もあれば、両者がより競争的になる州もあるとい

and others becoming more competitive.

Despite this, the terms "red state" and "blue state" have become widely recognized slang for describing the **political geography** of the United States. They are often used in discussions of American politics, maps of the country, and are frequently used by members of the media to describe the likely outcome of elections.

## Judicial system (composition of courts and jury system)

The United States **judicial system** is made up of **courts and judges** responsible for interpreting the law, deciding legal cases, and applying punishments within the United States. It consists of federal and state courts.

At the federal level, the judicial system is run by the United States Supreme Court, which is the highest court in the country. Below the Supreme Court are the lower federal courts, which include the United States Courts of Appeals and the United States District Courts. The **courts of appeals** are responsible for judging cases that have already happened, while the **district courts** are responsible for hearing original cases.

The federal courts are responsible for interpreting **federal laws**, including the United States Constitution. They also have the power to judge cases involving **federal crimes**, disputes between states, and cases involving parties from different states or countries.

At the state level, each state has its own judicial system. The highest court in each state is usually called the **state supreme court**. Below that are a system of smaller courts, but like the supreme court, they have the power to judge whether certain people or groups have violated the **laws of the state** or the **state constitutions**.

Overall, the United States judicial system is designed to be

うことです。

　とはいえ、「赤い州」と「青い州」とい
う表現はアメリカの**政治的地理**を表す俗
語として広く認知されています。アメリカ
の政治や地図について議論する際に使わ
れることが多く、メディアが選挙結果を
報じるときにも頻繁に使われています。

直近の上院選挙の勝者を
色分けした地図
赤は赤い州＝共和党
黒は青い州＝民主党

## 司法制度（裁判所の構成と陪審制度）

　アメリカの**司法制度**は、国内における法の解釈、訴訟
事件の判決、刑罰の適用を担う**裁判所および裁判官**で構
成されています。それには連邦裁判所と州裁判所があり
ます。

　連邦レベルでは、国の最高裁判所にあたる連邦最高裁
判所が司法制度を運営しています。最高裁判所の下には
連邦控訴裁判所と連邦地方裁判所からなる連邦下級裁
判所が設置されています。**控訴裁判所**がすでに判決済み
の審理を担当するのに対し、**地方裁判所**は第一審の審理
を担当します。

連邦最高裁判所

　連邦裁判所は、合衆国憲法を含む**連邦法**の解釈を行い
ます。また、**連邦犯罪**に関わる事件や州間の論争、異な
る州や国の当事者が関わるケースを裁く権利を有してい
ます。

　州レベルでは、それぞれの州に独自の司法制度があり
ます。各州の最高裁判所は通常、**州最高裁判所**と呼ばれ
ます。その下に小さな裁判所がいくつもありますが、こ
れらの裁判所も最高裁判所と同様に、特定の人々や集団
による**州法**や**州憲法**の違反を判断する役目を担っていま
す。

　概して、アメリカの司法制度は、政治的な影響を受け

independent of the **other branches** of government, ensuring that the law remains neutral, without political influence.

### Are Supreme Court Justices Great?

The Supreme Court is composed of nine "**justices**", or **judges**, who are chosen by the President and agreed on by the Senate. In that way, they are perhaps the most powerful Americans in government who are not elected by the people.

**Supreme Court justices** are chosen for life, which means they serve on the Court until they retire or die. This is meant to protect them from political pressure and make sure they judge the law independently.

These justices have incredible power. They are responsible for interpreting the meaning of the Constitution, and they can reject laws or actions that they think go against the **basic values** of the United States. The Supreme Court also has the final word on **legal disagreements** between the federal government and the states or between different branches of the federal government.

Supreme Court justices are appointed based on their education, career experience, and **legal views**. They are expected to be clear and logical in their decision-making, and their decisions are closely watched by those who study the law, politicians, and the American people.

## Local Politics (Laws by Region)

Supreme Court decisions and presidential elections may dominate the national news, but local politics tend to have more of an actual effect on the life of the average American. Local officials like mayors and **city council members** make decisions about important issues such as education, public safety, transportation, and housing.

Beyond that, there are **regional laws** that apply to specific geographic areas. Regional laws are created by state and local

るEnExpr... 

ることなく法の中立性が保たれるよう、政府の**他の部門**から**独立**するように配置されています。

## 最高裁判所判事は偉いの？

　最高裁判所は9人の「**判事**」で構成され、大統領が選任した後、上院が承認します。そうした意味では、彼らはおそらく国民によって選出されない、政府で最も大きな権力を持つアメリカ人なのです。

　**最高裁判所判事**の仕事は終身制で、自ら引退するか亡くなるまで法廷での義務を果たします。これは彼らが政治的圧力から守られ、独立した立場で法を判断できるようにするためです。

　こうした判事には驚くほどの権限が与えられています。彼らには憲法の意味を解釈する責任があり、アメリカの**基本的価値**に反すると考えられる法律や行動を拒否する権利があります。連邦政府と州、あるいは連邦政府の異なる部門同士の**法的意見の相違**についても、最高裁が最終決定権を握っています。

　最高裁判事は学歴、職歴、また**法的な見解**を考慮して任命されます。明確で理論的な意思決定が期待され、その決定は法律を研究する人々や政治家、またアメリカ国民によって注意深く見守られています。

2022年4月、ケタンジ・ブラウン・ジャクソン氏が、最高裁の233年の歴史の中で初めて黒人女性の判事となった。2024年現在の最高裁長官は、ジョン・グローバー・ロバーツ・ジュニア氏である。9人の判事は現在、保守派判事が5人、リベラル派判事が4人という構成になっている。

## 地方政治（地域ごとの法律）

　最高裁の決定や大統領選挙は全国的なニュースで取り沙汰されますが、実際のところ、一般のアメリカ人の生活により影響を与えるのは地方政治です。市長や**市議会議員**のような地方公務員は教育、治安、交通、住宅などの重要な課題について決裁します。

　その他にも、特定の地域に適用される**地域法**があります。地域法とは、豊かな森林を持つ地域の環境問題や、短

governments to deal with issues that are unique to a particular area, such as environmental concerns in a place that has a lot of forests, or economic development in an area that has attracted many new businesses in a short time. By definition, these laws vary from state to state and even from one city or county to another.

For example, in some states, it is legal to purchase and possess certain types of guns, while in others, such as California, there are **more strict rules** about gun ownership. Similarly, the legal age to purchase and consume alcohol varies from state to state, with some states allowing it at 18 while most require young adults to wait until they are 21.

In addition, local governments may create "**ordinances**", which are local laws about specific concerns within the community. These may include rules about parking, noise levels, pet ownership, and what types of businesses are allowed.

It's important to remember that while regional laws are all different, they cannot directly go against federal laws and the Constitution of the United States. Therefore, if a regional law conflicts with a federal law, the federal law wins. Of course, local governments and police may choose not to force their citizens to follow federal laws that they disagree with, so the situation is even more complicated than it might seem.

## About the School District

There is perhaps no part of local politics more important to the average American than the **running of a school district**.

A school district is an area within a state or region that is responsible for providing **public education** services to students. School districts are typically run by a group of elected members who are responsible for making decisions related to the district's educational programs, budget, and employees. Most of the money for a school district typically

期間で新規事業誘致を行った地域の経済開発など、その地域特有の問題に対処するために、州や地方自治体が制定する法律です。当然のことながら、これらの法律は州ごと、また市や郡によっても異なります。

　例えば、特定の銃の購入や所持を合法としている州がある一方で、カリフォルニア州のように銃の所有を**厳しく規制**している州もあります。同様に、アルコールの購入や摂取についての法定年齢も、州によって違いがあり、ほとんどの州では21歳まで待たなければならないのに対し、18歳で許可している州もあります。

　さらに、地方自治体は地域社会での特定の懸念事項について、地域法としての「**条例**」を制定することがあります。こうした条例には駐車場、騒音レベル、ペットの飼育、事業の許認可などの規定が含まれます。

　地域法は地域によって異なりますが、連邦法や合衆国憲法に直接、抵触することはできないということも覚えておくべきでしょう。つまり、地域法と連邦法が対立するときは、連邦法が優先されます。もちろん、地方自治体や警察は、自分たちが賛成しない連邦法を市民に守らせようとはしないため、状況は見かけ以上に複雑になることがあります。

### 学区について

　一般のアメリカ人にとって、**学区の運営**ほど重要な地方政治はないでしょう。

　学区とは、州またはその地域で、生徒に**公の教育**を提供する責任がある地区のことです。学区は通常、選挙で選ばれたメンバーによって運営され、地域の教育プログラム、予算、職員に関する決裁を行います。その資金のほとんどは、学区内で収められた**固定資産税**でまかなわれます。そ

comes from the **property taxes** collected within its boundaries. As a result, parents and residents within the school district tend to have very strong opinions about how their tax money is spent.

School districts vary widely in terms of quality and resources. Some districts are wealthy and able to provide a wide range of academic and **out of school opportunities**, while others struggle with limited money, leading to vast differences in educational outcomes. School choice is an issue that people often debate, because some believe that parents should have the right to choose the school that best fits their child's needs, while others argue that school choice only causes struggling schools to do worse while wealthy schools do better.

The role of standardized testing is also a source of debate. While some people believe that standardized tests are a useful tool for measuring student progress and making sure that schools are educating students properly, others argue that they can lead to **a narrow focus on test preparation** rather than broader educational goals.

Given the rise in gun violence over the last 20 years, school safety is a growing concern for many parents and teachers. Recent school shootings and other crimes have led to calls for **increased security**, but some people worry that guards and other security systems can create a sense of fear and get in the way of the educational process.

Finally, there is a continuing discussion about how best to prepare students for success in the 21st century. With the spread of computer technology into every part of our lives, some push for a focus on **STEM education** (science, technology, engineering, and math), while others argue that a **well-rounded education** including reading and writing, social sciences, and arts is needed for developing critical thinking skills and preparing students for a changing world.

のため、学区の保護者や住民は自分たちの税金の使われ方について、強い意見を持つ傾向があります。

　学区は、その質や資源という点で大きな違いがあります。多様な学びや**校外学習**を取り入れている裕福な学区もあれば、限られた資金で奮闘している学区もあり、教育成果にも大きな違いが見られます。学校選択はよく議論される問題で、保護者は自分の子供のニーズに合った最適な学校を選ぶ権利を持つべきだ、という意見がある一方で、学校を選択できるようにすると裕福な学校はますます良くなり、そうでない学校はより悪くなる、と主張する人もいます。

　標準テスト(SAT)の役割も、よく議論されます。このテストは、生徒の学力の向上を測定し、学校が生徒を適切に教育しているかを確認するために有効なツールである、という意見がある一方で、教育目標が広範囲ではなく、**テスト対策の偏重**につながるという意見もあります。

　ここ20年間の銃乱射事件の増加を受けて、学校の安全対策も多くの保護者や教師たちにとってますます大きな関心事となっています。近年の校内での銃乱射事件やその他の犯罪により、**安全性の強化**を求める声が高まる中、警備員やその他の警備システムが恐怖感を煽り、勉強の妨げにならないかと心配する人もいます。

　最後に、21世紀に生徒が成果を上げるためにはどのような準備したら良いのか、という議論が続いています。生活の至るところにコンピューター・テクノロジーが浸透している中、**STEM教育**（科学、技術、工学、数学）に重点を置くべきという意見もあれば、論理的思考を養い、変化する世界に対応できる生徒を育てるには、読み書き、社会科学、芸術など**総合的な学習**に重点を置くべきだという意見もあります。

# アメリカの移民の
# 歴史と現在

西への開拓者は幌馬車に家財道具を
のせ移動した。ときには急流を筏で渡
ることもあった。

　メルティング・ポットとい
う言葉は「人種のるつぼ」と
訳します。アメリカは文字通り「人種のるつぼ」なのです。

　先住民であるネイティブ・アメリカンを除けば、この国の住人はほぼ海外か
らの移住者か、その子孫です。例えば、ニューヨークは17世紀前半にはニュ
ーアムステルダムと呼ばれていました。最初の移住者がオランダ人だったか
らです。その後、同地がイギリスに占領されニューヨークと改名されました。

　アメリカの多くの都市にはこのように移民を象徴するような名前がついて
います。

　カリフォルニアからアメリカ南西部にかけての都市がスペイン語の名残を
とどめているのは、メキシコを経由してスペイン系の人々が入植したからに
他なりません。さらに、南部の都市、ニューオーリンズは「オルレアン」とい
うフランスの名前に由来しています。実際ニューオーリンズからミシシッピ
川をさかのぼり、カナダに至る地域は19世紀初頭までフランスの植民地でし
た。フランスを統治していたナポレオンが、この地を1803年にアメリカ合衆
国に売却したのでした。ルイジアナという名前も、フランスのルイ王朝の土
地という意味に他なりません。

　このように、アメリカは当初ヨーロッパ各地からの移民によって大きくなり
ました。彼らの多くは母国での貧困や迫害を逃れてきた人々で、特に初期の
移民者の多くは、カトリック系の国で迫害されていたプロテスタントでした。

その後、東欧やロシアなどから、ユダヤ系の人々も移住してきます。カトリック系の移住者も多くいます。その代表的な例が、イギリスの植民地政策のなかで苦しんでいたアイルランド系や、内戦などで生活を脅かされていた南イタリアの人々でした。彼らは、19世紀の半ばから20世紀にかけて大挙して新大陸の土を踏みました。そのため、19世紀の半ばには、東海岸の都市はそうした移民でいっぱいになったのです。

　そこで、国が奨励したのが中西部からカリフォルニアやオレゴンなどへの開拓でした。特に、オレゴンはイギリスと領有権を争っていたために、政府は入植者に無償で土地を提供することで、既成事実をつくろうとします。人々は6カ月以上かけて未開の地を横断してオレゴンに向かったのです。1840年代ごろのことでした。当時の人口の十人に一人がこの開拓に挑み、その中の十人に一人が旅の途中で命を落としたという過酷な旅だったのです。

　一方、同じ頃、南部では大地を開拓するために、アフリカから連れてこられた奴隷が使役されます。黒人がこうした凄惨な過去を背負っていることは周知の事実です。

　やがて、19世紀後半になると中国や日本からの移住者も増え始めます。1869年に開通した大陸横断鉄道の工事を担ったのも中国からの移民でした。

　しかし、ヨーロッパ系の人々からみれば、こうしたアジアからの移民は自らの土地や職業を奪いかねない危険な存在にうつります。また、南北戦争によって解放された黒人も、人種的偏見に加えてこうした既得権を脅かす存在になってしまいます。

　同じヨーロッパ系の人々でも、カトリック系やユダヤ系の人々と、プロテスタント系の人々の間にも拭えない対立がありました。移民の力によってアメリカ社会が豊かになった以上、異なる人種との共存の課題は最も大切で、無視することのできないテーマなのです。

　現在、アメリカでは全ての差別や偏見を撤廃するために公民権法が定められ、異なる人種や、様々な背景を持つ人々の平等が法的に保障されています。とはいえ、今でも差別に基づく犯罪が報道されているのも事実です。「人種のるつぼ」たるアメリカは、全ての人が集まり多様性を尊重して社会を発展できるかどうかの実験場であるといっても過言ではないのです。

# Part 2

# Let's Go to America

*Preparing for a Visit*

# アメリカへ行こう

出発前の準備

# VISA or Permanent Residence/Citizenship?

**Key Words** Visa, Undocumented, Deportation, Waiver, Green Card, Lottery, Citizenship

## To enter the country

Everyone who travels to America needs a visa. There are two main types: immigrant visas and non-immigrant visas.

**Immigrant visas** are for individuals who wish to live in the United States for a long time. These visas are often called "green cards" because they are usually printed on green-colored paper. There are a variety of ways to get an immigrant visa, including support from families or businesses in the United States, and the **Diversity Immigrant Visa Program**, which randomly chooses individuals from countries with low rates of immigration to the United States.

**Non-immigrant visas** are for those who wish to temporarily visit, study, work, or do business in the United States. These visas are issued for **a set period of time**, which can range from a few days to several years, depending on the type of visa and the reason for traveling to the United States. Some common types of non-immigrant visas include the B-1/B-2 tourist visa, the F-1 student visa, the H-1B work visa, and the J-1 exchange visitor visa.

To get either type of visa, individuals must fill out a **visa application** and go through a selection process, which includes an interview with a government worker at a US office in the country the person wishes to travel from. The process for getting a visa can

# ビザか永住権 / 市民権か？

**キーワード** ビザ、書類のない、国外追放、免除、グリーンカード、抽選、市民権

## 入国するには

　アメリカに渡航する人は誰でもビザが必要です。ビザには主に、移民ビザと非移民ビザの2種類があります。

　**移民ビザ**は、アメリカでの長期滞在を希望する個人向けのビザです。このビザは緑色の紙に印刷されるため「グリーンカード」と呼ばれています。移民ビザを取得するには、アメリカにいる家族や企業からサポートを受ける方法や、移民率の低い国から個人を無作為に選出する**移民多様化ビザ抽選プログラム**に応募する方法などがあります。

　**非移民ビザ**はアメリカに一時的に訪問、就学、就労、またはビジネスをする個人向けのビザです。ビザの種類やアメリカへの渡航理由に応じて数日から数年までの**一定期間**について発給されます。一般的な非移民ビザには、B-1/B-2観光ビザ、F-1学生ビザ、H-1B就労ビザ、J-1交流訪問者ビザなどがあります。

　どのビザを取得する場合も、個人は**ビザの申請書**を記入した上で、渡航元の国にあるアメリカの事務所で政府職員と面接をするなどの手続きが必要です。ビザを取得するための手順は個人の出身地や申請するビザの種類、

グリーンカード抽選は毎年10月から1カ月程度の間が応募期間で、翌年の5月ごろに当選の結果が発表される。

be different depending on the where an individual is coming from, the type of visa being applied for, and other factors. It's important to note that having a visa does not make it certain that a person will be able to enter the United States; individuals must still go through the **immigration system** upon arrival in the United States.

## Unlawful Aliens

**Illegal immigration** is one of the most debated issues in the United States. The arguments surrounding illegal immigration in the US are often heated and polarized, with different groups holding different views on the subject. There isn't even agreement about what people who enter and live in the United States illegally should be called. Some refer to those people as "**undocumented immigrants**", others say "illegal aliens", while most simply refer to them as "illegal immigrants".

When people discuss illegal immigration in the United States, they tend to talk about the economy.

It is a well-known fact that illegal immigration **provides a source of cheap labor** that benefits many Americans. After all, illegal immigrants from poor countries take on jobs that many Americans are not willing to do, and that helps keep the **cost of goods and services** low. However, having a supply of people willing to work for less money drives down wages for low-skilled workers and puts a strain on public services, such as healthcare and education, since illegal immigrants generally do not pay income taxes.

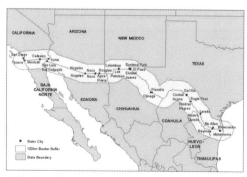

国境の壁の地図

その他の要因によって異なります。また、ビザを取得したからといって、確実にアメリカに入国できるわけではありません。アメリカに入国する際にも、**入国審査**を受けなければなりません。

## 不法滞在者について

　**不法移民の問題**はアメリカで最も議論されていることのひとつです。不法移民についての議論は、各グループにそれぞれ異なる見方があるため、しばしば白熱し、極論になりがちです。アメリカに不法入国をし、滞在し続ける人々のことをどう呼ぶのかさえ、意見が一致していません。「**書類のない移民**」と呼ぶ人もいれば、「**不法な外国人**」と呼ぶ人もいますが、たいていはただ単に「**不法移民**」と呼んでいます。

　アメリカの不法移民についての議論になると、人々はよく経済について言及します。

　不法移民が**安価な労働力を供給**することで、多くのアメリカ人が利益を得ていることは周知の事実です。貧しい国から来た人が、アメリカ人のやりたがらない仕事を引き受けることで、**商品やサービスのコスト**が低く抑えられています。しかし、低賃金でも働く人は、たいてい所得税を支

国境の壁

The other issues around immigration are more reflective of different American political views. For example, supporters of stricter immigration policies argue that illegal immigrants are more likely to commit crimes, and that this puts American citizens at risk. However, others point out that illegal immigrants actually have a lower crime rate than the general population. In this case, both sides will often ignore data that does not support their own point.

Some Americans believe illegal immigration is a threat to the safety of America as a country, since it makes it easier for dangerous individuals like terrorists to enter the country. Others argue that the vast majority of illegal immigrants are simply looking for a better life and do not pose a threat to **national security**.

In many ways, the debate comes down to one idea: whether it is good to **deport** illegal immigrants, sending them back to their home countries. Supporters of deportation argue that it is necessary to enforce the rule of law and protect American jobs. However, opponents of deportation argue that it is cruel to break up families and deport people who have been living and working in the United States for years.

Illegal immigration in America is a **moral debate**, in that many of the general facts are agreed on by both sides, but the conclusions about what to do in the face of those facts can be completely different. When speaking to Americans, it is best to be neutral on the topic of illegal immigration if you want to avoid upsetting anyone.

## Visa Waiver Program

The US Government's Visa Waiver Program (VWP) allows citizens from **certain countries** to travel to the United States for business or vacations without obtaining a visa. Instead, travelers must

払っておらず、そのために低技能労働者たちの賃金が下がったり、医療や教育などの公共サービスに負担がかかることもあるのです。

　その他の移民問題は、アメリカの政治的見解の違いをよく反映しています。例えば、移民政策の厳格化を支持する人は、不法移民は犯罪に関わる可能性が高く、そのことでアメリカ市民が危険にさらされると言います。しかし、不法移民は一般市民よりも犯罪率が低いと指摘をする人もいます。この場合、どちらの側もたいていは、自分たちの主張に反するデータを無視しているのです。

　また、不法移民はテロリストのような危険人物の入国を容易にし、アメリカの安全を脅かすと主張する人もいます。ほとんどの不法移民はただ単により良い生活を求めているだけで、**国家の安全保障**を脅かすようなことはないという意見もあります。

　これらの議論は多くの場合ひとつの意見に集約されます。それは、不法移民を**強制送還**し、母国へ送り返すべきかどうか、ということです。強制送還を支持する人は法の支配を強化し、アメリカの雇用を守るべきだと主張します。しかし、強制送還に反対する人は、家族を離れ離れにし、長年アメリカで暮らし働いてきた人々を国外追放するのは残酷だと主張しています。

　アメリカの不法移民についての議論は**道徳的な課題**であり、一般的な事実について、両者の意見は一致しているにも関わらず、それらの事実を前にして何をすべきかについての結論は平行線のままです。アメリカ人との会話で、不法移民について話す際は、誰かの気分を害さないためにも中立の立場でいるのが良さそうです。

## ビザ免除プログラム

　アメリカ政府によるビザ免除プログラム（ＶＷＰ）は、**特定の国**の市民に対してはビザなしでビジネスや休暇目的でアメリカに渡航することを認めるものです。その代わ

apply through the Electronic System for Travel Authorization (ESTA) before they travel.

Currently, there are 39 countries participating in the VWP, including Australia, Canada, France, Germany, Japan, South Korea, and the United Kingdom. To be eligible for the VWP, a country must meet **certain requirements** related to security and police cooperation, passport security, and border management.

Travelers entering the United States under the VWP are allowed to stay for up to 90 days, but they cannot stay beyond that period. They also cannot change their status to another visa category while in the United States.

It's important to note that even if a traveler is eligible for the VWP, they may still **be denied entry** to the United States if they do not meet the admission requirements or if they have a criminal record.

## Student Visa (Visa Requirements)

The student visa program in the United States allows foreign citizens to come to the US and study at high schools or universities. The two most common types of student visas are the F-1 visa and the J-1 visa.

The F-1 visa is intended for students who are interested in academic programs, including language training programs. To receive an F-1 visa, a student must first be accepted by a US school that has permission to work with foreign students. The student must then apply for an F-1 visa at a US embassy (government office) in their home country.

The J-1 visa is for students in programs that promote **cultural exchange** between the US and other countries. To be eligible for a J-1 visa, a student must first be accepted into an exchange program that is approved by the US government.

り、渡航者は渡航前に電子渡航認証システム（ESTA）による申請を行わなければなりません。

　現在、オーストラリア、カナダ、フランス、ドイツ、日本、韓国、英国などを含む39カ国がVWPに参加しています。VWPに入るためには安全面、警察間での協力体制、パスポートの安全性、国境管理などに、**一定の要件**を満たさなければはなりません。

　VWPでアメリカに入国する旅行者は、最長90日間の滞在が認められており、それより長く滞在することはできません。またアメリカに滞在中、他のビザ・カテゴリーに変更することもできません。

　なお、たとえVWPの対象者であっても、入国条件を満たしていなかったり、過去に犯罪歴がある場合は、アメリカへの**入国を拒否される**こともあり得ます。


## 学生ビザの要件

　アメリカの学生ビザプログラムは外国の市民がアメリカに来て、高校や大学で学ぶことを認めています。最も一般的な学生ビザは、F-1ビザとJ-1ビザのふたつです。

　F-1ビザは、語学研修を含む学問的なプログラムに関心のある学生を対象としています。F-1ビザを取得するには、まず留学生の受け入れができるアメリカの学校に入学を認められなければなりません。その後、学生は自国の米国領事館（政府事務所）でF-1ビザを申請します。

　J-1ビザは、アメリカと他国の**文化的交流**を促進するプログラムに参加する学生を対象としています。J-1ビザを取得するには、まずアメリカ政府から承認された交流プログラムへの参加が認められなければなりません。

Both the F-1 and J-1 visas allow students to work on-campus for up to **20 hours per week** while school is in session. Students may also be allowed to get jobs outside of school, such as internships or practical training programs.

It is important to know that obtaining a student visa is a process that can take several months. Applicants must provide documents with information about their family's income, proof of their plans to return to their home country after their studies are complete, and may be required to attend an interview.

## Practical Training

Practical training is a program that allows international students studying in the United States to gain work experience in their fields of study. This program is designed to provide students with an opportunity to apply the academic knowledge they have learned in the classroom to **real-life work settings**.

In the United States, international students who hold F-1 student visas can participate in practical training programs. These programs take two forms: Curricular Practical Training (CPT) and Optional Practical Training (OPT).

Curricular Practical Training (CPT) allows students to work in their field of study while they are still enrolled in school. CPT is usually a required part of the school curriculum, and students must receive academic credit for their work.

Optional Practical Training (OPT) lets students work in their field of study after they have completed their **academic program**. OPT can be used for up to 12 months after graduation, and students can apply for a visa extension if they meet certain requirements.

Just like every other part of the Visa program, this process can take several weeks or months, so it's important for students to plan ahead and apply early.

　F-1ビザ、またはJ-1ビザを持つ学生は、学校の授業が
ある間であれば、**週に20時間**まで校内で働くことができま
す。また、インターンシップやプラクティカルトレーニング
（実務研修）といった学校外での就労も認められています。
　学生ビザの取得には、手続きに数カ月を要することを
忘れてはいけません。また、申請者は家族の収入に関す
る情報や、学業修了後の帰国の予定を示す書類を提出し
なければならず、面接がある場合もあります。

## プラクティカル・トレーニングについて

　プラクティカル・トレーニングは、アメリカで学ぶ留学
生に、専攻分野での実務経験の機会を提供するプログラム
です。教室で学んだ学問的知識を**実際の仕事の場**で生かす
機会を与えることを目的としています。

　F-1ビザを持つ留学生は、このプログラムに参加するこ
とができます。プログラムにはカリキュラー・プラクティ
カルトレーニング（CPT）とオプショナル・プラクティカ
ルトレーニング（OPT）の2種類があります。
　カリキュラー・プラクティカルトレーニング（CPT）は、
まだ在学中の学生に自身の専門分野で働くことを許可す
るものです。CPTはたいてい学校のカリキュラムの一環と
して用意されており、学生には就労による単位の取得が義
務づけられています。
　オプショナル・プラクティカルトレーニング（OPT）は、
学生が自身の**専攻プログラム**を修了した後、その分野で働
くことを許可するものです。OPTは卒業後、最長12カ月
まで有効期間があり、一定の要件を満たせばその後ビザを
延長することもできます。
　他のビザプログラムと同様に、これらは手続きに数週間
から数カ月を要することがあるため、学生は事前の計画と
早めの申請が必要です。

## Work Visa Types and Conditions

There are several types of work visas available in the United States, each with its own set of conditions and requirements. The most common types of work visas are as follows:

**H-1B visa:** This visa is for foreign workers at certain jobs that require at least a college degree. The job must be offered by a US employer, and the foreign worker must have the necessary education, training, and experience to perform the job.

**L-1 visa:** This visa is for international companies to move their employees to the US for a short time. The employee must have worked for the company for at least one year before being eligible for the L-1 visa.

**TN visa:** This visa is for Canadian and Mexican citizens coming to the US to work in certain professional occupations. The job must be listed under the North American Free Trade Agreement (NAFTA), and the applicant must have the necessary qualifications and experience.

**O visa:** This visa is for individuals with **extraordinary ability** or achievement in the arts, sciences, education, business, or athletics. The applicant must have national or international recognition for their achievements.

**P visa:** This visa is for athletes, artists, and entertainers coming to the US to perform in a specific event or competition. The applicant must be recognized nationally or internationally for their talent.

To be eligible for any of these work visas, the applicant must meet **certain requirements**, such as having a job offer from a US employer and passing a medical examination. The specific conditions for each visa are all different, so it is important to speak with a **qualified immigration expert** for assistance.

## 就労ビザの種類と条件

　アメリカの就労ビザにはいくつかの種類があり、それぞれに条件や要件が定められています。最も一般的な就労ビザは以下の通りです。

　**H-1Bビザ**：このビザは少なくとも大学卒業以上の学歴を必要とする特定の職業に従事する、外国人労働者向けのものです。アメリカの雇用主の下で働くことを前提に、労働者は職務を遂行するための教育、訓練、経験を有していなければなりません。

　**L-1ビザ**：このビザは国際的な企業が、社員を短期間アメリカへ移住させるためのものです。L-1ビザを申請するには、社員は少なくとも一年以上その会社で就労していなければなりません。

　**TNビザ**：このビザはカナダとメキシコの国籍を持つ者が、アメリカで特定の専門職に就く際に発給されます。職業は北米自由貿易協定（NAFTA）に記載されているものでなければならず、申請者はその職業に求められる資格や経験を有していなければなりません。

　**Oビザ**：このビザは芸術、科学、教育、ビジネス、スポーツの分野で**並外れた能力**または業績を有する個人向けのものです。申請者は国内や国外において、その業績を認められていなければなりません。

　**Pビザ**：このビザはスポーツ選手、芸術家、芸能人などがアメリカに来て、特定のイベントや競技に参加する時のものです。申請者は国内や国外において、その才能を認められていなければなりません。

　どの就労ビザを取得する場合も、申請者はアメリカの雇用主の下で働くことや、健康に問題がないことなど、一定の**要件**を満さなければなりません。具体的な要件はそれぞれのビザによって異なるため、**資格を持つ移民専門家**に相談すると良いでしょう。

## Route to Permanent Residence

Becoming a permanent resident of the United States, also known as a Green Card holder, can be a lengthy and complex process. Here are some general steps to follow:

Determine if you qualify, then file an "immigrant petition." Once you determine your eligibility, you or your sponsor must file an **immigrant petition** with US Citizenship and Immigration Services (USCIS). This step is where you make the reasons for your immigrant status clear.

At that point, you will most likely need to wait some time before you can apply for a Green Card. The application process includes filling out government forms, providing personal documents, and attending an interview.

If you are approved, the USCIS will schedule an interview to help decide if you will receive a green card. During the interview, you will be asked questions about your personal history and the reason for your visit to the US. The USCIS will then review your application and make a decision. If you are approved, you will receive your Green Card, which gives you the right to live and work permanently in the United States.

Note that the above steps are a general guide and the process can change depending on your specific situation.

### Lottery for Permanent Residence

The Diversity Immigrant Visa Program (DV Program) mentioned earlier, is also known as the Green Card Lottery. It is a program that offers a chance for individuals from **countries with low rates of immigration** to the United States to obtain permanent residence, also known as a green card.

The **lottery** is held once a year, usually in October, and is open to

## 永住権への道

　グリーンカード保持者と言われる、アメリカの永住権保持者になるには、長く複雑な手順を踏まなければなりません。ここでは、その一般的な手順について紹介します。

　まず、自身に資格があることを確認し、「移民請願書」を提出します。この**請願書**はあなたか、あなたのスポンサーが米国移民局（USCIS）に提出します。この段階では、あなたが移民である理由を明確にします。

　ここで、グリーンカードを申請できるようになるまでしばらく待つ必要があります。申請手続きには、政府書類への記入や、個人書類の提出、面接などが含まれます。

　申請が許可されれば、USCISはあなたのグリーンカード保持について審査をするための面接を予定します。面接ではあなたの個人的な経歴や渡米の理由などについての質問があります。その後は再度、申請書の確認が行われ、決定が下されます。晴れて承認が得られた場合は、グリーンカードを受け取り、あなたはアメリカで永久に居住、就労することが可能になります。

　以上は一般的な手順であり、そのプロセスはそれぞれの状況によって異なることに留意しなければなりません。

### 永住権抽選について

　前述の移民多様化ビザ抽選プログラム（DVプログラム）は、グリーンカード抽選(宝くじ)としても知られています。これは、アメリカへの**移民率が低い**国の人々に永住権（グリーンカード）取得の機会を提供するプログラムです。 ☞p. 75参照

　**抽選**は通常、年に一度、10月に行われ、高校卒業以上

people who have at least a high school education or two years of work experience at a certain job. To apply for the lottery, applicants must submit an electronic form during the entry period, which usually lasts for one month. The application requires personal information, education and work history, and a photograph.

At the end of the entry period, the government has a **random drawing** of applicants to select winners. The winners are then notified and must go through a more detailed application process, which includes an interview, background checks, and **medical examinations**. If they pass all the requirements, they are granted a green card.

It's important to note that winning the lottery does not guarantee that an individual will receive a green card. The number of visas available through the lottery is limited, and more winners are selected than there are available visas. Therefore, winning the lottery only provides the **opportunity to apply** for a green card, and it's still important to meet all **eligibility requirements** and pass all required checks and examinations.

## Eligibility and testing for citizenship

Now, if you want to vote in the United States, that means becoming a **full citizen**. This is the final step beyond being a green card holder, and it demands the most work.

First, you must be at least 18 years old when starting the process, having held a Green Card for at least five years before applying to be a citizen, or three years if the Green Card was obtained through marriage to a US citizen. You need to have been present in the United States for at least half of that time, without leaving for extended periods.

Applicants must demonstrate good character, so anyone with a **criminal record** will not be considered.

の学歴があるか、または定められた職種で二年以上の就労
経験のある人が対象になります。応募には通常、１カ月間
の応募期間があり、電子フォームを提出します。申請には
個人情報、学歴、職歴、写真が必要です。

　応募期間が終了すると、政府は**無作為に抽選**を行い、当
選者を決めます。通知を受けた当選者には、さらなる申請
プロセスが待っており、面接や身元調査、**健康診断**などが
控えています。全ての要件に合格後、グリーンカードが発
給されます。
　当選したからといって、グリーンカードが発給されるわ
けではないことに注意してください。抽選プログラムで発
給できるビザ数には限りがあり、その数よりも多くの当選
者が選ばれるからです。つまり、抽選で選ばれることは、
ただ単にグリーンカードを**申請する機会**を得たということ
であって、全ての**資格要件**を満たし、必要な検査や試験に
合格しなければいけないことには変わりありません。

## 市民権取得のための資格と試験

　さて、アメリカで選挙に投票をしたい場合は、**完全な市
民**になる必要があります。市民権を得るということはグ
リーンカード保持者にとっての最終ステップでもあり、
それには多くの労力を要します。
　まず、市民権の申請を開始する時点で少なくとも18歳
以上であること、申請より前に少なくとも5年間グリーン
カードを保持していること、アメリカ市民との結婚によ
ってグリーンカードを取得した場合は、少なくとも3年
間それを保持していることが条件となります。また、こ
れらの期間の最低でも半分の期間は長期不在なしにアメ
リカに滞在していなければなりません。
　申請者は善良な人格であることを証明する必要があ
り、**犯罪歴のある人**は対象外となります。

You must pass tests demonstrating the ability to read, write, and speak basic English, and show your knowledge of US government, history, and laws. The test consists of 100 questions, and you must answer at least 60 questions correctly, so it's not quite as difficult as getting an A in school.

In addition to these requirements, you must also show that you understand the main points of the U.S. Constitution. Once the application is approved, you attend a special ceremony and take the **Oath of Allegiance** (promising to follow the rules of the United States) in order to become a US citizen.

## About Dual Citizenship

**Dual citizenship** in the United States refers to a person being considered a citizen of two countries at the same time. This means that the individual holds citizenship in the United States and at least one other country.

This means that people who are born in the United States to foreign parents or who become citizens of another country through marriage or other ways may still keep their US citizenship.

However, dual citizenship can affect things like paying taxes, **serving in the military**, and becoming a member of the government. It is important for people with dual citizenship to know the laws of both countries to avoid doing anything illegal.

Overall, dual citizenship can provide people with particular opportunities and benefits, like traveling more freely between both countries, but it also comes with certain responsibilities and restrictions.

　基本的な英語の読み書き、会話能力を証明するテストに合格し、アメリカの政府、歴史、法律に関する知識も証明しなければなりません。テストは100問で、そのうち60問に正解すればいいので、学校でAの成績をとるほど難しいわけではありません。

　また、申請者はこれらの要件に加え、アメリカ合衆国憲法の主なポイントを理解していることを示す必要もあります。申請が受理されれば、宣誓式に出席し、**忠誠の誓い**（アメリカのルールに従うことを約束する）を述べ、アメリカ市民となります。

### 二重国籍について

　アメリカにおける**二重国籍**とは、同時にふたつの国の市民であることを意味します。アメリカの市民権を持ちながら、少なくとも、もうひとつ別の国の市民権も持つということです。

　外国人の両親のもとにアメリカで生まれた人や、結婚やその他のきっかけで他国の市民権を得た人々は、継続してアメリカの市民権を保持することができます。

　しかし、国籍をふたつ持つということは納税、**兵役**、政府の一員になる時などに影響が生じる可能性があります。二重国籍を持つ人々は、違法にならないよう、両国の法律を良く理解しておくことが大切です。

　つまり、二重国籍を持つことは、両国間を自由に往来できるといった特別な機会が得られ、利点になることもありますが、同時に一定の責任や制限を負うということでもあるのです。

# 2 Transportation

Key Words  Check-in, Frequent Flyer Programs, Transit Cards, Rideshares, Auto Insurance, Driver's License

## Airplane

As we have discussed, the United States is a big place. When you're going from one city to another, it is usually easiest (and often cheapest) to fly. Thus, air travel in the United States is a common and popular form of transportation. The United States has a **well-developed airport system**, with many airlines operating throughout the country.

Most major cities in the US have at least one airport, with some cities having multiple airports for different regions. The busiest air travel cities in the US include Atlanta, Los Angeles, Chicago, and Dallas.

The major air travel companies in the United States are American Airlines, Delta Air Lines, United Airlines, Southwest Airlines, and Alaska Airlines. These airlines provide a wide range of flights, from **short domestic trips** to long international flights. Smaller airlines often have cheaper tickets, but those are almost always balanced out by having to pay for luggage, stop in other cities on the way, etc.

To travel by air in America, you must first buy a ticket. 24 hours before the flight, there is usually a "check-in" process where you provide some personal details to the airline. Once at the airport, you can go through security, and boarding the plane. Passengers

# 2 交通機関

キーワード チェックイン、マイレージ・プログラム、交通カード、シェアサイクル、自動車保険、運転免許証

## 飛行機

　これまで見てきたように、アメリカは広大な国です。あなたがもし、ある都市から別の都市へ移動するなら、最も簡単な（そして、たいていは最も安価な）方法は飛行機を利用することでしょう。飛行機は、アメリカではよく使われる人気の交通手段です。**発達した空港システム**により、多くの航空会社が全米に就航しています。

　アメリカのほとんどの主要都市に少なくともひとつは空港があり、地域ごとに複数の空港がある都市もあります。空の往来が最も盛んな都市はアトランタ、ロサンゼルス、シカゴ、ダラスなどです。

　アメリカにはアメリカン航空、デルタ航空、ユナイテッド航空、サウスウエスト航空、アラスカ航空といった主要な航空会社があります。これらの航空会社は、**短距離の国内線**から長距離の国際線まで幅広いフライトを提供しています。小規模な航空会社ほど、航空券代が安い傾向がありますが、その場合、荷物代を支払ったり、中継の都市へ立ち寄ったりと、結局はほぼ同額になります。

　アメリカで飛行機を利用するには、まずチケットを購入します。たいていフライトの24時間前には、「チェックイン」手続きが可能で、そこで個人情報を開示します。空港に到着後、セキュリティチェックを受け、飛行機に

空港によっては巨大なものもあり、利用する前にある程度、施設のレイアウトや設備を理解しておくと良い。また非常にネットワークが発達している分、混み合っているのも事実。フライトの遅延やキャンセルもよくあることなので、備えておくと良い。

will always be asked to show their ticket and **identification** (passport or driver's license) at check-in, security, and when trying to get on the plane.

During the flight, passengers may be provided with in-flight entertainment and snacks. However, the services offered on a flight are very different from company to company, so if you have a certain need (such as Wi-Fi or charging ports), you should check with the airline to confirm that those will be available on your flight.

Air travel in the United States is a convenient and efficient way to travel, although sometimes bad weather in one part of the country can cause problems all over as planes and crews get delayed. When traveling by air, it is best to have an emergency plan in case of your flight being canceled.

## Mileage

Airlines offer "frequent flyer" programs to their customers to encourage them to continue flying with their airline. These programs are designed to reward customers with benefits based on their **flying activity**.

Here's how frequent flyer programs work in the United States:

To get started, you just sign up for a frequent flyer program with your favorite airline. This is almost always free and can be done online or at the airport.

Once you've signed up, you can start earning points (called miles) when you fly with the airline or its business partners. The number of points you earn is based on the **distance flown**, price of ticket, and your total points earned at the time. Some airlines also offer ways to earn miles through credit card spending, shopping, or other partnerships.

As you gain points, you can move up the ranks of the program and earn a higher status. This comes with more benefits such as **free**

搭乗します。チェックイン時とセキュリティチェック時、また搭乗時には、必ずチケットと**身分証明書**（パスポートか運転免許）を提示しなければなりません。

　飛行機の中では、機内エンターテインメントや軽食を楽しむこともできます。ただし、そうしたサービスは航空会社によって大きく異なるため、特別に必要なもの（Wi-Fiや充電ポートなど）がある場合は、自身のフライトでそれらが利用できるかを航空会社に確認すると良いでしょう。

　アメリカの空の旅は、便利で効率的ですが、時には一部地域の悪天候の影響が全米に及び、機材や乗務員に遅れが出ることもあります。飛行機で旅行をする際は、フライトがキャンセルされた場合に備え、緊急時の予定を立てておくと良いでしょう。

## マイレージについて

　各航空会社は、顧客に長く自社のサービスを利用してもらおうと「マイレージ」プログラムを提供しています。これらのプログラムでは、顧客は自分たちの**搭乗実績**に応じて特典を得ることができます。

　ここでは、アメリカのマイレージ・プログラムの仕組みを紹介します。

　まず、好きな航空会社のマイレージ・プログラムに登録します。登録はたいてい無料で、オンライン、もしくは空港で行うことができます。

　登録が完了すると、その航空会社や提携航空会社のフライトを利用する度にポイント（マイルと呼ばれます）が貯まります。獲得できるポイント数は**飛行距離**や航空券代、それまでに獲得したポイントの合計数などで決まります。クレジットカードの利用やショッピング、その他提携会社を通じてもポイントが獲得できる航空会社もあります。

　ポイントが貯まるごとに、より上のランクへ上がっていき、さらに高いステータスを得ることができます。**手荷物**

日本の航空会社であれば、ANAのスターアライアンス、JALのワンワールドなどアメリカの航空会社と提携してポイントが貯まるものがある。

**luggage**, getting on the plane earlier than other passengers, and more. Once you've earned enough points, you can use them to buy rewards such as free flights, better seats, hotel stays, and car rentals.

Remember, many frequent flyer programs have **expiration dates** for points. If you don't earn or spend points within a certain period, your points may go away.

If there is one airline you like more than others, joining their frequent flyer program is a good way to save money. Just make sure that you read the frequent flyer contract carefully to understand how points are earned and spent, because once you join an airline it is best to stay with them for a long time.

## Railroads

Although railroads were important in the early economic development of the United States, they have received little investment since the 1950s. When it comes to **passenger travel**, there are honestly only a few regions where traveling by train is practical. Cities in the American Northeast are connected by rail networks. Outside of those places, though, train travel is generally unpopular. Why is that?

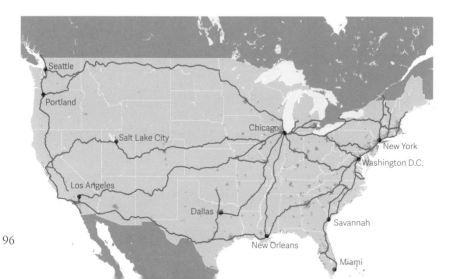

代が無料になったり、他の乗客よりも早く搭乗ができたり、その他にも多くの特典が得られます。十分なポイントが貯まれば、無料航空券や、座席のアップグレード、ホテルの宿泊やレンタカーなどの特典を購入することも可能です。

　多くのマイレージ・プログラムにはポイントに**有効期限**があるので気をつけてください。一定期間内にポイントを獲得、または使用をしなければ、そのポイントが消滅してしまうこともあります。

　もし、お気に入りの航空会社があるなら、マイレージ・プログラムに加入するとお得です。ただし、プログラム加入後は、その会社を長く利用することがベストなので、マイレージの契約書はよく読み、ポイントの獲得方法や使用方法を理解しておきましょう。

## 鉄道

　鉄道は、アメリカの初期の経済発展に重要な役割を果たしましたが、1950年代以降はほとんど投資されなくなりました。**人々の輸送手段**という意味で、列車の利用が実用的である地域は、正直なところ、ごく少数に限られています。アメリカ北東部の都市は、鉄道で結ばれていますがが、それらを除けば、列車はあまり人気のある移動方法とは言えません。それはなぜでしょう？

通称アムトラックと呼ばれる全米鉄道旅客公社が運営する鉄道が全米を結んでいる。ただ遅延が多く、運賃も高い、かつ本数が少ないなど概ね不便を極めている。ボストンとニューヨークを結ぶ路線であっても車両は古く、快適とは言えない状況だ。

←Amtrak（アムトラック）の鉄道網。1971年に設立され、北米の鉄道網は約3万7,000キロメートル。ニューヨークとシカゴ、ワシントンD.C.とロサンゼルスを結ぶなど長距離路線を中心に約200の路線を運行している。平均速度は80キロ程度で、全米を移動するにはあまり向かないだろう。

Most importantly, the **rail system** in the United States is limited compared to other countries, making it difficult for passengers to travel to many destinations by train. In many parts of the country, trains do not run often, and there are very few choices of where to travel to. Because the US is such a large country and even individual cities are quite spread out, it is not always possible to walk to a train station. People do not want to have to take a bus or other form of transportation to a train station, so they usually skip them.

Unlike many other countries, the United States does not have a complete **high-speed train system**. The few high-speed rail lines that exist serve specific routes and usually do not connect major cities. Furthermore, much of the rail system in the United States is old and in need of repair or replacement. This can lead to delays and safety concerns.

Also, rail travel in the United States faces competition from other kinds of transportation, such as cars, buses, and airplanes. Most Americans prefer driving or flying, which can make it difficult for rail travel to compete.

You might think that all these problems with trains would make traveling by rail cheap in the US. Unfortunately, that is not the case. Rail travel in the United States can be expensive, particularly for long-distance trips. Combined with everything discussed above, this leads to mostly empty passenger trains all over the country.

## Luxury Train Travel

Luxury train travel in the United States offers a different way to explore the country's landscapes while enjoying high level services.

There are number of companies that have routes through beautiful parts of the US, including the Rocky Mountains, the Grand Canyon,

最も重要な点は、アメリカの**鉄道網**が他の国々に比べ限られているため、乗客が様々な目的地へ行くのが難しいということです。国内のほとんどの地域では列車はそれほど走っておらず、その行先についてもほとんど選択肢がありません。アメリカは大きな国で、個々の都市が点在していることもあり、列車の駅まで歩いていくことさえままなりません。人々は駅へ行くためにバスを使ったり、他の交通手段を使ったりしたくないので、列車に乗ろうとしないのです。

また、他の多くの国々と違い、アメリカには**高速鉄道システム**が完全には整っていません。現在ある数少ない高速鉄道も、特定の路線を走っており、主要都市を繋いではいないのです。さらに、鉄道システムのほとんどは古く、修理や交換が必要です。そのため、遅延や安全面での懸念もあります。

アメリカの鉄道は、車、バス、飛行機といった他の交通手段との競争にもさらされています。ほとんどのアメリカ人は車か飛行機を好むため、鉄道は競合するのが難しい状況です。

これほどの問題を抱えた鉄道なら、その旅行費用は安いはずだと思われるかもしれません。しかし、残念ながら実際はそうとは言えません。アメリカでの鉄道の旅は、特に長距離になると高額です。これらのことを全て踏まえ、現在もほとんどの列車は空席のまま国中を走っているのです。

## 豪華列車の旅について

アメリカの豪華列車の旅は、一流のサービスを楽しみながら、風景を堪能できる一味違った体験です。

ロッキー山脈、グランドキャニオン、北西部の森林地帯など、多くの会社がアメリカの美しい地域に路線を走らせ

豪華列車
「カリフォルニア・ゼファー号」はシカゴからサンフランシスコまで3泊4日で走る長距離列車で、途中、コロラドやユタ州の景色を楽しめる。
「エンパイア・ビルダー号」はシカゴからシアトルまで走り、ミシシッピ川やグレートプレーンズの景色を楽しめる。
「サンセット・リミテッド号」は、オーランドからロサンゼルスまで走り、ニューオーリンズやテキサスの砂漠などの景色を楽しめる。

and the Northwest forests. Most companies provide private rooms, **dining**, and special cars for viewing nature while you travel.

Overall, luxury train travel in the United States offers an unforgettable way to experience America's landscapes, although it can be extremely expensive.

## Buses and subways

Getting around through **public transportation** is common in the Northeast, particularly in cities, but it is less common elsewhere, and almost impossible in rural areas.

Buses are used in many US cities, offering cheap transportation. Bus systems are typically run by city or **regional governments**, and many offer routes throughout the city, as well as to surrounding suburbs and towns. Passengers can typically pay for their **fare** with cash or a pre-paid transit card, and many systems offer cheaper fares for seniors, students, and low-income residents. Keep in mind, many Americans see city buses as dangerous to ride, and they are not a popular choice among middle and upper income citizens.

Subways, also known as metros or undergrounds, are a more popular form of public transportation in the US cities where

ボストンの地下鉄

ています。どこの会社も個室や**食事**を用意し、特別列車からは美しい自然を眺めることができます。

　概して、豪華列車の旅は大変高額ではあるものの、アメリカの風景を堪能できる忘れられない旅となるでしょう。

## バスと地下鉄

　**公共交通機関**を利用して移動することは、北東部の、特に都市部では一般的ですが、その他の地域ではまれで、地方にいたってはほとんど不可能です。

　バスはアメリカの都市部ではよく利用され、値段も手頃です。バスのシステムは通常、市や**地方自治体**によって運営されており、その多くは市内全域に限らず周辺の郊外や町へも路線を伸ばしています。乗客はたいてい、現金、またはプリペイド式の交通カードで**運賃**を支払いますが、高齢者や学生、低所得者には安い運賃を設定しているシステムがほとんどです。ただ、アメリカ人の多くは市バスを危険な乗り物と考えており、中・高所得者層の人々は、あまり好んでバスを利用しないということを覚えておきましょう。

　メトロ、またはアンダーグラウンドとも呼ばれる地下鉄は、公共交通機関の発達したアメリカの都市部では、

ニューヨークを走るバス

they can be found. Subway systems are typically faster and more efficient than buses, especially during peak hours when traffic can slow down buses.

Subways typically require passengers to purchase a **fare card** or ticket before entering the station. Once inside the station, passengers can swipe their ticket or card to enter the platform and board the train. Like buses, many subway systems offer deals to different groups of citizens.

While buses and subways are common forms of public transportation in US cities, the quality of these services is very different depending on the city and region. Some cities, such as New York and Boston, have well-developed subway and bus systems that serve millions of riders each day, while other cities have much more limited systems.

## Cabs/ Rideshares

Cabs and rideshare apps (Uber and Lyft are most popular) in the United States are transportation services that use private drivers for a single person or group. However, there are some differences in the way they operate.

Cabs, also known as taxis, are managed by local governments and use drivers with **special licenses and permits**. Cab companies typically own dozens of vehicles, and passengers can raise a hand to get picked up on the street, call for a car, or make a reservation in advance.

### [Rideshare Apps]

Rideshare apps like Uber and Lyft are technology companies that connect passengers with drivers who use their **personal cars**. Drivers must pass a personal history check and have a driver's license and insurance. Passengers use the app to request a ride, and

より頻繁に利用されています。地下鉄のシステムは通常、バスよりも速く便利で、交通渋滞の発生するピーク時には特に助かります。

　通常、地下鉄を利用するには、駅に入る前に**運賃カード**か切符を購入します。駅に入ると、乗客は切符、またはカードを改札に通し、プラットホームから電車に乗り込みます。バスと同様に、地下鉄のシステムでも、市民のグループごとの料金が設定されています。

　アメリカの都市部では一般的な公共交通機関であるバスや地下鉄ですが、そのサービスの質は都市や地域によって大きく異なります。ニューヨークやボストンのように、システムが発達していて、毎日何百万人もの人々が利用する都市もあれば、限られたシステムしかない都市もあります。

## タクシー / ライドシェア

　アメリカのタクシーとライドシェア（UberとLyftが最も人気があります）は、どちらも個人のドライバーが、ひとり、または複数の乗客にサービスを提供するものです。ただ、それらの運営方法にはいくつかの違いがあります。

　キャブとも呼ばれるタクシーは、地方自治体によって運営されており、ドライバーは**専用の免許や許可を**取得しています。タクシー会社はたいてい、何十台もの車両を所有しており、乗客は通りで手を挙げたり、電話で呼んだり、また事前に予約をしたりします。

[ライドシェアアプリ]

　UberやLyftといったライドシェアのアプリは、乗客と**自家用車**を使用するドライバーをつなぐテクノロジー系の会社が運営しています。ドライバーは個人経歴の審査に合格し、運転免許証の提示と、保険への加入が求め

the app matches them with a **nearby driver**. The fare is decided based on the distance and time of the trip and paid through the app.

When a passenger requests a ride, the app sends a notification to nearby drivers. Once a driver accepts the ride, the passenger can see the driver's name, photo, and license plate number. Passengers can also track the driver's progress and estimated time of arrival. After the ride, passengers can **rate** their driver and provide feedback.

In general, cabs have been disappearing from US cities over the last 10 years. They can still be found in the Northeast, but in the rest of the country you should expect to use a rideshare app if you need to go somewhere without an effective public transportation network (which is most places).

## Automobile

Renting a car in the United States is a fairly simple process. First, you choose a rental car company and make a reservation either online or over the phone. Make sure to provide your personal information, including your name, driver's license number, and credit card information.

Once you arrive at the rental car location, you will be asked to choose a car from the available inventory. Most rental car companies offer a range of vehicle sizes and types. The rental car company will ask you to provide a driver's license, **proof of car insurance**, and a credit card for payment. If you do not have your own insurance, the rental car company will offer to sell you insurance for an additional fee.

られます。乗客はアプリを使って乗車のリクエストをし、アプリは**近くのドライバー**とマッチングを行います。運賃は距離と時間に応じて計算され、支払いもアプリを通して行われます。

　まず、乗客が乗車のリクエストをすると、アプリは近くにいるドライバーにそれを通知します。ドライバーが乗車の承諾をすると、乗客はドライバーの名前や写真、ナンバープレートを確認することができます。ドライバーの運転状況や到着予定時刻の追跡も可能です。車を降りた乗客は、ドライバーの**評価をしたり**、フィードバックを送ることもできます。

　一般的に、この10年間でタクシーはアメリカの都市部から姿を消しつつあります。北東部ではまだタクシーが見られる所もありますが、その他の地域でもし有効な公共交通機関がない場合は（ほとんどの地域がそうです）どこへ行くにしてもライドシェアアプリを利用した方が良いでしょう。

## 自動車

　アメリカで、レンタカーを利用する手順はいたって簡単です。まずは、レンタカー会社を選び、オンラインか電話で予約をします。氏名、免許証番号、クレジットカード情報など、個人情報は必ず伝えましょう。

　レンタカー営業所に着いたら、貸し出し可能な車の中から車を選びます。ほとんどの会社は様々なサイズやタイプの車を用意しています。運転免許証、**自動車保険の証明書**、クレジットカードの提示も求められます。自身で保険に加入していない場合は、追加料金を払うことで保険を販売してもらうこともできます。

アメリカの主要レンタカー会社はハーツ、エイビス、ダラー、スリーピー、バジェット、ナショナルなど。それぞれ所有車の種類、料金、契約内容が異なるので、事前に把握しておくと良い。また営業所のロケーションも調べておくと良い。

When taking possession of the car, you will need to sign a rental agreement that outlines the **terms and conditions of the rental**, including the length of time, the daily cost, and any extra fees. Before you drive away, make sure to carefully check the vehicle for any damage. If you notice anything, take a picture, and report it to the rental car company before leaving.

When returning the car, make sure to **refill the gas tank** to where it was when you first got it. If you don't, the rental company will most likely charge a fee for refilling it themselves. Return the car to the **designated location** and remember to remove all personal belongings from the vehicle.

The final bill will be charged to your credit card, and a receipt will be provided to you. Most importantly, make sure to get confirmation that you returned the car before leaving. Either a paper receipt or an email confirmation are fine, but both are preferred. There have been many reports of rental companies claiming to have not received the car back and trying to charge customers for the full cost of the vehicle. Don't be afraid of seeming rude; get your receipt!

 **Useful Note**

You may have heard that you must be 25 years old to rent a car in the US, but many companies now rent certain cars to drivers as young as 21. In New York or Michigan you can rent a car when you are 18, but that is probably not a good idea to do as a foreign teenager without much driving experience.

車を受け取る際は、レンタル期間や1日あたりの料金、また追加料金など、**レンタカーの利用条件**が記載された契約書にサインをする必要があります。出発前に、車にキズがないかを入念にチェックしましょう。もし気になることがあれば、写真を撮り、出発前にレンタカー会社に報告をします。

車を返却する際は、最初の受取時の状態まで必ず**ガソリンを補充**します。そうしないと、給油代を請求されるかもしれません。**指定された場所に車を返却**し、私物を全て持ち出すことを忘れないでください。

最終的な金額がクレジットカードに請求され、領収書が発行されます。最も重要なことは、レンタカー会社を後にする前に確かに車を返却したという証明書を発行してもらうことです。紙でも、メールでも構いませんが、両方あると良いでしょう。車が返却されなかったと言い張り、顧客に車両代金の全額を請求しようとするレンタカー会社が相次いでいます。厚かましいと思われることを恐れず、領収書をもらいましょう！

### ★ 役立ちメモ

アメリカでレンタカーを利用するには25歳以上でなければならない、と聞いたことがあるかもしれませんが、現在、多くの会社は顧客が21歳以上であれば特定の車を貸し出しています。ニューヨーク州やミシガン州では、18歳でもレンタカーを借りることができますが、運転経験の乏しい10代の外国人にはお勧めとは言えません。

## About International License

To get an international driver's license in the United States, you must first have a driver's license from your home country, be at least 18 years old, and have a passport. The United States government has given two organizations the **power to issue** international driver's licenses: the American Automobile Association (AAA) and the American Automobile Touring Alliance (AATA). You can locate the nearest branch of either organization online or by contacting them directly.

You will need to provide the following documents to apply:

· A completed application form, which you can obtain from the AAA or AATA website or branch location,
· a copy of your valid US driver's license,
· two passport-sized photos of yourself,
· and a fee for the international driver's license, which varies depending on the organization you use

Once you have completed the application form and gathered the necessary documentation, you can submit your application in person at a branch location or by mail. Processing times may vary, so be sure to check with the organization for their estimate.

If your application is approved, you will receive your international driver's license either in person at the branch location or by mail. The international driver's license is valid for one year from the **date of issue.**

It is important to note that an international driver's license is not a substitute for a **valid driver's license**. You must have a valid driver's license from your home country to be eligible for an international driver's license, and you must carry both licenses with you while driving in the United States. Additionally, the international driver's license is not accepted in all countries, so be sure to check the driving laws of the countries you plan to visit.

## 国際免許について

　アメリカで国際免許証を取得するには、まず自国の運転免許証を所持していること、18歳以上であること、そしてパスポートを所持していることが必要です。アメリカ政府はアメリカ自動車協会（AAA）とアメリカ自動車ツーリング連盟（AATA）というふたつの団体に国際免許証**発行の権限**を委ねています。どちらの団体も、オンラインで検索するか、直接連絡をして、最寄りの支部を見つけることができます。

　国際免許の申請には以下の書類が必要です。

・AAAまたはAATAのウェブサイト、または支店から入手した記入済の申請書、
・有効なアメリカの運転免許証のコピー、
・パスポートサイズの写真2枚、
・国際運転免許証発行のための手数料（利用する団体によって異なる）。

　申請書を記入し必要な書類を揃えたら、直接支部へ行くか郵送し、提出をします。手続きにかかる日数は場合によって異なるので、提出先の団体に確認しておくと良いでしょう。

　申請が承認されると、直接支部へ行くか郵送かのどちらかで国際免許証を受け取ることができます。国際免許証の有効期限は**発行日**から一年間です。

　ただし、国際免許証は、**有効な運転免許証**の代用になるわけではないことに留意してください。国際免許証を所持するためには、自国の有効な運転免許証を持っていなければならず、アメリカで車を運転する際には両方の免許証を携帯していなければなりません。さらに、国際免許証は、どの国でも有効というわけではありませんので、訪問予定国の運転に関する法律を必ず確認しましょう。

日本で国際免許を先に取得することも考えよう。手持ちの免許証、パスポート、写真などを準備し、運転免許試験場か警察署の運転免許課で申請する。30分もかからずに免許証は受け取ることができる。アメリカで運転する場合は、国際免許だけでなく日本の免許証も必要なので注意。

## Bicycles (shared bikes)

Bike share programs are public transportation systems that allow individuals to rent bicycles for a short period of time, typically a few hours, for a fee. These programs have **gained popularity** in cities as a convenient and **environmentally friendly** mode of transportation.

In the US, bike share programs are typically operated by private companies in partnership with local governments. They involve a network of stations throughout a city, each with thousands of bicycles that can be rented and returned at any station.

To use a bike share program, users usually need to sign up for a membership, which can be done online or at one of the bike share stations. Members are then given access to the bikes by using a code or an electronic key. Users can rent a bike for **a set amount of time**, usually for 30 minutes to an hour, and return it to any bike station in the network.

Bike share programs can be a convenient way to **get around cities**, particularly for short trips or for commuting to work. The bikes are a sustainable mode of transportation, as they do not produce emissions and do not require the use of **fossil fuels**.

These programs have helped to promote biking as a transportation option and have contributed to reducing traffic and improving air quality in urban areas. You might consider using one of these programs if you are sight-seeing in an area with **low traffic**. When the weather is nice and you're interested in getting exercise, they can be a lot of fun!

## 自転車（シェアサイクル）

　バイクシェア・プログラムは個人が料金を支払い、短時間（たいていは数時間）自転車を借りることができる公共交通システムです。便利で**環境に優しい**交通手段として、都市部で**人気を集めて**います。

　アメリカのバイクシェア・プログラムは、一般的に地方自治体と提携する民間企業によって運営されています。都市全体に広がるステーション網には、通常、数千台の自転車が設置されており、どのステーションでも、自由に自転車をレンタルしたり返却したりすることができます。

　バイクシェア・プログラムを利用するには、通常オンラインか直接ステーションで、会員登録をする必要があります。会員登録後はコード番号や電子キーを使って、自転車を利用します。自転車の利用時間は**一定時間**（たいていは30分から1時間）に定められており、どのステーションでも、レンタルまたは返却をすることができます。

　バイクシェア・プログラムは、特に短時間の外出や通勤などで、**街を移動する**のに便利です。排気ガスを出すこともなければ**化石燃料**を使用する必要もない、持続可能な交通手段なのです。

　これらのプログラムはまた、交通手段の選択肢として自転車を普及させ、都市部の渋滞を緩和し、大気環境を改善することにも貢献しています。**交通量の少ない**地域を観光する際は、こうしたプログラムのひとつを検討してみると良いかもしれません。天気の良い日にエクササイズをしたい気分であれば、きっと楽しい体験になるはずです！

# 3 Communication

(**Key Words**) Landline, Conferencing, PO Box, SNS, Tracking, Certified Mail

## Phones

Telephones are used for a variety of purposes in America, including making and receiving calls, sending text messages and emails, accessing the internet, taking photos and videos, and using various apps for communication, entertainment, and productivity. The widespread use of telephones has also led to the development of many related industries, such as telecommunications, software development, and e-commerce.

**Mobile phones** have become so common that it is considered rare to see a **home phone**, also called a "landline". Phone lines are often included with internet and TV services in America, but they are almost never used at this point.

### Computer or Mobile

The choice between using mobile phones or computers to chat in the US ultimately depends on the individual's preferences, needs, and circumstances. Both devices have their advantages and disadvantages.

Mobile phones offer the convenience of portability and can be used anywhere at any time. They are also often **equipped with** various messaging apps, such as WhatsApp, Facebook Messenger, and iMessage, which allow for easy and instant communication with

112

# コミュニケーション

**キーワード** 固定電話、会議、私書箱、SNS、追跡、書留

---

## 電話

通話の発着信、テキストメッセージやEメールの送信、インターネット接続、写真や動画の撮影、コミュニケーション、エンターテインメント、便利なアプリの使用など、携帯電話は様々な目的で使われています。携帯電話の普及は、電気通信やソフトウェア開発、電子商取引などを含む多くの関連産業の発展にもつながりました。

**携帯電話**があまりに一般化したことで、「固定電話」と呼ばれる家庭用の電話を見かけることは珍しくなりました。アメリカではインターネットやテレビに付属していることの多い電話回線も、現在ではほとんど使われなくなりました。

### パソコンかスマホか

アメリカでチャットするのにスマートフォンを使うかパソコンを使うかは、完全に個人の好みやニーズ、状況によります。どちらのデバイスにも長所と短所があるからです。

スマートフォンは持ち運びが便利で、いつでもどこでも使用することができます。また、たいていはWhatsAppやFacebook Messenger、iMessageなどの各種アプリが**搭載**されており、素早く簡単に他人とコミュニケーションを取るこ

others. Mobile phones also often have a **camera built-in**, which can be useful for sharing photos and videos with others during chats.

On the other hand, computers offer a larger screen and keyboard, which can be more comfortable to use for extended periods. They also have more advanced features and capabilities, such as screen sharing and video conferencing, which can be useful for work-related communication or **remote learning**. Additionally, computers tend to have better internet connectivity and faster processing speeds, which can make chatting and other online activities smoother and more efficient.

For quick and informal chats, mobile phones may be more convenient, while for more complex communication tasks, such as **work-related tasks**, a computer may be more appropriate. Additionally, some people may prefer to use both devices depending on the situation.

## Email

Email is frequently used in the workplace to communicate with coworkers and customers. It is often used to share information, manage projects, and exchange ideas. Companies may use email to promote their products or services, provide special offers to customers, and communicate with their subscriber.

Email is also commonly used for personal communication, such as **staying in touch** with friends and family members who live far away. It can also be used to send invitations, make plans, and share news.

Many schools in the United States use email as a **primary means** of communication with students. This includes sending out **class schedules**, assignments, and important announcements. These days, it is common for a school email to be linked to special websites and programs that work together to manage classwork and communication between teachers and students.

とができます。**カメラが内蔵**されていることも多く、チャットをしながら相手と写真や動画を共有することも可能です。

　一方、大きな画面とキーボードのあるパソコンは、長時間でも快適に使用することができます。画面共有やウェブ会議など、より高度な機能や性能も備わっており、仕事上のコミュニケーションや**リモート学習**には最適です。また、パソコンはインターネットが繋がりやすく処理速度も速いため、チャットやその他のオンライン活動をよりスムーズで効率的に行うことができます。

　手軽でカジュアルなチャットには、スマートフォンの方が、**仕事に関する作業**など、より複雑なコミュニケーションにはパソコンの方が適しているかもしれません。状況に応じて両方を使う人もいるでしょう。

## Eメール

　Eメールは、職場の同僚や顧客とのコミュニケーションによく利用されます。また、情報の共有やプロジェクトの管理、アイデアの交換などにも利用されるでしょう。Eメールを活用して製品やサービスの宣伝、顧客への特別なオファー、購読者とのコミュニケーションなどを行う企業もあります。

　Eメールは遠方に住む友人や家族と**連絡を取り合う**など、個人的なコミュニケーションにもよく使用されます。招待状を送付したり、プランを練ったり、ニュースを共有したりするのにも便利です。

　多くのアメリカの学校は、生徒へ連絡事項を伝える**主な手段**としてもEメールを活用しています。**時間割**や課題、重要な連絡事項を、Eメールを使って伝えます。最近では、学校のEメールが指定のウェブサイトやプログラムにリンクすることで、授業の課題を知らせたり教師と生徒のコミュニケーションを管理したりすることが一

Email is an essential tool for communication in the United States, and it is the most widely used by individuals, businesses, and organizations of all kinds.

## Don't Use Carrier Mail Addresses

Using **carrier mail addresses**, such as a post office (PO) Box or a street address with "Unit" or "Suite" numbers, can seem like a convenient option for receiving mail in the US. However, there are several reasons why it may not be a good idea to rely on these types of addresses.

For one thing, carrier mail addresses are often not accepted by certain organizations and institutions. Some banks, credit card companies, and government agencies require a **physical street address** rather than a PO Box or a Unit/Suite number. This can lead to issues with mail delivery and important documents being lost or delayed.

Secondly, carrier mail addresses may not provide enough security for information. Unlike a physical street address, a PO Box or a Unit/Suite number can be opened by anyone who has the key or code. This could potentially put private information at risk, such as **financial statements**, **legal documents**, and personal data.

Finally, using a PO Box or a Unit/Suite number may give the impression that a business or individual is not stable, since they do not seem to have a **permanent address**. This could impact business relationships and potential opportunities.

While carrier mail addresses may be convenient in certain situations, it is important to consider the potential issues before relying on them completely. It may be better to use a physical street address for important personal or professional mail.

般的です。

　アメリカでEメールは、コミュニケーションに欠かせないツールであり、あらゆる分野の個人や企業、団体によって広く利用されています。

## 郵便物受取用住所を使わないで

　郵便局の私書箱（P.O.Box）や「Unit」「Suite」を含む**郵便物受取用住所**は、アメリカで郵便物を受け取るのに便利な方法と思われるかもしれません。ですが、この種の住所に頼ることが得策でない理由がいくつかあります。

　ひとつは、郵便物受取用住所は、特定の組織や機関では受け付けていないということです。一部の銀行やクレジットカード会社、政府機関は、私書箱やUnit、Suite番号ではなく、**実際の番地のある住所**を要求しています。そのため、郵便物の配達に問題が生じたり、重要な書類が紛失、または遅延したりすることがあります。

　また、郵便物受取用住所は、情報に対するセキュリティーが十分とは言えません。物理的な番地とは異なり、私書箱やUnit、Suite番号は鍵やコード番号さえあれば誰でも開けることができます。そのため、**財務書類**や**法的文書**、個人データなどの個人情報が危険にさらされる可能性があります。

　最後に、私書箱やUnit、Suite番号を使用する企業や個人は、**定住所**を持っていないように見え、不安定な印象を与えるということがあります。これでは、ビジネス関係や、潜在的なビジネスチャンスを無駄にしてしまう可能性もあるでしょう。

　このような理由から、郵便物受取用住所は場合によっては便利ですが、これだけを利用するのなら、問題があるかもしれないことを知っておくべきです。プライベートでも仕事でも、重要な郵便物を取り扱う際は、実際の住所を使用した方が良いでしょう。

私書箱

P.O.BoxとはPost office boxのこと。アメリカには郵便局が提供する私書箱と民間のものがある。双方、一長一短があり、もし借りる場合は自分のニーズに合った方を選ぶと良い。本文にもあるように、私書箱は住所として正式に使用できない場合もあるので注意が必要。

## SNS

Americans are gradually using social networking services for a variety of personal and professional roles that used to be filled by phones, email, and texting. When you meet people in the US, there's a chance that they will prefer to communicate using these apps rather than direct texting.

Social networking services have also taken on an important role in Americans' **professional lives**, allowing individuals to connect with **potential employers** or business partners. Platforms such as LinkedIn are popular for this purpose. Americans also commonly use SNS to share news and information as well as opinions and ideas.

These apps are also known to be filled with advertisements, whether they are direct commercials, corporate accounts, or **normal seeming people who are paid to represent a company**. When using SNS in America, you should be aware that your browsing and shopping data is most likely being collected by companies to use in advertisements.

### Line is Unique to Japan

You are of course familiar with the Line communication system that is widely used in Japan for both personal and professional communication. Many businesses use Line as a way to communicate with customers and clients, and it is also commonly used for group chats and social networking. In addition, the app has become an important **tool for emergency communication** during natural disasters, as it allows users to quickly send and receive information and check on the safety of friends and family.

While there is no app in America that provides all the features Line does, the Discord app might be the closest. Unfortunately, it is not as popular as many other social networking services, lowering its value slightly.

## SNS

　アメリカ人はこれまで電話やEメール、テキストメッセージで行ってきたことを、プライベートでも仕事でも、徐々にSNSに置き換えるようになってきています。アメリカで出会う人が、テキストのやり取りでなくアプリを使ったコミュニケーションを好むこともあるはずです。

　SNSは、アメリカ人の**仕事の場**でも重要な役割を担っており、個人が**将来の雇用主**やビジネスパートナーとつながるための手段にもなっています。LinkedInは、そうしたサービスを提供するプラットフォームとして人気です。SNSは、ニュースや情報、意見、アイデアなどの交換にも活用されています。

　これらのアプリは、直接的なコマーシャル、企業アカウント、**あたかも一般ユーザーのように見せて企業から金をもらって宣伝する人**など、様々な広告であふれています。アメリカでSNSを利用する際は、自分の閲覧経歴や買い物履歴などのデータが企業に収集され、広告配信に使われていることを知っておくべきです。

2002年にアメリカで設立され、2003年から正式にサービスが開始されたLinkedIn。プロフェッショナルなネットワーキングと仕事探しのための最も影響力のあるプラットフォームとされる。自己学習、キャリア開発ができる学習プログラムも充実しており、世界中で何百万もの個人や組織が利用している。

### LINEは日本だけのもの

　個人間でもビジネスでも、日本ではLINEというコミュニケーションシステムが広く使われています。LINEは、顧客やクライアントとのコミュニケーション手段として、多くの企業で利用されており、グループチャットやソーシャルネットワーキングとしても頻繁に活用されています。さらに、情報を素早く送受信し、友達や家族の安否を確認することのできるので、自然災害時の**緊急連絡用ツール**としても欠かすことのできないものになっています。

　LINEが持つ全ての機能を提供できるようなアプリはアメリカにはありませんが、Discordというアプリは最もそれに近いかもしれません。残念ながら、他の多くのSNSほどは普及していないため、使い勝手は悪いかもしれません。

## Postal and courier

In the United States, the competition between government and private **delivery services** has been going on for several decades. Government delivery services are mainly provided by the United States Postal Service (USPS), while private delivery services are provided by companies such as FedEx, UPS, and DHL.

One of the main areas of competition between these two types of delivery services is in the **package delivery market**. Private companies have been able to compete with USPS in this area by offering faster delivery times, more reliable tracking, and more flexible delivery options. Additionally, private companies have been able to offer lower prices due to their ability to use technology to make their delivery networks more efficient.

However, USPS still **dominates** the mail delivery market, particularly for first-class mail and standard mail. This is largely due to its mission of providing universal service to all Americans, no matter how distant they are from cities, at a reasonable price. USPS is also able to provide certain services, such as **certified mail** and **international mail**, that private companies may not be able to offer at the same prices.

Think of it this way: the USPS is best used if you want safety and reliability, while private companies are best used for their low prices and speed.

## 郵便と宅配便

　アメリカでは、政府系の宅配サービスと民間の**宅配サービス**の競合が、数十年にわたり続いています。政府系の宅配サービスは主にアメリカ合衆国郵政公社（USPS）、民間の宅配サービスはFedExやUPS、それにDHLなどが行っています。

　これらふたつの宅配サービスの主な競合分野のひとつに**小包の配達市場**があります。民間企業は、より短い配達期間と信頼のおける追跡システム、それに柔軟性の高い配達オプションによりUSPSと競い合ってきました。また、テクノロジーを駆使し配達網をより効率化することで、低価格も実現してきました。

　とはいえ、特に第一種郵便や普通郵便については、USPSは依然として市場を**支配**しています。これは、都市からどれほど離れていても、全てのアメリカ人に全国均質のサービスを低価格で提供する、というUSPSの使命によるところが大きいと言えます。USPSはまた、**書留郵便**や**国際郵便**といった民間企業が同じ価格で提供するには難しいような特定のサービスも行っています。

　安全性と信頼性を求めるならUSPS、低価格とスピード性を求めるなら民間サービスと考えるといいかもしれません。

United States Postal Serviceのことで日本の郵便局にあたる。ファーストクラスメール、プライオリティメール、大型荷物など、各種サービスがある。

街中を走り回るUSPSのトラック

# 4 Lodging

**Key Words** Privacy, Concierge, Authentic

## Hotels and Airbnb

The choice between staying at a hotel or an Airbnb in the US mainly depends on your budget, need for privacy, and overall desired mood of your vacation.

Hotels are typically considered more expensive than Airbnb rentals, especially in major cities or popular tourist destinations. However, hotels offer a range of extra services that may not be available in an Airbnb, such as room service, concierge services, fitness centers, and pools.

In contrast, Airbnb rentals are often cheaper and provide a more authentic **local experience**. They offer a range of options, from entire apartments or homes to private rooms in someone else's home. This allows you to have a more **personalized experience**, such as having access to a kitchen to cook your own meals or getting insider tips on the best local spots to visit.

Another factor to consider is the level of privacy you prefer. While hotels provide a level of privacy with daily housekeeping and key cards for rooms, Airbnb rentals can offer either more privacy by giving you the entire space to yourself, or less privacy if it is a shared space.

**4**

# 宿泊

キーワード プライバシー、コンシェルジュ、本物の

## ホテルとAirbnb

アメリカでホテルに泊まるかAirbnbに泊まるかは、主に予算、プライバシーが必要かどうか、どんな休暇にしたいかによって決まります。

ホテルは一般的に、特に大都会や人気の観光地では、Airbnbよりも高額であると考えられています。ですが、ホテルではルームサービスやコンシェルジュサービス、フィットネスセンター、プールなどのAirbnbにはないサービスを受けることができます。

対照的に、Airbnbはより手頃な価格で本格的な**地元の体験**を楽しむことができます。アパートや一軒家をそのまま借りるものから、他人の家の個室を借りるものまで、多様なオプションが用意されています。そのため、キッチンを使って自炊をしたり、地元のベストスポットを教えてもらったり、より**個人的な旅行体験**ができます。

考慮すべきもうひとつの点は、あなたがどの程度プライバシーを気にするか、ということです。ホテルのプライバシーが、毎日のハウスキーピングや部屋のカードキー程度に守られている一方で、Airbnbのプライバシーは、全スペースを借りることでよりプライバシーを確保することもできれば、共有スペースがありほとんどプライバシーを確保できないこともあるのです。

Airbnbは2008年に始まった民泊サービスで、Air Bed and Breakfastの略。現在世界191カ国で事業を展開していて、多くの旅行者にユニークな民泊体験を提供している。Bed and Breakfast（B&B）は18世紀ごろにイギリスで発祥したと言われる民泊の一種。

With Airbnbs, you must also consider the **extra fees** that typically don't exist with hotels. The most significant one is the cleaning fee, which for Airbnbs can be anywhere from $100-$300 **per stay**. You must review the purchase agreement carefully before deciding which option is actually cheaper in the end.

## Vacation rentals (long-term stay option)

Vacation rental homes, also known as vacation homes or holiday homes, are properties that are rented out to travelers looking for a place to stay during their vacation or holiday. These homes are typically **set up with all the furniture and appliances** you would expect in a normal home, including spaces like kitchens, living rooms, bedrooms, and bathrooms, as well as features like pools, hot tubs, or yards.

In the United States, vacation rental homes have become increasingly popular over the years as an alternative to traditional hotels and resorts. This is mainly because, for **a long term stay**, vacation rental homes can be more **affordable** than hotels, especially for larger groups or families. Renting a home can be more **cost-effective** than booking multiple hotel rooms, and the ability to cook meals in a full kitchen can save money on dining out. Furthermore, by paying for a block of time rather than individual nights, it is possible to get a better per-night price.

Vacation rental homes offer more privacy and space than hotels and many Airbnbs. Guests can enjoy their own bedrooms and bathrooms, and many homes have outdoor spaces like patios, decks, or yards where they can relax. Also, vacation rental homes are often located in **residential neighborhoods**, giving guests a more authentic experience of the local culture and lifestyle. Even Airbnbs are sometimes located in more typical tourist areas, so they do not necessarily give the same kind of experience.

　Airbnbでは、通常のホテルにはない**追加料金**についても考慮しなければなりません。最も代表的なものは清掃費で、一度の**滞在**につき100ドルから300ドルかかる場合もあります。最終的にどちらの方が低額になるかを見極めるためにも、前もって利用契約書に目を通しましょう。

## バケーションレンタル（長期滞在向け）

　バケーション・レンタルハウスは、バケーション・ハウスやホリデー・ハウスとも呼ばれ、休暇や休日の滞在先を探している旅行者に貸し出される物件のことを言います。これらの物件にはたいてい、普段の生活に必要な**家具や電化製品が全て備え付け**てあり、キッチンやリビングルーム、ベッドルーム、バスルームに加え、プールや浴槽、庭付きの物件もあります。

　アメリカでは、従来のホテルやリゾートに代わるものとして、バケーション・レンタルハウスの人気が高まりつつあります。**長期滞在**をする際、特に大人数のグループや家族連れの場合は、ホテルよりもバケーションレンタルの方が**手頃**だからです。複数のホテルの部屋を予約するよりも家を借りる方が、**費用対効果が高く**、また外食をするよりもキッチンで食事を作った方が経済的です。一泊ずつではなくまとまった期間の料金を支払うことで、一泊ごとの料金を低く抑えることも可能です。

　バケーション・レンタルハウスは、ホテルや多くのAirbnbに比べ、プライバシーやスペースをより確保することもできます。宿泊客は自分たちのベッドルームやバスルームを独占することができ、ゆっくりとくつろげるパティオやデッキ、庭などの野外スペースのある物件も多くあります。また、**住宅街**に位置することも多いため、宿泊者は地元の文化やライフスタイルに触れ、より本物に近い体験をすることが可能です。Airbnbは、時には典

民泊新法の施行で、2018年から日本でも民泊営業が可能になり、近年、バケーションレンタルの人気も高まっている。

If you are planning to stay somewhere for a week or more, and particularly if you have a larger group traveling together, renting a vacation home is probably your best option.

型的な観光地に位置していることがあるため、必ずしも
このような体験ができるとは限らないのです。
　あなたがもし、どこかに1週間以上滞在する予定があ
るのなら、そして特に大人数で旅行をする場合は、バケ
ーション・レンタルハウスはベストな選択肢でしょう。

# 5 Restaurants

**Key Words** Price fix (fixed price), Formal, Semi-formal, Fast-casual, Gratuity

## Fine dining

"Fine dining" restaurants in the US typically have high-quality food, a formal atmosphere, and polite, professional servers. These restaurants often have a separate wine list at the table, beautiful table settings, and decorative art.

Fine dining restaurants often have "prix fixe" or price fix menus, meaning customers choose from a set menu with multiple courses, rather than ordering dishes separately. The menu usually includes several options for each course, often with an emphasis on **local and seasonal ingredients**, and may change at times to reflect the availability of **fresh ingredients**.

The dress code for fine dining restaurants is typically formal or semi-formal, with men wearing dress shirts and pants (no jeans), with jackets and ties at the nicest places. Women's dress codes are generally more flexible in terms of what is considered formal fashion, but dresses are almost always fine. Reservations are usually required, and the staff provides a high level of attention to detail and personal service throughout the meal.

Fine dining restaurants in the US usually range from classic French and Italian establishments to modern restaurants that show off the latest **cooking techniques and trends**. These restaurants

# 5 レストラン

**キーワード** プリフィックス(固定価格)、フォーマル、セミフォーマル、ファストカジュアル、グラチュイティ

## 高級レストラン

　アメリカの「高級レストラン」では通常、質の高い料理、フォーマルな雰囲気、礼儀正しくプロフェッショナルなスタッフがそろっています。テーブルには特別なワインリストが用意され、装飾品も見事です。

　高級レストランでは、料理を個別に注文するというより、いくつかのコースメニューから料理を選ぶ「プリフィックス(またはプライスフィックス)」のメニューが用意されています。各コースにはたいてい、いくつかの選択肢があり、**地元の食材や季節の食材**に力を入れていたり、**新鮮な食材**があればそれらに変更されたりすることもあります。

　高級レストランのドレスコードは通常、最上級の店であればフォーマルかセミフォーマルで、男性はドレスシャツとパンツ(ジーンズはNG)にジャケットやネクタイを着用しなければなりません。女性のドレスコードは、何をもってフォーマルかにもよりますが、より柔軟で、ワンピースのようなものであればたいてい問題はないでしょう。多くの場合、予約が必要で、食事中はスタッフが細部まで気を配りきめ細やかなサービスを提供してくれます。

　アメリカの高級レストランはクラシックなフレンチやイタリアンから、最新の**料理技術や流行**を取り入れたモダンなレストランまで様々です。**都市部**に位置すること

tend to be located in **urban areas** and can be quite expensive, with prices for a multi-course meal landing anywhere between several hundred and several thousand dollars.

Although they are expensive, making room in your budget for the occasional trip to a fine dining restaurant can certainly be worth the experience.

## Restaurant Reservations

Making a reservation at a restaurant in the US typically involves calling the restaurant or using their online reservation system to secure a table for a specific date and time. People have gotten used to doing everything online, but when it comes to making restaurant reservations, calling to speak with a manager is actually the most simple method. Some restaurants do not make reservations over the phone and insist on you doing it online, but those systems can be confusing or unreliable, while a phone call is direct and clear.

After confirming that the restaurant will be open at the time you want, you'll need to call in and provide your name, phone number, and the number of people in your party. You may also be asked for special requests, such as **food allergies** or whether you would like to sit inside or outside. Once you've provided all the information they need, the restaurant will confirm your reservation either by phone or email.

Be sure to arrive at the restaurant on time for your reservation. If you're running late, it's always a good idea to call the restaurant and let them know. In general, restaurants will give you 10 or 15 minutes of extra time, but it's better not to risk it.

By the way, some restaurants may require a **deposit** or credit card information to secure a reservation, especially for larger groups or during busy times. They may also charge a fee for canceling, so be sure to check the restaurant's policies before making your reservation.

が多く、充実したコースは数百ドルから数千ドルと、か
なり高額にあることもあります。

　高価な出費にはなりますが、時には予算を確保し、高
級レストランへ行ってみるのも、きっと素晴らしい体験
になるでしょう。

## レストランの予約について

　アメリカでレストランの予約をするには、電話をするか、
店のオンライン予約システムで日時を指定するかが一般
的です。何かにつけてオンラインで済ませることに慣れて
しまっている人でも、レストランの予約ではマネージャー
と電話で話をするのが、実は最も簡単な方法です。中には
電話での予約を受け付けておらず、オンラインでしか予約
のできないレストランもありますが、それらのシステムは
分かりにくかったり信用ができなかったりするため、直接
電話をする方が確実でしょう。

　連絡を取ろうとする時間にレストランが営業している
ことを確認し、電話をして名前、電話番号、人数を伝えま
す。**食物アレルギー**や、室内の席またはテラス席など、特
別な希望を聞かれることもあるでしょう。必要な情報を全
て伝え終えると、レストランから電話やメールで予約の確
認が入ります。

　レストランの予約時間には遅れないようにしましょう。
もし、遅刻しそうな場合は電話でその旨を伝えましょう。ほ
とんどのレストランは遅刻をしても10分から15分の余裕
を見てはくれますが、そうならないことがベストでしょう。

　ところで、レストランによっては、特に人数の多い団体
客や忙しい時間帯の予約を確保するために、**先払い**やクレ
ジットカード情報を要求する店もあります。また、キャン
セルの際に手数料が発生する場合もありますので、予約前
にはレストランのポリシーを確認しておきましょう。

## Casual restaurants

Most restaurants in the US offer a relaxed, informal dining experience. Whether they are **fast-casual establishments** where customers order at the counter and then seat themselves or sit-down restaurants where customers are seated and served by waiters, casual restaurants are by far the most common kind across America.

The atmosphere of casual restaurants in the US is comfortable and welcoming, with a focus on providing a relaxing and enjoyable place to eat. The decor of these restaurants depends on the type of cuisine and the restaurant's target customers.

The menu of a casual restaurant typically includes a wide variety of dishes, from appetizers and salads to entrees and desserts. Many casual restaurants in the US offer American cuisine, but there are also many options for international cuisine, such as Italian, Mexican, Chinese, and Japanese. Reflecting **the diverse society in America**, it is also common for a restaurant to offer food from many different cultures.

In terms of price, casual restaurants in the US are more affordable than fine dining establishments, but prices **vary** depending on the restaurant's location and the quality of the food and service. Customers can expect to pay anywhere from $10 to $30 per person for a meal at a casual restaurant in the US. The general rule is that the closer you are to downtown in a large city, the more you can expect to pay.

If you want a nice dining experience that isn't too expensive while still being healthier than fast food, casual dining should be your choice.

## カジュアルなレストラン

　アメリカのほとんどのレストランでは、リラックスした雰囲気でカジュアルに食事を楽しむことができます。カウンターで注文を済ませた後、自分でテーブルにつく**ファスト・カジュアルタイプ**のレストランであれ、ウェイターに席を案内され注文を聞かれるタイプのレストランであれ、カジュアルなレストランはアメリカ全土で最もよく見られるレストランです。

　アメリカのカジュアル・レストランの雰囲気は気軽で親しみやすく、リラックスして食事が楽しめる場を提供することに重点が置かれています。レストランの内装も、料理の種類やターゲットとなる客層によって様々です。

　カジュアル・レストランのメニューはたいてい、前菜、サラダ、メイン料理、デザートなどバラエティーに富んでいます。アメリカ料理を提供するレストランも多くありますが、イタリア料理、メキシコ料理、中華料理、日本料理など様々な国の料理から選べます。**多様なアメリカ社会**を反映するように、レストランでも様々な文化を取り入れた料理が提供されています。

　価格は、カジュアル・レストランは高級レストランと比べ手頃ではあるものの、店の場所、料理やサービスの質によって**大きな違いがあります**。食事はひとりあたり10ドルから30ドルほどが相場でしょう。一般的には、大都会のダウンタウンに近ければ近いほど、価格は高くなる傾向があります。

　ファストフードよりも健康的で、かつ手頃で快適な食事を楽しみたいのなら、カジュアルなレストランはお勧めです。

ファスト・カジュアルとは、ファストフードと呼ばれるチェーン店より少し上の価格のレストラン。アメリカでは、チポトレ・メキシカン・グリル、パネラ・ブレッド、シェイク・シャック、スウィートグリーンなどがファストフードとカジュアルダイニングのギャップを埋める、便利で満足のいく食事ができる店と言われている。

## Burgers and Pizza

Burgers are a classic American food that has been popular for generations. They are typically made with a ground beef patty, lettuce, tomato, onion, cheese, and **condiments** like ketchup, mustard, and mayonnaise. This was originally a German dish, since "Hamburger" refers to Hamburg, a city in Germany. These days, burgers are combined with all kinds of cuisines, from Mexican to Indian. In **coastal cities**, there are even ramen burgers, which are made using pressed ramen noodles instead of wheat buns.

You can get a burger at almost any restaurant, whether it is fast food or fine dining. However, some of the best burgers are found at small, local places. These businesses can look old and cheap, but they often have been successful for generations because their burgers are good enough to attract loyal customers. Try eating at one of these places if you are interested in finding a truly **authentic American hamburger**.

Like burgers, pizza also began as a European dish, in this case from Italy. Over the last hundred years, it has become perhaps the most popular food in America, and it is available in three main styles. New York-style pizza is what you see on TV and in movies, with its wide, triangle shape and **fluffy crust**. Thin crust pizza is popular with people who want to eat slightly healthier, and it is a crispy style that is more like flat bread in other cultures. Chicago-style deep dish pizza is the least common type, as its incredibly thick, saucy, cheesy body is more like a large pie than a normal piece of pizza.

Most Americans prefer pepperoni, an Italian meat, as a topping on

## ハンバーガーとピザについて

　ハンバーガーは何世代にもわたり親しまれてきたアメリカの伝統的な食べ物です。たいていはひき肉のパティ、レタス、トマト、玉葱、チーズ、それにケチャップやマスタード、マヨネーズなどの**調味料**を加えて作られます。元々はドイツ料理で、「ハンバーガー」という名前もドイツの都市であるハンブルグに由来します。最近では、メキシコ料理からインド料理まで、ありとあらゆる料理がハンバーガーと組み合わされています。**沿岸部の都市**では、小麦のバンズの代わりに押し固めたラーメンを使用したラーメンバーガーまであるのです。

　ハンバーガーはファストフード店でも高級レストランでも、ほとんど全ての店で提供されています。ですが、最高のバーガーは時に地元の小さな店で見つけることができます。古びて安っぽくも見えるこうした店は、常連客を惹きつけて止まないバーガーのおかげで何世代にもわたって成功していたりします。**正真正銘のアメリカのハンバーガー**を食べるなら、ぜひこうした店へ行ってみると良いでしょう。

　ハンバーガーと同様に、ピザもヨーロッパ発祥（イタリア）の食べ物です。この100年間で、おそらくアメリカで最も人気のある食べ物となったピザには、3種類のスタイルがあります。ニューヨークスタイルのピザは、誰もがテレビや映画で目にしたことがあるもので、幅広の三角形の形と**柔らかい生地**が特徴です。薄い生地のピザは、健康的な食事を好む人々に人気があり、他の文化圏では、ほとんど平らに近いパンを使用したクリスピースタイルと呼ばれています。深めの焼き皿で焼くシカゴスタイルのピザは、最も珍しいタイプのピザで、驚くほどの分厚さにソースとチーズがたっぷり入った、ピザというよりは大きなパイのような形をしています。

　多くのアメリカ人が好むピザのトッピングは、イタリア

いくつかアメリカの人気ハンバーガー店を紹介しよう。ファイブ・ガイズ、In-N-Outバーガー、シェイク・シャック、ホワットバーガー、スマッシュバーガー、ハビット・バーガー、バーガービルなど、どの店も独自のメニューがあり、雰囲気も料理も楽しむことができる。

their pizza, but just about any vegetable or meat will do. Just make sure you ask what people want if you are ordering, because Americans can be quite **picky** about what goes on their pizza!

## Fast food, food court

Fast food refers to food that is quickly prepared and served in a restaurant or takeaway setting. Fast food restaurants in the US typically offer a limited menu of popular items such as burgers, **fries**, chicken, and ice cream, which can be ordered and served quickly.

No matter how they advertise, fast food restaurants are almost never a **healthy choice**. Beyond the **massive amounts of calories** in their food, they also contain high levels of salt and unhealthy fats and sugars. They are fine for customers who are in a hurry or on a tight budget, but you should not eat at them often.

Food courts in the US are found in shopping malls, airports, and other busy public places. There is normally a variety of fast food restaurants in a typical food court, often including well-known national chains as well as smaller local ones. Food courts offer a convenient way to grab a quick meal or snack while **on the go**. Like fast food though, you should note that the food offered here is made to be cooked and eaten quickly, and thus is generally not good for you.

## Food Trucks

Food trucks are mobile food sellers that work out of a truck or similar large vehicle. They have become popular in the United States in the 21st century, and are often found at festivals, concerts, and other outdoor events.

Food trucks offer the most unique food available, from

発祥のペパロニですが、ピザはどんな野菜や肉とでも良く
合います。もし、ピザを注文することがあれば、アメリカ
人はトッピングにとても**うるさい**ので、彼らのリクエスト
を必ず聞くようにしましょう！

## ファストフード／フードコート

　ファストフードとは、レストランやテイクアウト
店で素早く調理、提供できる料理のことです。アメリ
カのファストフード店では、たいていハンバーガー、
**フライドポテト**、チキンやアイスクリームなど、注
文したらすぐ出せるメニューに限定されています。

　どのように宣伝しようとも、ファストフード店が
**健康的な選択肢**とは言えません。**超ハイカロリー**で
あることに加え、塩分や体に悪い脂肪、糖分が大量に含
まれています。時間のない時や予算が限られている時は
まだしも、頻繁に利用するべきではありません。

　フードコートは、アメリカではショッピングモールや
空港、その他人の多く集まる場所に多くあります。名の知
れた全国チェーン店から地元の小さなチェーン店まで、
フードコートには多くのファストフード店が並んでいま
す。フードコートは**外出先**で手早く食事や軽食を取るの
に便利です。ただ、ファストフードと同様に、素早く調
理し食べられるよう用意された食事なので、体には良く
ありません。

## フードトラック

　フードトラックは、トラックや大型車で移動して食品
を販売する業者です。21世紀以降、アメリカで人気にな
り、フェスティバルやコンサート、野外イベントなどで
よく見かけるようになりました。

　フードトラックには、ハンバーガーやホットドッグと

Food truckは、日本ではキッ
チンカー（和製英語）とほぼ同
意。調理できる設備を整え、移
動して食品販売をする飲食店
のこと。

classic American food like burgers and hot dogs to more exotic options like sushi, falafel, and Korean barbecue. Many food trucks specialize in a particular type of cuisine, such as tacos or pizza, so the chefs in charge of them are free to experiment and try new things with their food.

フードトラック

Food trucks are often owned and operated by small business owners, and offer an affordable way for new business owners to get started. They are also popular with consumers who are looking for a convenient, affordable, and often unique dining experience. Eating at food trucks is a great way to support local businesses and meet other members of the community.

In the United States, food trucks must follow rules depending on the state and local area in which they operate. These **regulations** cover **health and safety standards**, so you can mostly trust food trucks to be clean and safe. That said, not all local governments pay careful attention to their food trucks, so you should use your best judgment when trying to decide if one is good to eat at.

## Take-out

The concept of take-out food goes very deep in American culture, and it has become increasingly popular over the years as an **affordable option** for people who are too busy to cook or who want to enjoy restaurant-quality food without the trouble of

いったアメリカでお馴染みの料理から、寿司やファラフェル、韓国式バーベキューなどの異国情緒あふれる料理まで、実にユニークなメニューが取り揃えられています。また、多くのフードトラックは、タコスやピザといった特定の料理に特化していることから、担当のシェフたちは自由に腕を振るって新しいメニューに挑戦することができます。

ファラフェルは中東のソウルフードで、ひよこ豆やそら豆をつぶして香辛料を混ぜ合わせて固め、食用油で揚げた料理。

　フードトラックを経営する事業主は、比較的小規模であることが多く、新規の事業主であっても少ない資金で事業を始めることができます。便利さや良心的な価格、面白い食事体験を求める人々にも人気があります。フードトラックを利用することは、地元の企業を応援することにもつながり、また地域の人々と交流する良い機会にもなります。

　アメリカでフードトラックを始めるには、営業をする州や地域によって異なる規則に従わなければなりません。これらの**規則**には**健康や安全に係る基準**が設けられていることから、フードトラックは清潔で安全です。とはいえ、全ての地方自治体が細心の注意を払っているわけではありませんので、利用するなら自身でよく見極めるようにしましょう。

## テイクアウト

　テイクアウトはアメリカでよく浸透しており、忙しく料理ができない人や手間をかけずにレストラン並みの食事を楽しみたい人の間で、**手頃な選択肢として年々人気**が高まっています。アメリカ人は、地域より個人の好みを

dining in. Since Americans tend to value their individual tastes over those of their community, eating good food at home in a private place has always been very attractive to them. Since the COVID-19 pandemic, takeout has become an even more common way for Americans to enjoy their favorite restaurant meals while social distancing and avoiding crowds.

Typically, take-out food is ordered either by phone or online, and customers can either pick up their orders at the restaurant or have them delivered to their location. There are a **handful of phone apps** that pick up food from restaurants and deliver it customers, although as always you should check to see what kinds of additional charges will be applied to the order.

## What about Tips?

Tipping culture in the United States is an important part of the **service industry**. In most US restaurants, it is expected for customers to leave a tip, which is an extra amount of money, **on top of** the cost of their meal.

The amount of a tip in a US restaurant is typically 15-20% of the total bill, but some people may tip more or less depending on the quality of service they received. The amount of the tip is left up to the customer, and is not included in the price of the meal. For waiters who are friendly and provide **constant service** like refilling drinks and checking on the table, a larger tip is common. On the other hand, if your waiter is rude or does not pay attention to you, it is socially accepted to remove some money from the tip.

The situation is a little complicated, though, because in many US states **servers** are paid a lower minimum wage than other workers, with the expectation that they will earn tips to **make up the difference**. This has led to a culture where tipping is expected to provide most of a server's income.

大切にする傾向があり、家庭というプライベートな空間で美味しい料理を楽しめることは、これまでもとても魅力的なことでした。コロナ禍以来、テイクアウトは、混雑を避けソーシャルディスタンスを保ちながらお気に入りのレストランの味を楽しむことのできる、より一般的な方法となりました。

　テイクアウトをするには通常、電話かオンラインで料理を注文し、レストランへ受け取りに行くか配達をしてもらいます。たくさんのアプリがこうした受取や配達のサービスを提供していますが、いつものことですが、注文の際はどのような追加料金が必要になるかを確認しておきましょう。

## チップはどうする？

　アメリカのチップの文化は、**サービス業**において重要な役割を果たしています。アメリカのほとんどのレストランでは、食事の代金に**上乗せをして**チップを渡すことが一般的です。

　チップの金額は、たいてい合計金額の15％から20％ですが、サービスの質によって多めにチップを渡す人もいれば少なめに渡す人もいます。いくらチップを渡すかは客に委ねられていますが、それらは食事の代金には含まれていません。飲み物を足したり、テーブルをチェックしたり、**常に行き届いたサービス**をしてくれたフレンドリーなウェイターには多めにチップを渡すことが一般的です。一方、失礼だったり、あまり気を配ってくれなかったウェイターに対しては、チップを少なめに渡すことも許されています。

　ただ、アメリカの多くの州の**ウェイターやウェイトレス**の賃金は、他の職種に比べ低く、チップはその**差を埋める**ものと考えられていることから、状況は少し複雑です。チップが彼らの収入のほとんどを賄っていると考える文化があるのです。

アメリカにおけるチップの習慣は、食文化の重要な一部で守られるべきと考える人もいれば、賃金の公平性や透明性の観点から反対を主張する人もいる。チップはサービスをしたその人だけに渡されるのか、プールしておいて厨房スタッフも含め、従業員皆で分配するのか、など問題も多い。

It is worth noting that while tipping is expected in most US restaurants, there are some exceptions. Some **high-end restaurants** may include a service charge in the bill, also called a "gratuity" which means that tipping is not necessary. In other cases, such as fast food or fast casual restaurants, tipping is not expected at all. **The general rule** is that if you sit down and are served by a waiter, you are expected to tip, unless it is already part of the bill as mentioned earlier.

　アメリカでは、ほとんどのレストランでチップを渡すことが当然とされていますが、例外もあります。一部の**高級レストラン**では請求額にサービス料が含まれている場合があり、これは「グラチュイティ（心づけ）」とも呼ばれるもので、チップは必要ないことを意味します。また、ファストフード店やファストカジュアル・レストランなどでもチップを渡す必要はありません。**一般的なルール**として、席に着いてウェイターからサービスを受けた場合は、前述のように既に請求額の一部となっている場合を除き、チップを渡す必要があるということです。

# 6 Shopping

**Key Words** Brick and Mortar, Megastore, Outlets, Consumer Protection, Institution

## Online shopping

Americans love to shop, and they do it in almost any way you can imagine.

Of course, the biggest trend in the last decade has been the shift toward online shopping, which is more convenient and sometimes cheaper than buying things in person. Many former **brick and mortar** (physical) businesses have set up online stores where customers can browse and purchase products from the comfort of their own homes. Online shopping also allows customers to compare prices and products from different businesses quickly. Most importantly, online shopping allows customers to find exactly what they want, instead of simply choosing from whatever a physical store has **in stock**.

Physical stores are still a popular option for shopping in the US. Theses businesses were hit hard by the Covid 19 pandemic, but they are actually recovering as Americans who were trapped inside for years return to in-person activities. Perhaps the most popular brick and mortars are supermarkets, where you can buy food as well as **kitchen and cooking supplies**. There are also megastores, such as Costco, where you can buy large amounts of household items at low cost, although you almost always need a membership to shop there.

# 6 ショッピング

・・・・・・・・・・・・・・・・・・・・・・・・・・・・・・・・・・・・・・・・・・・・・・・・・・・・・・・・・・・・・・・・

**キーワード** 実店舗の、メガストア、アウトレット、消費者保護、
機関

## オンラインショッピング

　アメリカ人は買い物が大好きですが、考えられるあら
ゆる方法でショッピングを楽しんでいます。

　ここ10年間におけるの最大のトレンドは、もちろん、
より便利で、時には実店舗へ行くよりも安く買い物がで
きるオンラインショッピングへのシフトです。かつて**実
店舗**（ブリック・アンド・モルタル）を構えていた企業の
多くが、自宅にいながら商品を閲覧したり購入したりで
きるオンライン・ストアを開設しました。オンライン・
ストアでは、色々な企業ごとの価格や商品を瞬時に比較
することができます。ただ単に実際にある**在庫**の中から
商品を選ぶのではなく、本当に欲しい商品を間違いなく
見つけられるということが最大の特徴です。

　実際に店へ行く買い物は、今もアメリカでは人気の選
択肢です。コロナ禍では大きな打撃を受けたものの、何
年もの間、自粛していたアメリカ人が対面の活動を再開
するにつれて、目に見えて回復しつつあります。最も親
しまれている実店舗と言えば、やはり食料品や**台所用品、
調理用具**などを取り扱っているスーパーマーケットでし
ょう。低価格で大量の日用品を購入することができるコ
ストコのような量販店もありますが、そうした店で買い
物をするには、たいてい会員になる必要があります。

brick（レンガ）と mortar（モ
ルタル）で作った実店舗での
ビジネスという意味。

アメリカにあるオンラインショップの代表的なものとして、AmazonやWalmartはよく
知られている。他にも電化製
品ならBest Buy、ファッション系ならNordstrom、Macy's、
健康・美容であればSephora、
家具ならIkea、書籍でBarnes
& Noble、Books-A-Millionな
どがある。

Other than these **everyday stores**, there are a number of less common shopping options available, depending on where you live. You might hear about "outlet malls", which stores offer discounted prices on brand-name products, often by selling extra or items that are otherwise in less demand. Farmers' markets are popular places to buy **fresh produce** and other **local products**. These markets typically operate in **open-air settings**, allowing customers to buy directly from the farmers and producers. Pop-up shops are businesses that appear for a limited time and often feature unusual products.

## America, a Paradise for Returned Goods

With all the shopping to do in America, it's a good thing that it's also one of the best places in the world when it comes to **returning a product** you no longer want or need. The US has strong **consumer protection laws**, which give consumers the right to return a product if it does not work, **does not match the description**, or is not of high enough quality. These laws protect consumers and provide them with a sense of safety when making purchases.

Many businesses in the US also allow customers to return products within a certain period of time for a **refund or exchange**. This encourages consumers to buy with confidence, knowing that they can return a product if it does not meet their expectations. Businesses in the US offer options such as free return shipping, in-store returns, and drop-off locations. This makes the return process quick and easy for customers.

Overall, the combination of strong consumer protection laws and generous rules from businesses make the US an excellent place for returning purchases.

　こうした**日用品を取り扱う店舗**以外に、地域によってはあまり知られていない買い物の選択肢があります。売れ残った商品や需要の少なかった商品をはじめとしたブランド品を割引価格で提供する「アウトレットモール」は聞いたことがあるかもしれません。ファーマーズマーケットは**新鮮な農産物**や**地元の特産品**を買い求める人々に人気のスポットです。通常は**野外**に設営され、農家や生産者から直接商品を購入することができます。ポップアップショップは、期間限定で設営される珍しい商品を扱うことの多いショップです。

## 返品天国、アメリカ

　色々なショッピングを満喫できるアメリカは、不要になった商品の**返品**もまた、世界で最も容易にできる国といえます。アメリカには強力な**消費者保護法**があり、商品が機能しなかったり、**説明と違っていたり**、質がよくなかったりした場合は、消費者はそれらを返品することができます。こうした法律は消費者たちを守り、物を購入する際の安心感を与えてくれるものです。

　多くの企業もまた、一定期間内であれば、商品の**返品や交換**を消費者に認めています。そうすることで、消費者は万が一商品が期待にそぐわなかった場合でも返品することができるという安心感を持って買い物をすることができます。返品送料が無料になったり、店舗での返品が可能であったり、持ち込み場所が設定できたり、その選択肢も様々です。返品手続きが素早く簡単にできるよう配慮されているのです。

　概して、強力な消費者保護法と企業の寛大な規定の組み合わせにより、アメリカは購入商品を返品するのに最適な国となっているのです。

アメリカの店には、このような返品受付の場がたいていある。

## Buying Souvenirs at the Supermarket

It might seem strange, but if you are interested in buying a souvenir from a town that you like, you might consider getting one at the local supermarket!

For one thing, supermarkets are easy to get to, making it no problem to stop by and pick up souvenirs during your busy travel time. There is also a cost benefit, since supermarkets offer souvenirs at lower prices compared to tourist shops, which are known for **over-charging**. This can be especially appealing to travelers who are concerned about their budget.

In addition to their high prices, **tourist shops** have a bad reputation for selling products that do not really represent local culture. Supermarkets, on the other hand, have mostly local customers and as a result may offer products that people in the area actually care about. This provides travelers with a chance to bring back souvenirs that reflect the culture and traditions of the region they visited.

Overall, purchasing souvenirs at a US supermarket can be a convenient, **cost-effective**, and authentic way for foreigners to bring back mementos of their travels to the United States.

## Cashless

Across America, cash is much less common than it used to be, but most places still accept it. The average American pays for most things with credit card, the most widely accepted forms of cashless payment in the US. You can apply for a credit card from a bank or financial institution and use it to make purchases online or at physical stores.

Debit cards are similar to credit cards, but they **are linked directly** to your bank account. When you make a purchase using a debit card, the **funds** are taken directly from your bank account.

## スーパーマーケットでお土産を買うことについて

奇妙に思われるかもしれませんが、気に入った町でお土産を買うなら、地元のスーパーマーケットへ行ってみてはどうでしょう！

ひとつには、スーパーマーケットは見つけやすく、時間のない移動中であっても、立ち寄って買い物ができるという手軽さがあります。スーパーマーケットでは、割高な観光客向けの店に比べ良心的な価格でお土産を買うことができるので経済的でもあります。予算を気にする旅行者にとっては特に魅力的でしょう。

また、**観光客向けの店**には、割高であることに加えて地元の文化を反映するような商品があまり揃っていない、という良くない評価もあります。その反面、スーパーマーケットには地元の顧客が多く集まるため、その地域の人々に普段から好まれている商品が並んでいます。スーパーマーケットであれば、旅行者は訪れた地域の文化や伝統が反映されたお土産を購入できるというわけです。

概して、アメリカのスーパーマーケットでお土産を買うことは、外国人にとって旅の思い出を持ち帰るための、**経済的**で間違いのない方法なのです。

## キャッシュレス

アメリカ全土で、現金は以前ほど使用されなくなりましたが、ほとんどの場所ではまだ使うことができます。ふつうのアメリカ人は、ほとんどの買い物をクレジットカードで行います。クレジットカードはアメリカで最も広く受け入れられているキャッシュレス決済です。クレジットカードは銀行や金融機関で申し込むことができ、オンラインや店舗での買い物に使用することができます。

デビットカードは、クレジットカードに似ていますが、銀行口座に**直接紐づけされています**。買い物をすると、その**代金**が直接銀行口座から引き落とされます。デビット

Debit cards are also widely accepted in the US, and many banks offer them to their customers for free.

Although the US is still well behind Japan, **mobile payments** have slowly become popular in the US in recent years. Applepay, Googlepay, and Samsung pay are the most widely used, and having one of them makes it likely that you will be able to use mobile payment, at least in cities. Stores that are part of larger chains commonly accept mobile payments, but as a rule you should not expect mobile payments to be available. Unless you are in a rural area, it is likely that you can pay with credit or debit card, so cash is not necessary except in rare cases.

## Sale times

When you are making big purchases in the US, it is a good idea to wait for some of the big annual sales.

Black Friday: This is the day after Thanksgiving and is widely considered to be the beginning of the holiday shopping season. Many businesses offer large discounts to bring shoppers into their stores, either in person or online.

Cyber Monday: This is the Monday following Thanksgiving and is focused on online shopping, so businesses offer special deals such as free shipping.

Prime Day: This is a shopping event created by Amazon for its Prime members, typically held in July. Since Amazon is by far the most popular online shopping site in America, this is a fairly well known sale.

Memorial Day: This is a government holiday on the last Monday in May, marking the beginning of summer. Many businesses offer Memorial Day sales and discounts on outdoor equipment,

カードもまたアメリカで広く普及しており、多くの銀行が無料でそのサービスを提供しています。

　日本にかなり遅れは取っているものの、**モバイル決済**は近年アメリカでも徐々に浸透しつつあります。Apple PayやGoogle Pay、Samsung Payが最も普及しており、これらのうちどれかを持っていれば、少なくとも都市部ではモバイル決済ができます。大型のチェーン店ではたいていモバイル決済をすることができますが、絶対というわけではありません。ただ、地方以外ではクレジットカードやデビットカードが使用できるため、よほどでない限り現金は必須ではないでしょう。

## セール時期

　アメリカで大きな買い物をするのなら、年に何度かの大きなセールを待つと良いでしょう。

　**ブラックフライデー**：サンクスギビングデーの翌日で、ホリデーショッピング・シーズンの始まりとされています。買い物客を呼び込もうと多くの企業が実店舗でもオンラインでも大幅な値下げを行います。

　**サイバーマンデー**：サンクスギビングデーの翌月曜日で、企業はオンラインショッピングに特化し、送料無料などの特別割引を行います。

　**プライムデー**：アマゾンがプライム会員に向けて開催するショッピングイベントで、通常7月に開催されます。アマゾンはアメリカで最も人気のあるオンラインショッピング・サイトであるため、このセールは大変よく知られています。

　**戦没将兵追悼記念日（メモリアルデー）**：夏の始めにあたる5月の最終月曜日で、祝日です。多くの企業がこの日にセールを開催し、アウトドア用品や家具、キャンプ用

furniture, and camping supplies.

**Labor Day**: This is another government holiday that falls on the first Monday in September and is a popular time for retailers to offer end-of-summer sales on items like the ones mentioned above.

**Back-to-School Sales**: This is a period in late summer when businesses offer discounts on school supplies, clothing, and electronics to prepare students for the upcoming school year.

You don't have to buy things at these sales, but they are a reward for patient and careful shopping. Just make sure that the items on sale cannot actually be had for a lower price during the rest of the year, because some businesses have been known to trick customers with **exaggerated "deals"**.

具などが値引きされます。

　**勤労感謝の日（レイバーデー）**：9月の第1月曜日にあたる祝日で、小売店が前述のような商品について夏の終わりのセールを開催することで知られています。

　**バック・トゥ・スクールセール**：夏の遅い時期に、企業が学校の新学期に向けて学用品や衣類、電化製品などを値引きするセールです。

バック・トゥ・スクール
セール

　必ずしもセール時期に買い物をする必要はありませんが、時期を見て賢く買い物をする価値はあります。ただ、**大げさな「お買い得」**セールをうたって顧客をだます企業もあるため、セール中の商品が同じ年に、より安い価格で手に入るようなものではないかを確認しましょう。

# 7

# Activities

**Key Words** Yoga, Trendy, Broadcast, Projection, Cord-cutting, Cable TV, Satellite TV, Tax Deduction

## Exercise

There are many forms of exercise that are popular in the United States. Running and walking are **easy-to-do forms of exercise** that can be done anywhere, at any time. They are great for improving heart health, burning calories, and **reducing stress**. Just remember, not all US cities have sidewalks, so make sure to plan a safe route in advance. Furthermore, many locations in America are quite far apart compared to in Japan or Europe, so walking to a destination is simply not always a practical option.

**Weight training** is popular among Americans who are looking to increase their size and/or strength. It can be done at home, but the cost and difficulty of setting up a home gym means many Americans decide to join gyms with monthly memberships.

For Americans interested in reducing stress and improving their overall mental and physical health, yoga is a form of exercise that combines stretching, breathing, and meditation to improve **flexibility**, strength, and balance. Yoga studios can be found around the country, but they are not as common as traditional gyms. You are most likely to find Americans interested in Yoga on the coasts and in larger cities.

Although people ride bicycles in the cities and countryside, cycling is most popular in the American suburbs. This is because

# 7 アクティビティ

......................................................................

**キーワード** ヨガ、流行、放映、映写、コード・カッティング、ケーブルテレビ、衛星放送、税額控除

## エクササイズ

　アメリカで人気の運動は様々です。ランニングやウォーキングは、場所や時間を選ばず**手軽にできる運動**です。心臓の健康状態を改善し、カロリーを消費し、**ストレスを軽減する**のに最適です。ただ、アメリカの全ての都市に舗道があるわけではないので、事前に安全なルートを確認しておく必要があります。さらに、日本やヨーロッパと比べ、アメリカでは多くの場所が離れているため、歩いて行くのは必ずしも現実的ではありません。

　**ウエイトトレーニング**は、体格を良くしたり筋肉を鍛えたい人に人気です。自宅で行うこともできますが、自宅にジムを構えるとなると費用も手間もかかることから、多くの人は月会費を支払ってジムへ通います。

　ストレスを軽減し、心身共に健康を目指したい人にとって、ストレッチや呼吸法、瞑想などを組み合わせたヨガは、**柔軟性**や体幹、バランス感覚を鍛えるのに最適です。ヨガスタジオはアメリカ各地で見られますが、従来からあるジムほどには普及していません。沿岸部や大都市へ行けば、ヨガ好きのアメリカ人に会えるでしょう。

　都会でも田舎でも自転車に乗る人はいますが、サイクリングが最も親しまれているのはアメリカの郊外です。

155

cities are filled with car traffic, and that crowding can making riding a bike unsafe. On the other hand, America is so large that the distances between locations in rural areas are difficult to travel on a bike. Thus, the suburbs are something of a paradise for **bicycle riders**.

Finally, swimming is popular mainly among older Americans, since it places less strain on the joints while being great for heart health. Even on the coasts, swimming in the ocean for exercise is not very common, so most Americans who want to swim will get a gym membership. Some wealthy areas have nice local pools, but that is not common and should not be expected.

## Trendy Exercise Class

In addition to traditional forms of exercise, there are many trendy exercise options in the US that have gained popularity in recent years. Some of these options include:

High-Intensity Interval Training (HIIT) is a type of workout that involves **short bursts of intense exercise** followed by brief periods of rest. HIIT is popular because it's a time-efficient way to get a full-body workout in a short amount of time.

CrossFit is another high-intensity workout that combines weight training, gymnastics, and other exercises. It's popular because while it is **challenging**, it can still be adapted to any fitness level. As a result, it is popular with beginners and those who are not confident about their athletic skills.

Finally, SoulCycle is a form of **indoor cycling** that focuses on creating a community and a **sense of belonging**. It's popular because of its high-energy atmosphere and motivational instructors. Many Americans struggle to stay motivated when it comes to exercise, so having a small community of friends is quite helpful. In America, fitness and exercise is often viewed as a social activity, so don't be surprised if you are invited to the gym by new friends.

都会は車の往来が激しく、サイクリングをするには危険であることがその理由です。また、アメリカは国土が広いため、田舎のあちこちを自転車で移動することは大変です。そのため、**サイクリングをする人**にとって、郊外はパラダイスなのです。

最後に、水泳は関節への負担が少なく心臓にも良いため、アメリカの高齢者たちに特に人気があります。海岸沿いであっても、運動のために海で泳ぐことは一般的ではないので、ほとんどの人はジムに通っています。一部の富裕層が住む地域には地元に立派なプールがある場合もありますが、どこにでもあるわけではなく期待はできません。

## 流行のエクササイズクラスについて

従来のエクササイズに加え、アメリカでは、近年人気になったエクササイズが多くあります。ここでは、そのいくつかを紹介します。

高強度インターバル・トレーニング（HIIT）は、**負荷の高い短時間の運動**と短い休憩を組み合わせて行うワークアウトです。短時間ながら全身運動ができる、時間効率の良いエクササイズとして人気があります。

クロスフィットは、ウエイトトレーニング、体操、その他のエクササイズを組み合わせて行う高強度のワークアウトです。**大変ではありますが**、どんなレベルの運動にも対応できることが魅力です。そのため、初心者や運動神経に自身のない人にも人気があります。

最後に、ソウルサイクルは**室内で行うサイクリング**で、コミュニティーや**仲間作り**に重点を置いています。エネルギーにあふれた雰囲気と、モチベーションを上げてくれるインストラクターが人気です。こと運動に関しては、モチベーションの維持に苦戦するアメリカ人にとって、小さなコミュニティーで仲間を作ることは良い刺激になります。フィットネスやエクササイズを社交的な活動として捉え

ソウルサイクルスタジオ

## Sports

As you almost certainly know, The United States is a nation of sports lovers, and there are many popular televised sports in the country. In fact, live sports are by far the mostly highly rated television programs in the country, particularly as other forms of entertainment have grown over the years.

The National Football League (NFL) is the most popular sports league in the United States, with an estimated 180 million viewers tuning in to watch the Super Bowl each year. NFL games are broadcast on major networks such as CBS, NBC, and Fox, and Sundays during the football season are like mini-holidays for many Americans. If you are at a bar or restaurant with a football game on television, be prepared for **loud, emotional reactions** from local viewers.

The National Basketball Association (NBA) is another popular sports league in the US. The NBA season runs from October to June and is broadcast on major networks such as ABC, ESPN, and TNT. Basketball is not quite as popular as football, but it is loved by young Americans and is particularly popular in cities because it can be played in **crowded urban areas**.

Major League Baseball (MLB) was historically the most popular sport in the US, but it has struggled to

アメフトの試合

られているアメリカでは、新しい友人にジムに誘われることがあっても決して意外なことではありません。

## スポーツ

　広く知られているように、アメリカはスポーツ愛好家の国で、多くの人気スポーツがテレビで放映されています。実際、毎年様々なエンターテインメントが登場する中、スポーツ中継は国内で最も視聴率の高い番組となっています。

　ナショナル・フットボール・リーグ（NFL）はアメリカで最も人気のあるスポーツリーグで、毎年1億8,000万人もの視聴者が、スーパーボウルの中継にチャンネルを合わせています。NFLの試合はCBSやNBC、Foxなどの主要ネットワークで放映され、シーズン中の日曜日は、多くのアメリカ人にとって、さながらミニホリデーとなります。アメフトの試合中継をしているバーやレストランにいる時は、地元客たちの**大きな声や感情的なリアクション**に遭遇すること覚悟しておきましょう。

　全米バスケットボール協会（NBA）もまた、アメリカで人気のあるスポーツリーグです。NBAのシーズンは10月から6月で、試合はABC、ESPN、TNTなどの主要ネットワークで放映されます。バスケットボールはアメフトほど人気があるわけではありませんが、若者の間や、**混雑した都市部**でもプレーできることから、特に都会で人気があります。

　メジャーリーグベースボール（MLB）は歴史的に見てもアメリカで最も人気のスポーツですが、若い人々の間では野球離れが進んでいます。とはいえ、MLBの決

毎年2月上旬の日曜日に開催される。当日は、Super Bowl Sundayと言う。第1回目は1967年1月に開催された。

find fans in the younger generations. The World Series, which is the championship series of MLB, is still one of the **most-watched** sporting events in the country. Part of baseball's problem in America is that, compared to basketball, it requires a great deal of open space to play, as well as special equipment and at least a few friends.

Speaking of special equipment and difficulty finding places to play, Hockey is either one of the most popular sports in America or completely forgotten, depending on who you ask. The National Hockey League (NHL) is the main professional ice hockey league in the US, with games being broadcast on major networks, but its ratings are not as high as football, basketball, or baseball. Hockey is also seen as something of an **upper class sport**, since a full set of equipment costs hundreds or even thousands of dollars and paying for time at ice rinks can get expensive as well.

Soccer is extremely popular among young people in America, with many children in the suburbs playing in youth leagues growing up. However, that experience does not really translate to interest in soccer as a TV product, as the sport has always struggled to **draw an audience** in America. Major League Soccer (MLS) has been growing in popularity in the US over recent years, and many networks show English, German, or Italian games for serious fans, but the sport still trails the previous four in overall viewers.

Golf and tennis are also fairly popular sports, but they are usually played casually. They are less common to see on television, and are sometimes looked at as upper-class sports that aren't open to the **general population**.

勝シリーズであるワールドシリーズは、今なお全米で**最も視聴率の高い**スポーツイベントのひとつです。アメリカにおける野球の難点は、バスケットボールに比べ、プレーをするのに広大な敷地が必要であること、また専用の用具や少なくとも数人の仲間が必要だということでしょう。

　専用の用具や特別な場所で言えば、アイスホッケーは、アメリカで最も人気のあるスポーツとも言えますが、人によっては全く興味のないスポーツとも言えます。ナショナルホッケーリーグ（NHL）はアメリカの主要なアイスホッケー・プロリーグで、その試合は主要ネットワークでも放送されますが、アメフトやバスケットボール、野球ほど視聴率は高くありません。アイスホッケーは用具を一式揃えるのに数百ドルから数千ドルもの費用がかかること、またアイスリンク代が高額であることから、**上流階級のスポーツ**というイメージがあります。

1942年当時、すでに人気のスポーツだったアイスホッケーの試合

　サッカーはアメリカの若者に特に人気があり、主に郊外に住む子供たちが少年リーグに入ってプレーして育っています。ただ、その経験がテレビで放映されているサッカーへの関心につながることはあまりなく、アメリカのサッカー放映は、たいてい**視聴者集め**に苦戦しています。メジャーリーグサッカー（MLS）は、近年人気が高まりつつあり、多くのネットワークが本格的なファン向けに英語やドイツ語、イタリア語で試合を放映していますが、それでもまだ、全体としては前述の4つのスポーツに遅れをとっているのが現状です。

　ゴルフやテニスも、とても人気のあるスポーツですが、たいていはあまり注目を浴びずにプレーされています。テレビで目にする機会も少なく、**一般庶民向け**というよりは上流階級者向けのスポーツというイメージがあります。

## Super Bowl of National Events

The Super Bowl typically takes place on the first Sunday in February and is the final game of a months-long football season that begins in the fall.

The Super Bowl has become much more than just a football game. It has become a **national phenomenon** that brings people together, regardless of their cultural backgrounds or even interest in football. It is estimated that over 100 million people in the United States alone tune in to watch the game each year, making it the most-watched event every year.

The Super Bowl also has a significant impact on the US economy. It is estimated that over $6 billion is spent on Super Bowl-related expenses, such as food, beverages, merchandise, and travel. The Super Bowl also generates **significant revenue** for the host city, as fans from all over the country flock to the host city to attend the game and participate in related events.

Beyond its economic significance, the Super Bowl is also an important event for advertisers. The game is known for its **high-profile commercials**, which often feature celebrities and memorable advertisements. Companies are willing to pay millions of dollars for the opportunity to advertise during the Super Bowl, as they know that millions of people will be watching.

Americans host Super Bowl parties filled with light gambling and heavy amounts of American food. They are highly informal, and parties tend to be equally split between guests who want to watch the game and those who are mostly interested in socializing.

Overall, the Super Bowl has become a symbol of American culture and a significant event for sports fans, advertisers, and the US economy.

## 国民的イベントのスーパーボウル

　通常、2月の第一日曜日に開催されるスーパーボウルは、秋から数カ月に及ぶアメリカンフットボール・シーズンの最終試合にあたります。

　スーパーボウルは単なるアメフトの試合以上のものとなっています。文化的背景やアメフトへの関心の枠を超えて、人々をひとつにする**国民的現象**となっているのです。毎年、そのゲームを観ようと、アメリカだけでも1億人以上の人々がテレビにくぎ付けになり、最も高い視聴率を誇ると言われています。

　スーパーボウルのアメリカ経済への影響は絶大です。食品、飲料、グッズや旅行などを含めたスーパーボウル関連の出費は60億ドルを超えると言われています。国中のファンたちが観戦や関連イベントのために集まるスーパーボウルは、その開催都市にとっても**大きな収入源**なのです。

　経済的な影響だけでなく、スーパーボウルは広告主たちにとっても重要なイベントです。試合中に流されるコマーシャルは、有名人を起用したりインパクトの強い内容にしたりと、この試合は**注目度の高い宣伝**で知られています。数えきれないほどの人が観戦するスーパーボウルで、宣伝を行うために企業は何百万ドルもの出費をいとわないのです。

　アメリカ人は、軽く賭けたり、大量のアメリカ料理を持ち寄ってスーパーボウル・パーティーを開きます。パーティーはカジュアルなもので、試合の観戦が目的の人と、社交の場を楽しみたい人が、それぞれ半数くらいであることが一般的です。

　概して、スーパーボウルはスポーツファンや広告主、アメリカの経済にとって重要なイベントであるとともに、アメリカ文化の象徴なのです。

スーパーボウルでは、毎年異なるNFLスタジアムを使用する。
2024年（第58回）は推定約2億1,000万人（アメリカ人の約3分の2）が視聴した。歴代最も勝利したチームは、ピッツバーグ・スティーラーズが6回、ニューイングランド・ペイトリオッツが6回、ダラス・カウボーイズが5回、サンフランシスコ49ersが5回となっている。

多くの人々が集まるスーパーボウルの試合

## Films

Movie theaters in the United States have a rich culture that has evolved over the years. From the early days of silent films to the modern era of digital blockbusters, movie theaters have been an important part of American entertainment.

One of the defining features of movie theaters in the US is their popularity as a **social gathering place**. Going to the movies is often seen as a fun group activity, whether it's a date, a family outing, or a night out with friends. As such, theaters are designed to hold very large crowds, with multiple screens and show times throughout the day.

Another aspect of US movie theater culture is the emphasis on the **movie-going experience itself**. Theater owners often invest heavily in luxuries such as comfortable seating, high-quality sound systems, and **state-of-the-art projection technology** to create an unforgettable experience for moviegoers. Many theaters also offer special events such as midnight screenings, theme nights, and Q&A sessions with filmmakers to attract and retain customers.

Food and drink are another key part of the movie theater experience in the US. Moviegoers can expect to find a wide range of snacks and drinks available for purchase, including popcorn, candy, soda, and even hot dogs and nachos. Although prices for these items can be high, they are the primary source of income for theaters, which actually do not make much money from ticket sales themselves.

Finally, US movie theaters have faced significant challenges in recent years due to the rise of **streaming services** and the COVID-19 pandemic. However, the industry remains strong, with many theaters adapting to the changing times by showing classic films and cutting ticket prices even further. Despite the challenges,

## 映画

　映画館には、アメリカが長年にわたり培ってきた豊かな文化があります。映画がまだ無声だった創成期からデジタル大作となった現代に至るまで、映画館はアメリカのエンターテイメントの重要な一部を担ってきました。

　アメリカにおける映画館の特徴のひとつに、**社交の場**としての人気があります。デートであれ、家族との外出であれ、また友達との夜遊びであれ、映画館を訪れることは楽しいグループ・アクティビティなのです。大勢の観客を収容できるよう設計された映画館では、一日を通じ複数のスクリーンで映画が上映されています。

昔から親しまれてきたミズーリ州の古い映画館

　映画館におけるアメリカ文化のもうひとつの側面として、**鑑賞体験そのものに重点が置かれているということ**があります。映画ファンに忘れられない体験をしてもらおうと、映画館のオーナーはしばしば、快適な座席、高品質のサウンドシステム、**最先端の映写技術**などの高価な設備に投資します。また、映画館は深夜上映やテーマナイト、映画製作者とのQ&Aセッションなど、観客を呼び込み、維持するための特別なイベントも提供しています。

　飲食もまた、映画館体験の重要な要素です。映画ファンはポップコーンやキャンディー、ソーダ、さらにはホットドッグやナチョスなど、様々なスナックや飲み物を買うことができます。これらの商品は割高と思われるかもしれませんが、チケット売上では収益が十分ではない映画館にとっては主要な収入源なのです。

　最後に、アメリカの映画館は近年の**ストリーミングサービス**の台頭やコロナ禍によって大きな困難に直面しています。名作映画を上映したり、チケット代を割引したりすることで、多くの映画館は時代の変化に適応しており、映画業界は生き残っています。課題はあるものの、少なく

the culture of movie theaters in the US remains a beloved part of American entertainment culture, at least for now.

## Cord Cutting

Cord-cutting refers to the practice of canceling traditional cable or satellite TV subscriptions in favor of streaming services that allow viewers to access TV shows, movies, and other video content over the internet.

The trend of cord-cutting has gained popularity in the US in recent years, as many people have sought to reduce their **monthly expenses** and gain more flexibility in their viewing options. With the rise of streaming services such as Netflix, Hulu, Amazon Prime Video, Disney+, and others, viewers have more choices than ever before for accessing video content.

Cord-cutting can be seen as a response to the increasing costs of traditional cable and satellite TV subscriptions, which often require viewers to pay for hundreds of channels they never watch. By subscribing to streaming services, viewers can choose to pay only for the content they actually want to watch.

Cord-cutting has also been fueled by the increasing availability of high-speed internet connections, which make it possible to stream **video content in high-definition** without buffering or interruptions. As a result, many viewers are choosing to watch TV shows and movies on their computers, smartphones, or smart TVs instead of traditional cable or satellite boxes.

Overall, cord-cutting has **disrupted** the traditional TV industry and forced providers to adapt to changing consumer preferences. It has also created new opportunities for content creators and streaming services to reach audiences directly, without the need to go through powerful business partners.

とも今のところは、映画館における文化はアメリカのエンターテイメント文化の一部として愛され続けています。

## コード・カッティングについて

　コード・カッティングとは、インターネット経由でテレビ番組や映画、またその他の映像コンテンツにアクセスできるストリーミングサービスを選択するため、従来のケーブルテレビや衛星放送の契約を解除することです。

　近年、アメリカでは、多くの人々が**月々の出費**を減らしたり、より柔軟に観たいものを選べるようになったことから、コード・カッティングの人気が高まっています。Netflix やHulu、Amazonプライムビデオ、Diney+といったストリーミングサービスの台頭により、視聴者たちは映像コンテンツにアクセスするための選択肢を、以前より多く持つようになったのです。

　コード・カッティングは、観もしない何百ものチャンネルに料金を支払う従来のケーブルテレビや衛星放送、またそれらの料金の高騰に対する反応とも言えます。ストリーミングサービスに加入することで、視聴者は本当に観たいコンテンツだけに料金を支払えるようになりました。

　高速インターネット接続の普及により、バッファリングや中断なしに**高画質のビデオコンテンツ**をストリーミングできるようになったこともまた、コード・カッティングの人気に拍車をかけました。そのようなことから、多くの人々はテレビ番組や映画を、従来のケーブルテレビや衛星放送ではなく、パソコンやスマートフォン、またはスマートテレビなどで視聴することを選んでいます。

　全体として、コード・カッティングにより、従来のテレビ業界は**混乱し**、プロバイダーたちも視聴者の嗜好に適応せざるを得なくなりました。また、コンテンツ制作者やストリーミングサービスにとっては、巨大なビジネスパートナーに頼ることなく、直接視聴者にリーチできる新たな機会ともなったのです。

テレビのリモコンからも自由にアクセスできるストリーミングサービス

バッファリングとは、データの送受信における処理速度や転送速度の差を補うため、または通信の減速や中断に備えて、データを一時的に記憶領域に保存しておくこと。動画再生の前にある程度のデータが貯まるまで待ち、その後再生が開始される。

## Performing arts

The performing arts in the United States are incredibly **diverse** and include a wide range of **disciplines**, from theater to dance, as well as many more.

Theater is one of the most prominent performing arts in the US and includes both Broadway productions in New York City and **smaller regional theaters** throughout the country. Many of the most famous American playwrights, such as Tennessee Williams and Arthur Miller, have made **significant contributions** to the American theater tradition.

Dance is also an important performing art in the US, with many prominent ballet and modern dance companies located throughout the country. Some of the most famous American dancers and **choreographers** include Martha Graham and Alvin Ailey.

While theater and dance can be found anywhere in America, performing arts like opera and ballet are most likely only going to be found in the larger cities, as the interest in these art forms is not high enough in most areas.

### Tax Savings with Art Support

In the US, **tax savings** can be achieved through art support by making charitable donations of art to qualifying **non-profit organizations**.

According to law, individuals who donate artwork to qualified charitable organizations may receive a **tax deduction** equal to the fair market value of the donated artwork. This deduction translates to money saved when the individual goes to pay their annual income taxes.

To qualify for the deduction, the donated artwork must be considered a "**collectible**" by the IRS, which generally includes paintings, sculptures, drawings, prints, and other works of art. The artwork must also be donated to a qualified charitable organization,

## 舞台芸術

　アメリカの舞台芸術は、驚くほど**多岐にわたっ**ており、演劇やダンスをはじめ様々な**分野**があります。

　ニューヨークのブロードウェイや全米各地の**小さな地方劇場**など、演劇はアメリカで突出した舞台芸術のひとつです。テネシー・ウィリアムズ、アーサー・ミラーをはじめとした多くの有名な劇作家たちは、アメリカの演劇の伝統に**大きく貢献**しました。

有名なニューヨークのブロードウェイ街 © Matt H. Wade

　ダンスもまたアメリカで主要な舞台芸術であり、著名なバレエ団やモダンダンス・カンパニーがアメリカ全土にはあります。マーサ・グレアムやアルヴィン・エイリーは、アメリカの最も有名なダンサーおよび**振付師**です。

　演劇やダンスは、アメリカのどの地域でも見られますが、オペラやバレエなどの舞台芸術については、関心のある地域は少なく、大都市でしか見ることができないでしょう。

### 芸術品支援による節税

　アメリカでは、対象となる**非営利団体**に美術品の寄贈をすることで、芸術品支援による**節税**をすることができます。

　法律によると、個人が適格な慈善団体に美術品を寄贈した場合、その公正市場価格と同額の**税額控除**を受けることができます。個人が所得税を納める際は、この控除により節税が可能です。

　控除対象となるには、寄贈された美術品がIRS（米国国税庁）によって「**収集品**」と見なされなければならず、これには主に絵画や彫刻、素描や版画、その他のアート作品が含まれます。また、寄贈される美術品は、美術館や大学、

such as a museum, university, or other public institution.

It's important to note that tax laws surrounding art support can be complex, and it's recommended to consult with a **tax professional** or financial advisor before making any donations or purchases.

## Museums

Museums in the US are diverse and cover a broad range of subjects and interests. Generally, though, the following types of museums can be found in most major cities.

Art museums: These museums feature collections of paintings, sculptures, and other forms of visual art from a wide range of artists and periods.

Natural history museums: These museums showcase exhibits about the **natural world**, including fossils, animal specimens, and interactive displays about ecosystems and the environment.

Science museums: Science museums feature exhibits and **interactive displays** about topics such as physics, biology, chemistry, and technology.

History museums: These museums focus on specific historical events or periods, including military history, cultural history, and the history of science and technology.

Children's museums: These museums are specifically designed for children and feature interactive exhibits and hands-on activities that encourage learning and exploration.

Ethnic and cultural museums: These museums focus on specific cultures, ethnic groups, or regions and showcase exhibits about art, history, and traditions.

Some of the most well-known museums in the US include

その他の公的機関などの適格な慈善団体に寄贈されなければなりません。

　芸術品支援をめぐる税法は複雑な場合があるので、寄贈や購入を行う前には**専門の税理士**やフィナンシャルアドバイザーに相談しましょう。

## 博物館

　アメリカの博物館は、様々なテーマや興味対象を扱っています。一般的には下記のような博物館がほとんどの主要都市にあります。

　美術館：幅広い時代の芸術家の絵画や彫刻、その他視覚的な作品が展示されています。

　**自然史博物館**：化石や動物標本、生態系や環境についての体験型の展示など、**自然界に関する展示**がされています。

　**科学博物館**：物理学や生物学、化学、テクノロジーなどのテーマに関する展示や**体験型の展示**がされています。

　**歴史博物館**：軍事史や文化史、科学技術史など、特定の歴史的事項や時代に焦点を当てた展示がされています。

　**子供博物館**：子供を対象とした、学習や探求を促すインタラクティブな展示や体験型のアクティビティが行われています。

　**文化民族博物館**：特定の文化や民族、地域に焦点を当て、それらの芸術や歴史、伝統などについて展示されています。

　アメリカで最も有名な博物館や美

メトロポリタン美術館

the Smithsonian Institution in Washington, D.C., the American Museum of Natural History in New York City, the Art Institute of Chicago, and the Getty Center in Los Angeles. Many cities and towns throughout the US also have smaller, local museums that focus on specific local topics or interests.

## Permanent Exhibitions on Weekdays

Permanent weekday museum exhibits are displays that are **open to the public** on a regular basis, typically during weekdays, and are designed to showcase a museum's collection or a particular theme or topic. These exhibits are usually set up in a specific section of the museum and are available for visitors to explore whenever they feel like it.

The term "permanent" refers to the fact that these exhibits are not temporary or traveling exhibits, which are typically displayed for a limited time and then moved on to other museums. Instead, **permanent exhibits** are designed to be a long-term part of the museum and are usually organized around a specific theme or subject.

Some examples of permanent weekday museum exhibits might include displays of **ancient artifacts**, natural history exhibits, art collections, or interactive science exhibits. These exhibits can provide visitors with an educational and engaging experience that can be enjoyed on a regular basis, making museums a popular destination for both locals and tourists.

Permanent weekday museum exhibits are often a central feature of a museum's collection and can be used to attract visitors and increase public awareness of the museum's mission and purpose. They can also serve as a way to highlight a particular cultural or historical impact, or to explain important scientific discoveries or advancements.

術館には、ワシントンD.C.のスミソニアン博物館、ニューヨークのアメリカ自然史博物館、シカゴ美術館、ロサンゼルスのJ・ポール・ゲティ美術館などがあります。また、全米の多くの都市や町には、地元のテーマや関心に焦点を当てた小規模の博物館があります。

## 平日の常設展について

　平日の常設展とは通常、平日に**一般公開**される展示のことで、その館のコレクションや特定のテーマ、トピックに沿ったものを展示することが目的とされています。これらの展示はたいてい、施設の特定のセクションに設けられ、来館者はいつでも好きな時に見学することができます。

　「常設」とは、期間限定の展示であったり、終了後に他の館へ移されたりするような、一時的な展示や巡回型の展示ではないということです。そのため、**常設展示**は博物館や美術館における長期的な役割を担うよう設定されており、その多くは特定のテーマや主題に沿って構成されています。

　平日の常設展の例としては、**古代遺跡**の展示や自然史の展示、美術品のコレクション、またインタラクティブな科学展示などがあります。このような展示により、来館者たちは教育的かつ魅力的な体験を定期的に楽しむことができるため、博物館や美術館は地元の人々や旅行者にとって人気のスポットとなっています。

　平日の常設展は、たいていその館の中心的存在となっており、来館者を呼び込んだり、館の使命や目的について人々の認識を高めたりする役割を果たしています。また、特定の文化や歴史について焦点を当てたり、重要な科学的発見や進歩について紹介したりする手段ともなっています。

# アメリカの国立公園を
楽しむ

東西を結ぶインターステートは偶数、
南北は奇数で表される

90 INTERSTATE

5 INTERSTATE

95 INTERSTATE

10 INTERSTATE

　アメリカの州をまたい
で縦横無尽に都市を結ぶ高速
道路をインターステート（州間高速
道路）といいます。高速道路の番号が偶数
であれば東西に、奇数であれば南北に延びています。

　たとえば、インターステート10号線は、カリフォルニアからフロリダまで、アメリカの南を横断するのです。同じように、10号線と交差して北に伸び、ラスベガスからソルトレイクシティを経てモンタナ州のカナダ国境までのびる高速道路は15号線です。

　この10号線と15号線に挟まれたアメリカ西部の広大な地域は、アメリカでも最も国立公園の多い地域となります。アメリカの国立公園は連邦政府がその雄大な自然とそこに生きる生物を管理していて、入園するには管理料を払うのが一般です。しかし、入園といってもそこは単なる公園というイメージでは測れない広さと、山や谷といった多彩な自然に彩られた巨大なパークです。

　ロサンゼルスから15号線を北上し、ラスベガスまで5時間、そこからさらに3時間も走れば、西部劇の映画の中に迷い込んだかのような砂漠とメサと呼ばれる奇岩が連なる地域に入っていきます。15号線から東に折れて

メサと呼ばれるテーブル状の大地

ゆけば、アメリカで最も有名な国立公園ともいえるグランドキャニオンや、その周辺にあるいくつもの国立公園のある地域に入ってきます。

　地球の創世記にまで遡れるような地層や、その奥を流れるコロラド川の渓谷、そんな渓谷を流れる川や風雨によって何万年、時には何億年もかけて形作られた岩や山は、訪れる人の目を奪います。

　この地域は、そうした自然の威容を畏怖して生活していたのが、アメリカン・インディアンの部族です。彼らが古代から居住しては移住した足跡が、数多くの遺跡として残っているのもこの地域です。彼らが今も守り続ける文化と雄大な大地とが溶け合うのがこの地域の特徴です。

　15号線をさらに北に行けば、19世紀半ばにアメリカに移住してきた人々が土地を求めて西へと移住した「オレゴントレイル」と呼ばれる開拓路が残る山岳地帯に入ります（p.71参照）。この過酷だった開拓路も今では、マウントティートンなど、ロッキー山脈の名峰が連なる国立公園となっています。広大な地域に温泉が散在するイエローストーンもこの近くです。1872年に、グラント大統領がアメリカ第1号の国立公園に指定したのがイエローストーンです。

ロッキー山脈

　国立公園を訪れながらそこを開拓した人々や、あるいはそこで自然を崇めてきた先住民の文化に目を向けるとき、アメリカという国と大地の底知れぬパワーを感じるのです。

　もちろん、国立公園はこの地域だけにあるわけではありません。東海岸から西海岸まで、アメリカには59の国立公園と、75の国立モニュメントがあります。国立モニュメントはアメリカの歴史を知る上で欠かすことのできない国家遺産が指定されているものです。

　アメリカの東から西、北から南へと国立公園を訪ねれば、地域ごとの多彩な自然の相違を味わえます。東海岸を例にとれば、紅葉の美しいメイン州の国立公園と、スワンプにワニが泳ぐフロリダの公園まで、95号線という一本のインターステートがつないでくれます。

　アメリカに旅行するときは、ぜひ広大な大地を高速道路で走りながら、国立公園を訪ねて旅することをおすすめします。

# Part 3

# Let's Live in America

*Living in the USA*

# アメリカに住もう

暮らしの常識

# Housing

Key Words Tenant, Screening, Dormitories, Roommate (vs. Flatmate), Explosive, Inspection, Closing, Bubble

## Where to live?

The relationship between **location and property value** in the US is strong, with the value of a property being heavily influenced by its location. In general, properties located in desirable areas, such as urban or suburban areas with good schools, low crime rates, access to services like shopping, dining, and entertainment, and being close to major employment centers, tend to be more valuable than properties in areas that lack those things. Additionally, properties that offer beautiful views or are located near natural features like lakes, mountains, or beaches may also have higher prices.

On the other hand, properties located in areas with **high crime rates** and poor schools, or near industrial or noisy areas, may have lower values.

California, Washington state, and the Northeast coast of America are known for being expensive. Places like the South and the Midwest have lower rents and home prices, but you need to be more careful about making sure the area you would be living in has all the things you want. Rural areas, on the other hand, almost always have cheap housing, but because of how big America is, that means you will be isolated most of the time.

# 住宅

**キーワード** 家主、審査、寮、ルームメイト(vs. フラットメイト)、高騰、検査、契約完了、バブル

## どこに住むか？

アメリカにおける**立地と不動産価格**の関係は深く、その価格は立地に大きく左右されます。一般的に都心部や郊外の、学校が充実し、犯罪率が低い、ショッピングや食事、娯楽などのサービスにアクセスしやすく、職場にも近いといった理想的な立地にある物件は、そうでない立地の物件に比べ価値が高い傾向があります。また、美しい景観が望める物件や、湖、山、ビーチなどの自然が近くにある物件も、価格が高くなる傾向があります。

一方、**犯罪率が高く**、学校が充実しておらず、または工業地帯や騒音地域が間近にある物件は価値が低くなりがちです。

カリフォルニア州、ワシントン州、アメリカ北東部の沿岸は物件価格が高いとされています。南部や中西部などは、比較的家賃も住宅価格も安いですが、住もうとする地域に必要なものが揃っているかを確認した方が良いでしょう。一方、地方であればたいていの住宅は安価ですが、アメリカは広いため大抵の場合、孤立してしまうことになります。

国内で人気のある居住地は、以下の都市が挙げられる。経済状況、雇用、生活水準、気候、自然環境などで評価された。
・カリフォルニア州：サンディエゴ、サンノゼ
・テキサス州：オースティン、ダラス
・コロラド州：デンバー
・ノースカロライナ州：シャーロット
・ワシントン州：シアトル

## Single-family and multi-family (condo and co-op)

**Single-family housing** refers to a home designed for one family or household, typically not attached to other buildings and located on its **own plot of land**. Single-family homes may range from small, 1 or 2 bedroom "**bungalows**" to huge mansions, and are typically owned by an individual or couple.

**Multi-family housing** refers to any building or structure that houses more than one family, generally split into separate units within the same building. Multi-family housing units may include apartments, condominiums, townhouses, and other similar structures.

While single-family housing and multi-family housing are distinct in terms of their design, ownership, and use, they are also related in several ways. For example, many families start out living in a multi-family home but may transition to single family housing as their needs change over time. However, it is also common for **retired Americans** whose children have moved out to switch from relatively large single family homes to smaller houses or apartments.

Unlike in Japan, it is more common for Americans to buy an **existing house** than build a new one. This means that houses are seen not just as homes, but as investments that usually increase in value over time and can help pay for retirement if sold. Property rental in the US is a common practice where landlords rent out their properties to tenants for a monthly fee.

Here are some key aspects of property rental in the US:

**Tenant Screening:** Before **renting a property**, landlords typically screen potential tenants by checking their credit score, employment status, rental history, and **criminal background**.

## 戸建住宅と集合住宅

　戸建住宅とは、一家族または世帯向けに設計され、普通は個人の所有地に建てられた独立した建物のことを言います。戸建ては寝室がひとつかふたつの「平屋」から、大邸宅まで様々で、個人か夫婦で所有されることが一般的です。

　集合住宅とは、一世帯以上が住む建物のことで、通常は建物内が個々のユニットに分かれています。アパート、コンドミニアム、タウンハウス、その他同様の構造をした建物を集合住宅といいます。

　戸建住宅と集合住宅は、その設計、所有権、用途などに違いはあるものの、いくつか関連性もあります。例えば、多くの家族は集合住宅から生活を始め、月日の経過とともにニーズが変化し、戸建住宅へ引っ越します。また、子供が独立し退職したアメリカ人は、大きめの戸建住宅から小さな家やアパートへ引っ越すこともあります。

　日本とは異なり、一般的なアメリカ人は新しく家を建てるのではなく、中古住宅を購入します。家は単に住む場所というより、時間とともに価値の上がる投資と捉えられており、売却すれば老後の生活費の足しになると考えているのです。家主が自身の所有する不動産を貸し出し、毎月の賃料を徴収する不動産賃貸も、アメリカでは一般的な形態です。

　ここでは、アメリカの不動産賃貸に関する一般的な事項を紹介します。

　入居審査：大家は通常、物件を貸し出す前に入居希望者のクレジットスコア、雇用状況、賃貸履歴、犯罪歴などを審査します。

アパートは通常、不動産管理会社や個人の家主などが所有する建物。居住者は建物内の１ユニットを賃借し、所有権は持たない。
コンドミニアムは、居住者が所有権を持つ集合住宅内の個々のユニットである。建物は集合住宅だが、各戸は独立して個人が所有する。
タウンハウスは個人所有の複数階建ての住宅で、隣接する物件と隣り合っているが、玄関はそれぞれ独立している。

**Lease Agreement:** Once a tenant is selected, the landlord and tenant sign a lease agreement that outlines **the terms and conditions** of the rental arrangement, such as the rental amount, payment due date, **security deposit**, duration of the lease, and maintenance responsibilities. Most **lease agreements** are for one year, but they can vary.

**Rent Payment:** Tenants are typically required to pay **rent** on a monthly basis, usually due **on the first day of the month**. Some landlords may offer a **"grace" period** of a few days before late fees are applied.

**Security Deposit:** Landlords may require tenants to provide a security deposit, which is usually equivalent to one month's rent. The deposit is held by the landlord and returned to the tenant at the end of the lease term, provided that the tenant has fulfilled all the terms of the lease. This is meant to cover the cost of any damage that the tenant does to the apartment. Unfortunately, landlords have been known to keep some or all of the security deposit for a variety of reasons. Since getting a security deposit back would involve a long and expensive legal battle, it is best to consider a security deposit to be gone as soon as it is paid. Any amount that is returned is essentially bonus money.

**Maintenance and Repairs:** The landlord is responsible for maintaining the property in a clean and safe condition and making any necessary repairs. However, tenants are also expected to maintain the property and report any issues or damages to the landlord as soon as possible.

**Eviction:** If a tenant **violates the terms** of the lease agreement, the landlord may initiate eviction proceedings to remove the tenant from the property. The specific eviction process varies by state and local laws.

　**賃貸契約**：入居者が決まると、大家と借主は、賃貸料、支払期限、**敷金**、賃貸期間、メンテナンスの責任など、**契約条件**が記された**賃貸契約書**にサインをします。ほとんどは一年契約ですが、例外もあります。

　**家賃の支払い**：借主は通常、**毎月1日に家賃を支払います**。延長料が発生する場合は、その前の数日間を「**猶予**」期間として設けている大家もいます。

　**敷金**：大家は通常、家賃の一カ月分にあたる敷金の支払いを要求します。大家が預かった敷金は、賃貸期間終了後、借主が賃貸条件を全て満たしていた場合に返還されます。敷金は借主が賃貸物件を傷つけてしまった際の費用をカバーするために使われます。とはいえ残念なことに、様々な理由をつけて敷金の一部、または全額を留保してしまう大家もいると言われています。敷金を返還してもらうには、長期にわたる高額な法廷論争が必要になることもあるため、敷金は支払った時点でもう返ってこないと考えた方が無難でしょう。もし、返還されることがあれば、その時はボーナスが入ったのだと思いましょう。

　**メンテナンスと修理**：大家は物件を清潔で安全な状態に保ち、また必要な修理を行う責任があります。同時に借主も、物件を維持し、問題や破損などがあった場合は速やかにそれらを大家に伝える必要があります。

　**立ち退き**：借主が賃貸契約の**条項に違反**した場合、大家は借主を物件から退去させるために立ち退きの手続きを開始することができます。具体的な手続きは、州法や地方法によって異なります。

## Tenant Screening

**Tenant screening** is a process used by landlords and property managers in the United States to learn more about the personal history and character of possible tenants before allowing them to rent a property. The process typically involves a background check on the tenant's credit, criminal history, **employment status**, and rental history.

The purpose of tenant screening is to ensure that landlords are renting to responsible and reliable tenants who will pay rent on time, take care of the property, and not pose a threat to other residents or the neighborhood. In many American cities, it is extremely difficult to **kick out a tenant** who stops paying rent, so landlords want to be as certain as possible before giving someone permission to live in their building.

Some common steps in tenant screening include:

**Application:** Prospective tenants are asked to fill out an application form that collects personal information such as their name, address, Social Security number, employment history, and personal or professional references.

**Credit check:** Landlords may use a **credit reporting agency** to obtain the tenant's credit report, which provides information about their credit history, debts, and payment history. This is important, because tenants with good credit scores have a history of paying what they owe. Also, a person with a high credit score will want to protect it by paying their bills, while a person with a very low credit score has less motivation to be **financially responsible**.

**Criminal background check:** Landlords may conduct a criminal background check to determine if the tenant has a criminal record that could lead to the tenant posing a risk to the property or other residents.

**Rental history:** Landlords may contact **previous landlords** to confirm the tenant's rental history and determine if they have a habit of paying rent on time and taking care of the property.

## 入居審査について

　**入居審査**とは、アメリカの家主や不動産管理業者が、物件を貸し出す前に、入居予定者の個人的な経歴や状況を詳しく知るために行う手続きのことです。手続きでは通常、入居者のクレジット、犯罪歴、**雇用状況**、賃貸履歴が審査されます。

　この審査は、家主から入居者について、家賃を期限内に支払うことや、物件を大切に管理し、他の住人や近隣の人々に危害を加えず、責任と信頼のおける賃貸ができることを確認するために行われます。アメリカの多くの都市では、家賃が払えなくなった**入居者を退去させる**ことは非常に難しく、そのため家主は入居者を迎える前にできる限り状況を把握しようとします。

　一般的な入居審査の手順は以下の通りです。

　**申込み**：入居希望者は申込書に、氏名、住所、社会保障番号、職歴、照会先となる個人や職場などの個人情報を記入します。

　**信用調査**：家主は**信用調査会社**に依頼をし、入居者のクレジットヒストリーや負債、支払履歴などについて記載された信用報告書を入手します。支払履歴が良好であれば、クレジットスコアが高いことを意味するため、この手順は重要です。また、クレジットスコアの高い人はそれを維持するために支払いをきちんと守ろうとしますが、逆に低い人は**経済的責任**を甘く見る傾向があります。

　**犯罪歴調査**：家主は入居者に犯罪歴がないか、また物件や他の住人に危害を及ぼす可能性がないかを判断するために犯罪歴調査を行う場合があります。

　**賃貸履歴**：家主は入居者の**以前の大家**に連絡をし、賃貸経歴を確認することで、その入居者に家賃を期日通り支払い、物件を管理する習慣があるかを確認することがあります。

過去の借入と返済の記録をクレジットヒストリーという。信用調査機関が延滞、債務不履行の有無、クレジットカードの利用状況などを調べ、一般的に300点から850点までの範囲でスコアを出す。ローンの借り入れ、クレジットカードの発行、賃貸契約に必ず必要になる。

**Employment confirmation**: Landlords may contact the **tenant's employer** to confirm their employment status and income to ensure that they will be able to afford the rent in the future.

It is important to note that the **Fair Housing Act** makes it illegal for landlords to discriminate against possible tenants based on their race, color, national origin, religion, sex, familial status, or disability.

## Dormitories or Apartments

Choosing between dorms or apartments as a college student depends on your personal preferences, budget, and lifestyle. Typically, dorms are more expensive than apartments, but the price may vary based on location and services provided. If you are on a **tight budget**, you may want to consider sharing an apartment with roommates to split the cost.

You also need to consider the location of the dorms and apartments in relation to your classes, campus services, and social activities. Living on campus may be more convenient, but apartments may be closer to **off-campus attractions** and entertainment. Generally, students who have cars find living in off-campus apartments to be relatively easy, although parking at universities is not always simple or cheap.

In a dorm, you may be assigned a roommate or roommates, which can be a great way to make new friends and have a social and academic support system. However, if you prefer more privacy, an apartment may be a better choice.

Dorms often come with amenities like meal plans, security, and cleaning services, while apartments mostly require you to take care of these things yourself. Consider whether you want the convenience of having these things provided for you or if you prefer more independence.

　**雇用確認**：家主は入居者の雇用先に連絡をし、雇用形態や収入を確認することで、入居者に将来的な家賃を支払う能力があるかを確認することがあります。

　なお、**公正住宅取引法**により、人種や肌の色、国籍、宗教、性別、家族構成、障害の有無によって入居者を差別することは違法とされていることを覚えておきましょう。

## 寮かアパートか

　大学生として、寮とアパートのどちらを選ぶかは、個人の好みや予算、ライフスタイルにより様々です。たいてい寮の方がアパートよりも高額で、住む場所や提供されるサービスによって異なります。もし、**予算に限り**があるなら、ルームメイトとアパートをシェアして費用を折半するのも良いでしょう。

典型的な寮の一室

　また、授業やキャンパス内のサービス、学校外での活動などによって寮やアパートの場所を検討することも大切です。キャンパス内に住めば便利かもしれませんが、アパートの方がより**学校外での楽しみ**が充実するかもしれません。車を持っている学生は、気軽にキャンパス外のアパートを選ぶ傾向がありますが、大学の駐車場は決して便利で安いというわけではありません。

　寮の場合はにはたいてい、ひとりまたは複数のルームメイトが割り当てられるため、新しい友達を作ったり、生活面または学業面での助けを得るには最適でしょう。ただ、プライバシーの方が重要というのであれば、アパートの方が良いかもしれません。

　たいてい寮には、食事プラン、安全対策、清掃など、アパートであれば自分で用意しなければならない環境が整っています。こうしたことが整えられている便利さか、自活するか、検討してみましょう。

Your lifestyle and personal preferences may also play a role in your decision. Do you like to socialize and be surrounded by people all the time, or do you prefer a quieter, more independent living situation? Do you like to **cook your own meals**, or do you prefer to have meals prepared for you?

In America, younger college students tend to live in dorms while they are still adjusting to life on their own and are excited about making new friends. As they get older, students pursue more independence and move into off-campus apartments with the friends they have made at college.

## Roommate

Living with a roommate in the US is a common way for people to save on rent and other **living expenses**. Roommates can be found through various means, such as online roommate matching services, **personal referrals**, or through social media groups.

One thing that sometimes confuses visitors to America is that "roommate" does not mean someone who you share an actual bedroom with. It refers to what people in the UK and some other countries typically call a "flatmate". Now, it gets a little complicated because a college roommate is usually someone you share an actual bedroom with, often freshman year. The general rule is that if a college student refers to a roommate, they might or might not mean someone they share a room with. Any other adults are most likely talking about someone they share an apartment with while sleeping in different bedrooms.

Anyway, once you have found a roommate, you will need to sign a lease agreement that outlines the terms of your living

　どちらに決めるかは、あなたがどんな暮らしをしたいの
か、何が好きかにもよるかもしれません。あなたは社交的
でいつも周りに人がいるのが好きですか？　それとも静か
で独立した暮らしの方が好きでしょうか？　**自炊**は好きで
すか？　それとも誰かに食事を用意してもらう方が好きで
すか？

　アメリカでは、一人暮らしに慣れておらず、新しい友
達も作りたいという若い学生は、寮で暮らす傾向がありま
す。そして年齢とともに自立心が育ってくると、大学でで
きた友達とキャンパス外のアパートへと引っ越します。


## ルームメイト

　アメリカでルームメイトと暮らすことは、家賃やその
他の**生活費**を節約するためによくする方法です。ルーム
メイトはオンラインのルームメイト・マッチングサービ
スや**個人の紹介**、ソーシャルメディアのグループなど、
様々な方法で見つけることができます。

　アメリカに来て、「ルームメイト」が実は個室を共有す
る人のことではないと知ると、混乱するかもしれません。
ルームメイトは、イギリスやその他の国では「フラット
メイト」と呼ばれています。混乱を招く理由は、カレッ
ジ・ルームメイトというと普通は新入生の時に個室を共
有する人のことを指すからでしょう。一般的な慣習とし
て、もし大学生がルームメイトについて言及した場合、
それは寝室をシェアしている人のことを指す場合もあれ
ば、そうでない場合もあるということです。ですが、そ
れ以外の大人であれば、ルームメイトとはアパートを共
有しながらも、別々の個室を使っている相手のことを指
す場合がほとんどなのです。

　いずれにせよ、ルームメイトが見つかれば、生活条件
などを記載した賃貸借契約書にサインをしなければなり

ルームメイトの定義は、同じ住
居で生活を共有する人。家賃
や生活費を分担し、キッチン
やバスルームを共有する。フ
ラットメイトはルームメイト
と同義。これに対し、カレッジ・
ルームメイトは、個室を共有
すること。キッチン、バスルー
ム、リビングルームなどは共
有スペースとして利用する。

arrangement. This may include details about rent payment, **utilities**, **chores**, and other responsibilities. It's important to make sure you understand and agree with all the terms before signing the lease.

When living with a roommate, it's important to communicate openly and honestly about expectations and boundaries. This can include things like how you'll split household chores, what time you typically go to bed or wake up, and whether or not guests are allowed.

It's also important to respect each other's privacy and personal space. This may mean setting guidelines for sharing common areas, like the kitchen or living room, or agreeing on a schedule for using shared spaces. Living with a roommate can be a great way to form new friendships and save money, but it requires open communication and **mutual respect** to make the living arrangement work smoothly. Americans tend to be fairly open and direct about their feelings, so conversations about those things are expected between roommates. As long as both parties are friendly and honest, most roommate issues can be solved without trouble.

## Purchase

First, remember that in America it is incredibly common to purchase a **used home**. In fact, almost 90% of new homeowners buy an **existing home** rather than building one. Because of this, the process of buying a home in America involves doing quite a bit of research into the history and construction of the home.

Before you start looking for a home, however, it's important

ません。契約書には家賃の支払いや**光熱費、家事**その他の責任などについて記されています。サインをする前に内容を理解し、全ての条件に同意できることを確認しましょう。

　ルームメイトと暮らすには、自分が思っていることや、自分の許容範囲について、率直に話すことが大切です。家事をどのように分担するか、就寝や起床の時間、ゲストを家に招いて良いかなどが含まれます。

　お互いのプライバシーや個人のスペースを尊重することも大切です。キッチンやリビングルームなどの共有スペースを使うときのガイドラインを決めたり、スケジュールを確認しておくと良いでしょう。ルームメイトとの同居は、新しい友人関係を築いたり、生活費を節約するのに素晴らしい方法ですが、快適な共同生活を送るためにはオープンなコミュニケーションと**互いの尊重**が欠かせません。アメリカ人はオープンで、感じたことを率直に表現する傾向があるので、生活に関するニーズなどもルームメイトとの間でオープンに話すと良いでしょう。両者がフレンドリー、かつ誠実である限り、ルームメイトとの問題はほとんど解決されるものです。

## 購入

　はじめに、アメリカでは**中古住宅**を購入することが驚くほど一般的であることを覚えておきましょう。実際、新らしく住宅を購入する人の約90%は、新築するのではなく**中古の家**を購入しています。そのため、アメリカで住宅を購入する際は、そのプロセスとして物件が過去どのように扱われてきたか、構造はどうかなど、かなり綿密に調べることになります。

　まず、家探しの前に予算について検討することが大切

アメリカの中古住宅は地域、築年数、広さ、状態、設備などの要因で価格が大きく異なる。2023年12月時点では、中古住宅の平均価格は約40万ドル（現行レートで約6千万円）。前年から約8％上昇している。

191

to figure out how much you can afford. This will depend on your income, credit score, and other financial factors. You can use **online mortgage calculators** to get an idea of how much you can afford. Once you have a budget in mind, you should get pre-approved for a **mortgage** from a lender. This will give you a better idea of how much you can actually borrow and will make you a more attractive buyer.

A **real estate agent** can help you find homes that meet your criteria and negotiate on your behalf. It's important to choose an agent who is knowledgeable about the local market and has a good reputation.

With the help of your real estate agent, start looking at homes that fit your budget and needs. You may want to make a list of "**must-haves**" and "**nice-to-haves**" to help narrow down your options. When you find a home you like, you will need to make an offer. Your real estate agent can help you determine a fair price and negotiate with the seller. Before closing on the home, you should have a professional home inspection to check for any issues that could affect the value or safety of the home.

Once everything is in order, you will need to sign a lot of paperwork and pay **closing costs**. This can include fees for the title search, appraisal, and attorney fees.

Overall, purchasing a home in the US can be a rewarding experience, but it's important to do your research, work with a trusted team of professionals, and be prepared for the process to take some time. The supply of available homes in **high-demand areas** is limited, and you should expect to make numerous offers before you successfully buy a home.

です。これはあなたの収入やクレジットスコア、その他の経済状況によって変わります。いくらまでなら出せそうか、**オンラインの住宅ローン・シミュレーション**を使って調べることができます。いったん予算が決まれば、貸し手から**住宅ローン**の事前承認を受けてみましょう。そうすることで、実際にいくらぐらい借りられるかがわかり、買い手として有利になります。

　**不動産業者**は、あなたの条件に見合う物件を見つけ、あなたに代わって交渉してくれます。地元の相場に詳しく、評判の良い業者を見つけましょう。

　不動産業者の助けを借りて、予算や希望に合う物件を探し始めます。選択肢を絞り込むために、「**なくてはならないもの**」と「**あったらいいもの**」のリストを作成すると良いでしょう。気に入った物件が見つかれば、申し込みをします。不動産業者は適正価格を算出し、売主との交渉をサポートしてくれます。最終判断をする前には、専門家による住宅検査を受け、価格や安全性に関わる問題点がないかを確認しましょう。

　全ての準備が整えば、多くの書類にサインをし、**不動産売買手数料**を支払います。これには所有権調査、不動産鑑定、弁護士費用などが含まれます。

　概して、アメリカでの住宅購入はいい経験になりますが、よく調べることと、信頼のおける専門家チームと協力すること、そして多少の時間がかかることを覚悟しなければなりません。**人気のあるエリア**の物件数は限られており、無事に住宅を購入するには何件も申し込みをしなければならないことも心得ておきましょう。

不動産業者への手数料は売買価格の6%、買い手と売り手から3％ずつ取るのが一般的。その他の諸費用として、検査費用、鑑定評価費用、登記費用、税金などが徴収される場合もある。

## Explosive Property Taxes

The term "explosive property taxes" refers to a situation where **property taxes** increase rapidly and significantly over a short period of time. There are several factors that can contribute to such an increase in property taxes, including changes in property values, **local government budgetary needs**, and state tax policies.

One common reason for explosive property taxes is a sudden increase in **property values**. When property values rise quickly, local governments may increase property tax rates to generate more revenue to fund public services such as schools, roads, and public safety. However, this can lead to a significant increase in property taxes for homeowners and businesses, particularly for those who have owned their properties for a long time and have not seen such increases before.

Another factor that can contribute to explosive property taxes is budgetary needs of local governments. When local governments face **budget shortfalls**, they may increase property tax rates to make up for the shortfall. This can be especially problematic if local governments have not managed their budgets effectively or if they have high levels of debt.

Finally, state tax policies can also contribute to explosive property taxes. For example, some states have laws that limit property tax increases to a certain percentage each year. If property values rise significantly in a given year, local governments may be forced to increase property tax rates significantly in subsequent years to make up for lost revenue.

Overall, explosive property taxes can be a **significant burden** for homeowners and businesses, and they can have a major impact on local economies and quality of life.

## 固定資産税の高騰について

　「固定資産税の高騰」とは、**固定資産税**が短期間で急激に上昇することです。このような固定資産税の上昇には資産価値の変化や**地方自治体による予算の必要性**、また州の税制によるものなど、様々な要因があります。

　固定資産税の高騰の一般的な要因のひとつに、**資産価値**の急激な上昇があります。資産価値が急激に上昇すると、地方自治体は学校や道路、治安などの公共サービスをより充実させるため、税収を獲得しようと固定資産税率を引き上げることがあります。これは住宅所有者や企業にとって、大幅な固定資産税の増額であり、特に長きにわたって不動産を所有し、それまでこうした引き上げを経験したことのなかった場合は大きな痛手となります。

　固定資産税の高騰のもうひとつの要因は、地方自治体による予算の確保があります。地方自治体は**予算不足**になると、それを補うために固定資産税率を引き上げることがあります。自治体が効率的な予算管理を怠っていたり、多額の負債を抱えていたりする場合は、特に問題となります。

　最後に、州の税制も固定資産税の高騰の要因となります。例えば、いくつかの州には年ごとの固定資産税の上昇率を一定に制限する法律があります。そのため、ある年に住宅の価値が一気に上昇したような場合、回収しきれなかった税収分を補うため、地方自治体に次年度以降の固定資産税率を大幅に引き上げさせることがあります。

　概して、固定資産税の高騰は、住宅所有者や企業にとって**大きな負担**となり、また地域経済や生活の質にも大きな影響を与えます。

住む場所によって税額は異なるが、平均税率は住宅価格の約1.1%。州別に見ると、テキサス州が1.9%、カリフォルニア州1.2%、ニューヨーク州で1.1%となっている。通常は年2回に分けて支払う。

## Sell the property

Selling a house in the US can be a complex process, but in general it is slightly easier than buying. As in the buying process, a good real estate agent can help you determine the right price for your house, market it effectively, and negotiate with potential buyers. Your agent will help you set a fair price for your house based on the local real estate market, the condition of your home, and other factors.

You should prepare your home for sale by cleaning, making necessary repairs, and staging your home to make it look attractive to **potential buyers**. Your agent will list your home on the local Multiple Listing Service (MLS) and other online platforms to attract potential buyers. Your agent will schedule showings for potential buyers to tour your home. When you receive an offer, your agent will help you review it and negotiate with the buyer to reach a mutually agreeable price.

Once you accept an offer, the buyer will typically have an **inspection** done and request any repairs before finalizing the purchase. At closing, you will sign the necessary paperwork and transfer ownership of the property to the buyer.

Note that the exact process can vary depending on the state and local laws and regulations, as well as the specific circumstances of your home sale. It's important to work closely with your real estate agent to navigate the process successfully.

### Real Estate Bubble

A **real estate bubble** refers to a situation where housing prices in a particular market rise rapidly to unusually high levels, fueled by a variety of factors. As the bubble grows, more and more people buy houses, hoping to make a profit from rising prices.

## 売却する

　アメリカで家を売るのは、複雑で大変なこともありますが、たいていは購入をするよりも簡単です。購入時と同じように、良い不動産業者が、あなたの家の価値を適正に判断し、効果的に売り出し、買い手との交渉をサポートしてくれます。地元の不動産の相場、家の状態、その他の状況に応じて適正な価格を設定してもらいましょう。

　家を売るにあたってあなたがすべき事は、部屋を掃除し、必要な修繕をして、**購入予定者**に気に入ってもらえるようホームステージングをすることです。不動産業者は、買い手を募るために地元のマルティプル・リスティング・サービス（MLS）やその他のオンラインプラットフォームにあなたの家を掲載します。希望者に対しては、物件の内覧も予定します。購入の申し込みがあれば、それらを確認するとともに、双方が納得のいく金額で契約ができるようサポートしてくれるでしょう。

　あなたが申し込みを受諾すると、買い手は通常、最終的な購入の前に**住宅検査**を行い、修理すべきところを提示します。必要な書類にサインをし、不動産の所有権を買い手に譲渡して契約完了となります。

　正確なプロセスは州や地域の法律および規則、またあなたの家の販売状況によって異なることに注意しましょう。不動産業者と連携をとりながら、上手くプロセスを進めることが大切です。

日本でもホームステージングという言葉が定着してきた。これは売り物件を家具や小物で飾り、購入希望者に住むイメージを持ってもらうための手法。早く、高く物件を売却するために費用はかかるが事前にやっておく方がいいとされる。

## 不動産バブルについて

　**不動産バブル**とは、ある市場の住宅価格が、様々な要因によって異常に高騰することです。バブルが拡大すると、多くの人々が価格上昇による利益を期待して次々と住宅を購入するようになります。

However, eventually, the market becomes full, and there are more houses being sold than people who want to buy them. At this point, prices begin to fall, and those who bought into the market at the height of the bubble may find themselves **owing more money** than their homes are worth.

The United States has experienced several real estate bubbles in recent decades. One of the most notable was the housing bubble of the mid-2000s, which was caused by a combination of **casual lending standards** and **low interest rates on loans**. The bubble burst in 2007-2008, leading to a global financial crisis and widespread economic problems that many economists feel the United States still has not fully recovered from.

Today, many experts believe that some US housing markets may be experiencing another bubble, as housing prices in many cities continue to rise rapidly despite **economic uncertainty**. While it's difficult to predict whether or when a new bubble will burst, it's important for both buyers and policymakers to be careful and not put themselves in financial danger.

　ところが、そのうち市場は飽和状態となり、家を買いたい人よりも売りたい人の方が多くなります。すると、住宅の価格は下落し始め、バブルの絶頂期に家を購入した人はその家の価値よりも**多額の借金**を背負うようになります。

　アメリカは、ここ数十年間で、何度か不動産バブルを経験しています。最も顕著だったのは、**融資基準の緩和**と**借入の低金利化**により引き起こされた2000年代半ばの不動産バブルです。2007年から2008年にかけてのバブル崩壊は世界的な金融危機と広範な経済問題を引き起こしたため、多くの経済学者は、アメリカはもう立ち直れないと考えたほどでした。

　今日、**不透明な経済状況下**で、多くの都市の住宅価格が上がり続けている現状を目にし、専門家の多くは、アメリカの住宅市場の一部が再びバブルに見舞われることを懸念しています。いつどのように、新たなバブルが崩壊するかを予測することは困難ですが、買い手も、また政策立案者も、経済的な危機に見舞われないよう注意することが大切です。

# 2 Financials

## Banking

If you are going to live in America for an extended period of time, you may want to do some **personal banking**. The first step is to choose a bank that suits your needs. Banks offer different types of accounts, services, fees, and interest rates, so it is a good idea to research and compare different options. After choosing a bank, you can open a checking and savings account by completing an application form and providing identification and proof of address. You will also need to make an **initial deposit**. Once your account is open, you can manage it through online or mobile banking, in-branch banking, or through automated teller machines (ATMs). You can **deposit and withdraw money**, pay bills, transfer funds, and view account statements. Most major US banks have all-digital banking now that you can do on a phone, so it is rarely necessary to go into a **physical bank** after the first time. Furthermore, banks usually don't charge fees for having a checking account these days, which is one less bill to worry about.

Major banks offer credit and debit cards that you can use for purchases or cash withdrawals. Credit cards allow you to borrow money from the bank, while debit cards use your account balance to pay for transactions. It is common for Americans to use credit

# ファイナンス

**キーワード** 当座、残高、ソーシャルセキュリティー・ナンバー、収入、投資

## 銀行

　もし、あなたが長期間アメリカで暮らすのであれば、**個人向け銀行口座の開設**を考えた方が良いでしょう。まずは、自分のニーズに合った銀行を選びます。口座の種類やサービス、手数料、利息は銀行により様々ですので、色々調べ、比較してみてください。銀行が決まれば、口座開設書に必要事項を記入し、身分証明書と住所証明書を提出後、当座預金と普通預金の口座を開設することができます。**初期入金**も必要です。口座開設後は、オンライン・バンキングやモバイル・バンキング、支店やATMで口座を管理することができます。**入出金**や請求書の支払い、送金や取引明細の確認なども可能です。最近では、こうした取引をスマートフォンで行うオール・デジタル・バンキングが、主要銀行のほとんどで導入されているので、最初に銀行へ行くことを除けば、わざわざ**実店舗**へ足を運ぶ必要もありません。さらに、最近の銀行では当座預金を保持していても手数料がかからなくなったため、出費を気にする必要もなくなりました。

　大手銀行には、買い物をしたり現金を引き出したりできる、クレジットカードやデビットカードのサービスがあります。クレジットカードは銀行からの借り入れが、デビットカードは預金からの決済が可能です。アメリカで

オール・デジタル・バンキングとは、銀行が提供するすべてのサービスがデジタルプラットフォーム上で完結すること。インターネット・バンキングやモバイルアプリを通じて口座の開設ができる銀行もある。時間と場所の制約を受けたくない顧客にとって非常に便利だ。

201

cards that offer rewards for certain kinds of purchases. If you like to eat out at restaurants, you might want to find a credit card that gives you bonus points for doing so. There are also cards that give you cash back for travel, which can be used on flights and hotels. Since credit card companies make their profits from people who don't pay their bills on time, these rewards are basically free for responsible users.

## Transfers and Personal Checks

There are several ways to transfer money between individuals in the US, including **personal checks**. The best method will depend on various factors, such as the amount of money you want to transfer, the urgency of the transfer, and your personal preferences.

Over the last decade, online payment services such as PayPal, Venmo, and Cash App have become the **most common ways** to transfer money between individuals. These services allow you to send and receive money quickly and easily using just an email address or phone number. You can link your bank account or credit card to these services, and they charge a small fee or commission for their services. Since most Americans do not like carrying cash or going to the trouble of **depositing a check**, this is how people generally prefer to receive money.

Bank transfers allow you to send and receive money directly from your bank account. Many banks offer free or low-cost transfers between accounts held at the same bank, and some banks also allow you to transfer money to accounts at other banks. This option is best for larger amounts of money and for those who prefer a more traditional banking method. It is also commonly used for **scheduled payments** and exchanges between professionals.

Personal checks are a traditional method of transferring money

は、特定の種類の買い物で特典が得られるクレジットカードを選ぶことが一般的です。レストランでよく外食をするのであれば、その時にボーナスポイントが付与されるクレジットカードを探すのも良いでしょう。また、航空券やホテルの支払いなど、旅行をすることでキャッシュバックを受けられるカードもあります。クレジットカード会社は、支払期日の守れない人々から利益を得ているため、信頼に足る利用者はこれらの特典を無料で利用できるのです。

## 送金と個人用小切手

　アメリカで、個人間の支払いをするには、**小切手を**含め様々な方法があります。送金金額、緊急性、個人の好みなど、時々の事情で最適な送金方法は異なります。

小切手

　PayPalやVenmo、Cash Appをはじめとするオンライン決済サービスは、ここ10年で個人間の送金の**最も一般的な方法**となりました。これらのサービスでは、Eメールアドレスか電話番号があれば、簡単に送着金をすることが可能です。銀行口座やクレジットカードをこれらのサービスに紐付けることで、少額の手数料や取引料でサービスを利用することができます。ほとんどのアメリカ人は現金を持ち歩いたり、わざわざ**小切手を換金したり**はしないので、この方法での支払いが一般的に喜ばれます。

　銀行振込では、銀行口座を使って直接送着金をすることが可能です。ほとんどの銀行では、同じ銀行間であれば手数料なしか、少額の手数料で送金ができ、他行の口座に送金ができる銀行もあります。金額が大きい場合や、従来の銀行間取引を好む場合は、この方法をとると良いでしょう。銀行振込はまた、**定期的な支払い**や専門家同士の資金のやり取りなどにもよく使われます。

　小切手は、個人間で資金のやり取りをするための昔なが

between individuals. To use a personal check, you simply **write a check** to the person you want to pay and give it to them. The recipient can then deposit the check into their bank account. However, checks can take several days to clear, and there is always the risk of a "bounced" check if you don't have enough money in your account. Although personal checks have become less common in America over the years, they are still used by older people and small businesses that want to have physical records of transactions.

**Wire transfers** are a secure and fast way to transfer money between individuals. Importantly, they can be used to transfer money domestically or internationally, and they typically clear within a few hours. However, wire transfers are often more expensive than other methods and may require you to visit a bank branch in person.

Ultimately, the best way to transfer money between individuals in the US depends on your personal needs and preferences. Consider the amount of money you want to transfer, the speed of the transfer, and any fees or commissions associated with each method before making your choice.

## Pay Attention to Payment

If you don't pay your **minimum credit card bill** on time, you'll likely be forced to pay a late fee. Depending on your credit card issuer, this fee can be anywhere from $25 to $50 or more.

Even if you make your minimum monthly payment on a credit card, you'll still be charged interest on the total amount you owe every month. Credit card interest rates can be quite high, with some cards charging upwards of 20% or more. Over time, these interest charges can add up and make it harder to **pay off your balance**. Basically, the most efficient use of a credit card is to increase the rewards points you get for purchases you would make anyway, then pay the card off in full every month. This allows you to take advantage of the credit card's

らの方法です。**小切手に記入**し、相手に渡すだけで支払い
をすることができます。受取人は、銀行で小切手を換金し
ます。ただ、小切手の決済には数日かかることがあり、ま
た口座に十分な預金がなかった場合は「不渡り」になるリ
スクもあります。近年、小切手はあまり使われなくなって
きていますが、年配の人や取引の記録を残しておきたい小
規模事業主などからは、今なお使用されています。

　**電信送金**は、個人間での送金を安全、かつ迅速に行うこ
とができます。重要な点は、国内外へ送金ができ、通常数
時間で決済がされるということです。ただ、他の方法より
も割高になることが多く、また銀行の支店へ出向かなけれ
ばならないこともあります。

　結局のところ、アメリカで個人間の送金を行うための最
善の方法は、個人のニーズや好みによって異なります。送
金の金額やスピード、そのための手数料や取扱料などをよ
く考慮してから選択しましょう。

電信送金は銀行同士が直接連絡を取り合って手続きを行う仕組みなので、特に海外に送金、または海外から受け取りたい場合は、安心感がある。

## 支払いには注意しよう

　クレジットカードの**最低請求額**を期限内に支払えなか
った場合は、延滞料が発生することがあります。この延滞
料は、カードの発行会社によっては25ドルから50ドル以
上になることもあります。

　たとえクレジットカードの最低請求額を毎月支払って
いても、支払いの完了していない総額部分には利息が発生
します。クレジットカードの金利は非常に高額で、中には
20％以上の利息がつくカードもあります。これらの利息
は、日を追うごとにどんどん膨れ上がり、**完済すること**が
難しくなります。多くの場合、クレジットカードの最も有
効的な使い方とは、普段なにげなくしている買い物の中で
ポイント還元を増やしつつ、毎月の請求額を完済すること

benefits without any of the negative effects.

Your payment history is also a key factor in deciding your credit score. Late payments have a negative impact on your score, making it harder to get approved for loans or credit in the future. Many people don't think about it, but you can also use a credit card to show future lenders that you are responsible with money. By paying your credit card bill on time each month, you develop a good credit score over time. A high credit score is **incredibly valuable** when it comes to taking out large loans, like those for a house or car. Scores that are high enough make banks more comfortable giving you a loan, and as a result they charge lower interest rates. So, even if you are not interested in getting the rewards from using a credit card, it is a good idea to use one at least sometimes in order to increase your credit score.

## Social Security

In the United States, a Social Security number (SSN) is a nine-digit unique ID number assigned to citizens, permanent residents, and temporary residents.

SSNs were first introduced in 1936 as a way to track workers' earnings for **Social Security benefit** purposes. Today, they are also used as a form of identification for many purposes, such as opening a bank account, applying for a credit card, and paying taxes.

When a person applies for an SSN, they must provide proof of identity, age, and citizenship or immigration status. Once the application is processed, the SSA assigns a **unique nine-digit number** to the individual, which stays with them for life.

The first three digits of the SSN are known as the "area number" and correspond to the geographic region where the person applied for their SSN. The next two digits are known as

です。そうすることで、クレジットカードのマイナス面ではなく、プラス面を活用できるからです。

　また、支払履歴はあなたのクレジットスコアを決める大切な要素です。支払が遅れるとスコアに悪影響を及ぼし、将来のローンやクレジットの審査が通りにくくなります。多くの人はあまり気にとめませんが、あなたがお金について信用に足る人物であることを将来の貸し手に示す際、クレジットカードの履歴を提示することもできるのです。毎月の請求額を期限通りに支払うことで、長期的に良好なクレジットスコアを保つことができます。良好なクレジットスコアは、家や車の購入などで大きな借入をする際、**驚くほどの価値**があります。銀行からの借入はより簡単に、金利もより低く抑えられるようになるのです。クレジットカードの特典に興味はなくても、クレジットスコアを上げるために、時々はカードを利用してはどうでしょう。

## 社会保障番号

　アメリカのソーシャルセキュリティー・ナンバー（SSN）とは市民、永住者、一時居住者に割り当てられる9桁の固有のIDナンバーのことです。

　SSNは**社会保障給付**のため、労働者の収入を追跡する方法として1936年に初めて導入されました。今日では、銀行口座の開設やクレジットカードの申請、税金の納付など、様々な目的で身分証明書として利用されています。

　SSNを申請するには、身元や年齢、市民権または在留資格の証明書を提出する必要があります。申請が下りると、SSA（社会保障局）から各個人に、**固有の9桁の番号**が割り当てられ、この番号は生涯変わりません。

　番号の最初の3桁は「地域番号」で、SSNが申請された地理的な範囲を表しています。次の2桁は「グループ番号」と呼ばれ、地域番号をさらに細分化するためのもの

the "group number" and are used to further break down the area number. The final four digits are the "serial number" and are assigned sequentially to each person within the group.

While SSNs are used for many purposes, it's important to keep them safe and secure to prevent **identity theft**. People are advised to avoid sharing their SSN unless it's absolutely necessary and to monitor their credit reports regularly for any suspicious activity. You must be 100% sure that an organization is trusted before providing your SSN, and never include it in texts or emails.

## Taxes

Taxes in the United States are collected by the federal government, state governments, and local governments to pay for **public services** such as education, healthcare, infrastructure, and national defense. There are several types of taxes in the US, including income tax, sales tax, and property tax. The federal government collects income taxes, while state and local governments collect sales tax and property tax.

Income tax is calculated based on how much money a person makes doing business, minus their **business expenses**. The tax rate changes depending on the level of a person's income, but the basic rule is that if you make money from any kind of business transaction in America, you almost certainly have to report it to the government.

State and local governments collect taxes to fund their own public services. Sales tax is the most common type of state and local tax, which is applied to the purchase of goods and services. Property tax is another common type of state and local tax, which is based on the value of owned real estate.

Individuals and businesses are required to **file tax returns**

です。最後の4桁は「通し番号」で、同じグループの人々
へ発行順に割り当てられます。

SSNは様々な目的に使用されるため、**個人情報の漏洩**
を防ぐために安全に保管されなければなりません。どう
しても必要な時以外は番号を人に伝えず、クレジットレ
ポートに疑わしい入出金がないことを定期的に確認しま
しょう。SSNを提示する際は、その相手先が100％信頼
できることを確認し、メールやテキストに番号を記載す
ることは控えましょう。

## 税金

アメリカの税金は連邦政府、州政府、そして地方自治体
が徴収し、教育、医療、インフラ、国防などの**公共サー
ビス**に充てられます。アメリカには所得税、売上税、固
定資産税など様々な税金があります。連邦政府が所得税
を徴収し、州政府と地方自治体が売上税や固定資産税を
徴収しています。

所得税は、ビジネスで得た収入から、それにかかった**経
費**を差し引いた金額に基づいて計算されます。税率は個
人の所得レベルに応じて異なりますが、もしあなたがア
メリカで何らかのビジネスをして収入を得た場合は、漏
れなく政府に報告することが基本のルールです。

州政府と地方自治体は、それぞれ公共サービスを行う
ために税金を徴収しています。売上税は州税および地方
税の最も一般的なもので、商品の購入や、サービスの提
供を受けた際にかかります。固定資産税も同様で、これ
は所有する不動産の価値に基づいて課税されます。

個人や企業は、所得を報告し税額を算出するために、毎

アメリカの売上税は、商品や
サービスにかかる税金である
点では消費税と同じだが、消
費税は全国一律に対して、売
上税は州ごとに税率が変わ
る。州によって5％〜10数％
程度の違いがある。

every year to report their income and calculate the amount of tax they owe. The deadline for filing federal income tax returns is usually April 15th, but in recent years that deadline can be extended to the fall if you request it in advance.

There are various **deductions** and credits available to individuals and businesses to reduce the amount of money they have to pay in taxes. Common deductions include money given to charity, interest paid on home loans, and state and local taxes paid. Federal income tax rates are structured into different tax brackets, with higher tax rates applying to higher levels of income. For example, in 2021, the tax rate for income between $0 and $9,950 was 10%, while the tax rate for income between $523,601 and $628,300 was 37%.

Overall, the US tax system is complex and can be challenging to navigate. It's important to consult with a tax professional or use tax software to be sure that taxes are filed correctly and to take advantage of all available deductions and credits.

## Buy Software or Hire an Accountant

When deciding whether to use tax software or **hire an accountant**, it's important to consider the how complex your tax situation is. If your finances are relatively simple, such as having only **one source of income** and no deductions or credits, then using tax software is probably a good option. However, if you have multiple sources of income, own a business, have investment income, or have major deductions or credits, it may be a good idea to hire an accountant who has the professional experience that you lack.

Remember, an accountant may be expensive, but the time you save by using one could easily **balance out** the cost. Moreover, making a mistake on your taxes can result in **expensive penalties**, so the best choice is usually to play it safe.

年確定申告を行います。連邦所得税の申告期限は通常4月15日ですが、近年は事前の申請により秋まで期限を延長することができます。

　納税額を抑えるために利用できる**控除**やクレジットは色々あります。一般的な控除には慈善事業への寄付金や住宅ローンの利子、州税や地方税の支払いなどがあります。連邦所得税の税率には、所得が高ければ高いほど税率も高くなる累進課税のシステム（タックスブラケット）が適用されています。例えば、2021年の場合、0ドルから9,950ドルの収入に対する税率は10％でしたが、52万3,601ドルから62万8,300ドルの収入に対する税率は37％でした。

　概して、アメリカの税制度は複雑で、完全に理解することは難しいかもしれません。正しく税金を申告、かつ利用できる控除やクレジットを最大限適用するためにも、税理士に相談をしたり、税務ソフトを活用したりすると良いでしょう。

### ソフトを買うか、会計士を雇うか

　税務ソフトを使うか、それとも**会計士を雇う**かを決める際には、自身の税務状況がどの程度複雑であるかを考慮することが大切です。**収入源が1箇所**で、控除もクレジットもない比較的単純な税務状況であれば、税務ソフトを使うと良いでしょう。ですが、収入源が複数だったり、会社を経営し、投資収入があり、また大きな控除やクレジットがあったりする場合は、経験のある会計士に依頼します。

　会計士を雇うには費用がかかりますが、そうすることで生まれたあなたの時間は、きっとそれに**見合う**はずです。さらに、誤った税務申告をすると**高額な罰金**を科される可能性もあるため、安全策を取ると良いでしょう。

アメリカの公認会計士は、U.S. Certified Public Accountantという。

## Investments

Investing in the US involves putting money into **different financial instruments** with the aim of generating a profit or return on the investment. The US has a robust and sophisticated financial system, which offers a wide range of investment opportunities to individuals and institutions alike.

Here are the key steps to understand how investing works in the US:

**Choose your investment vehicle:** Investors can choose from various **investment vehicles** such as stocks, bonds, mutual funds, exchange-traded funds (ETFs), options, and futures, among others. Each of these vehicles has its own characteristics, risk profile, and potential return.

**Open an investment account:** Investors need to open an **investment account** with a **brokerage firm** or financial institution to buy and sell securities. There are different types of investment accounts, including individual retirement accounts (IRAs), 401(k) plans, and taxable investment accounts.

**Research and analyze potential investments:** Before investing in any **security**, it is essential to conduct thorough research and analysis to understand the underlying fundamentals, risk factors, and potential returns. Investors can use various resources such as **financial statements**, company reports, market data, and expert opinions to make informed investment decisions.

**Buy and sell securities:** Once an investor has chosen a security, they can buy it through their investment account. The price of the security is determined by the market forces of supply and demand. Investors can also sell their securities in the open market to realize a profit or loss.

**Monitor and manage investments:** Investing requires ongoing

## 投資

　アメリカでの投資とは、利益や収益を得ることを目的に、**様々な金融商品**に資金を投じることを言います。アメリカには洗練された金融システムがあり、個人にも法人にも幅広い投資の機会があります。

　ここでは、アメリカの投資の仕組みを理解すべく、その主なステップを紹介します。

　**投資手段を考える**：株や債券、投資信託、上場投資信託（ETF）、オプション、先物など様々な**投資手段**から投資を選択します。その手段によって特徴やリスクプロファイル、予想できる利益は様々です。

　**投資口座を開設する**：証券を売買するために、**証券仲介業者**、または金融機関で**投資口座**を開設します。投資口座には個人退職口座（IRA）や401（K）プラン、それに課税対象となる投資口座など様々な種類があります。

　**投資先候補を調査、分析する**：どの証券に投資する場合も、その基本的な概要やリスク要因、ポテンシャルリターンを理解するため、徹底的な調査や分析を行うことは不可欠です。**財務諸表**、企業レポート、市場データ、専門家の意見など、様々なリソースを活用し十分な情報に基づいた投資判断を下します。

　**証券の売買**：証券が決まれば、投資口座を使って購入をします。証券の価格は、需要と供給という市場の力関係によって決まります。公開市場で証券を売却することで、利益を得ることもあれば、損失を出すこともあります。

　**投資の観察と管理**：投資では、その戦略が投資家の財

2023年の調査で、アメリカ人の約50~60％の人が何らかの投資をしていることがわかっている。最も一般的なのは株式投資で、その他、債券、投資信託、不動産などに、老後の資金、教育費の確保、資産形成などの理由で投資をしている。

monitoring and management to ensure that the investment strategy is aligned with the investor's financial goals and risk tolerance. Investors need to track the performance of their investments, stay up-to-date with market trends and news, and adjust their investment strategy accordingly.

**Pay taxes on investment gains:** In the US, investors are required to pay taxes on their investment gains, including capital gains, **dividends**, and **interest income**. The tax rate depends on the type of investment, holding period, and the investor's income level.

Investing in the US requires a good understanding of **financial markets**, investment vehicles, and risk management. It is crucial to conduct thorough research, work with a reputable financial institution or advisor, and diversify the investment portfolio to mitigate risk and maximize returns.

務目標やリスク許容度に適合しているかを確認するため
に、定期的な観察と管理を行うことが重要です。自身の
投資のパフォーマンスを見直し、市場の動向やニュース
を常に把握した上で、状況に応じて投資戦略を調整しま
す。

　**投資利益に対し納税をする**：アメリカではキャピタル
ゲインや**配当金**、**利子所得**などの投資利益に対し、税金
を支払う必要があります。税率は投資の種類や保有期間、
投資家の所得水準により異なります。

　アメリカで投資を行うには**金融市場**や投資手段、リス
ク管理についての十分な理解が必要です。リスクを軽減
しリターンを最大化させるためには、十分な調査を行い、
信頼できる金融機関やアドバイザーと協力して投資ポー
トフォリオを分散させることが極めて重要です。

# 3 Cars

**Key Words** Learner's Permit, DMV, Driver's Ed, Lease, Dealership, Title, Inspection, Registration

## Driver's license

If you are at least 16 years old and a **legal resident**, you can get a driver's license in the US. That's the good news. The bad news is that getting a license is a long, involved process, and you will most likely need help to make it happen. Most states will require you to get a **learner's permit**, which allows you to drive with another licensed driver in the car. This is useful for practicing the basics of driving a car, usually in **empty parking lots** (there are many of those in the US).

You can get a learner's permit by going to the Department of Motor Vehicles (DMV) and passing a **written test** of driving laws, as well as a simple **vision test**. Once you have a learner's permit, you can sign up for a driver's education class (commonly called "driver's ed"), where you will practice driving on the road with an instructor. After completing driver's education, you will continue to practice and study until you take your written and driving tests at the DMV. If you have the proper documents (generally proof of identity and where you live) and score highly enough on the tests, you will get your driver's license.

# 3 車

**キーワード** 運転練習許可証、車両管理局、ドライバーズ・エデュケーション、リース、ディーラー、権利証、検査、登録

## 運転免許証

アメリカでは、16歳以上の**合法的な居住者**は運転免許を取得することができます。これは良いニュースでしょう。ただ、悪いニュースは、アメリカで免許を取得するには長く複雑な手続きが必要で、誰かの助けなしにはほとんど不可能だということです。多くの州では、免許所持者に同乗してもらい、車を運転するための**運転練習許可証**を取得する必要があります。これは、運転の基本を練習するためのもので、たいていは**誰もいない駐車場**を使って練習をします（アメリカにはそのような駐車場が多くあります）。

運転練習許可証を取得するには、車両管理局（DMV）へ行き、運転法規についての**筆記試験**と簡単な**視力検査**に合格しなければなりません。運転練習許可証を取得すれば、ドライバーズ・エデュケーションのクラス（通称「driver's ed」）に申し込み、インストラクターと路上で運転の練習をします。ドライバーズ・エデュケーション終了後は、運転の練習と勉強を継続してからDMVにて筆記テストと実技テストを受験します。テストで十分な点数を獲得し、適切な書類（通常は身分証明書と住所証明書）を揃えれば、運転免許証が取得できます。

## Non-Driver's License

In the United States, a **non-driver's license** is an identification card issued by the state's DMV or a similar agency. It serves as an official form of identification for people who do not have a driver's license or who do not intend to drive a car.

A non-driver's license contains personal information like the individual's full name, address, date of birth, and a photograph. It is often used to perform **official tasks** such as opening a bank account, obtaining government assistance, or voting.

The requirements for getting a non-driver's license can be different depending on the state. Generally, individuals must provide proof of identity, residence, and Social Security number, as well as pay a fee. **Proof of residence** usually comes in the form of a bill or official document addressed to you personally, which is why many Americans still like to receive paper bills.

It can be useful to have a form of ID on you at all times, so if for any reason you cannot get a driver's license, a non-driver's license is a good alternative.

## Purchase or lease a vehicle

Purchasing a car in the US is a big decision and a major financial choice. Before you start shopping for a car, it's important to determine how much you can afford to spend. Consider your income and expenses carefully to determine a **realistic budget** for your car purchase. Once you have a budget in mind, start researching different car options that fit within that budget. Consider factors such as **fuel efficiency**, reliability, and safety ratings, as well as your personal preferences for size, style, and features. Look for car dealerships with good reputations and positive customer reviews. You can also consider buying from a private seller if you prefer, but there are less legal protections if you go that way. Before you

## ノンドライバーライセンスについて

　**ノンドライバーライセンス**とは、州のDMV、または同等の機関が発行する身分証明書カードのことです。これは、運転免許証を持たない人や、車の運転をするつもりのない人のための身分証明書となるものです。

　ノンドライバーライセンスには、個人の氏名や住所、生年月日、写真などの情報が表記されています。通常は、銀行口座の開設や政府からの補助の受領、投票など、**公的な作業**を行う際に使用されます。

　ノンドライバーライセンスを取得するための条件は州によって異なります。一般的には身分証明書、住所証明書、ソーシャルセキュリティー・ナンバーを提示し、料金を支払うことで取得できます。**住所証明書**は、宛先にあなたの住所が書かれた請求書や公文書がそれにあたるため、多くのアメリカ人は未だに紙の請求書を好みます。

　身分証明となるIDは、常に身に着けておくと便利なため、何かの理由で運転免許証が取得できない場合は、代わりとなるノンドライバーライセンスを持つと良いでしょう。

## 車の購入とリース

　アメリカで車を購入することは、気持ちの上でも経済的にも大きな決断です。車を買い求める前に、どのくらいの出費が可能かを考えます。あなたの収入や支出を考慮し、購入のための**現実的な予算**を決めましょう。予算が決まったら、その範囲内でどんな選択肢があるか調べます。**燃費**、信頼性、安全性などの要素に加え、サイズ、形、機能など、個人的な好みについても考慮します。好意的なカスタマー・レビューを得ている評判の良いカーディーラーを探しましょう。希望すれば個人からの購入も検討できますが、その場合は法的な保護が手薄になるかもしれません。購入を決める前には試乗し、車が自身の

commit to buying a car, take it for a test drive to make sure it meets your needs and feels comfortable to drive. Finally, you will have to negotiate a price with the dealership or seller. **Bargaining about price** is not common in most situations in America, but car prices are understood to be flexible. Do your research beforehand to ensure you're getting a fair price based on the car's condition, **mileage**, and market value, and assume that whoever you are buying from is willing to give you some discount to make the sale.

If you're not paying cash for the car, you'll need to get a loan from a bank, credit union, or the dealership itself. Compare rates and terms to find the best option for you, but once again interest rates will mostly depend on your credit score and income. If you are buying from an official dealership, you will need to do a lot of paperwork to complete the purchase. This will typically include signing a sales agreement, **registering the car**, and getting license plates. If you are buying it from an individual, you will just need the signed car "title", which is a form that shows official ownership.

## Maintenance

Legally owning and operating a car in the United States means you will be responsible for a number of things that need to be handled either annually or when you first make the purchase. To operate a car in the US, you must register it with the state in which you live. Registration typically involves filling out a form and paying a fee, which varies by state and is based on factors such as the type of car, its age, and its value. You will also need to provide proof of insurance and may need to provide proof of passing a **safety inspection**. Most states in the US require that cars pass a safety inspection before they can be registered. The inspection typically covers items such as brakes, lights, tires, and **emissions**. The frequency of inspections varies by state, with some

ニーズに合っているか、乗り心地が良いかなどを確認しましょう。最後に、ディーラーや販売者と価格の交渉をします。アメリカでは**値段の交渉**はあまり一般的ではありませんが、車については柔軟な対応が見込めます。車の状態、**走行距離**、市場価値に基づいた適正な価格が提示されているかを事前に確認し、どんな購入先でも多少の値引きが期待できると考えましょう。

現金で支払いをしない場合は、銀行や信用組合、または購入先のディーラーでローンを組む必要があります。金利や条件を比較し、最適なローンを選びますが、ここでもまた、あなたのクレジットスコアや収入が金利に影響してきます。正規ディーラーで購入をする場合は、購入手続きに多くの書類が必要です。売買契約書のサインや**車両登録**、ナンバープレートの取得などが必要になります。個人販売者から購入する場合は、「権利証」という車の正式な所有権を示す書類にサインをするだけです。

## メンテナンス

アメリカで合法的に車を所有し運転するには、最初の購入時以外にも毎年様々な手続きが必要になります。アメリカで車を運転するには、居住する州での登録が必要です。登録では通常、用紙を記入し手数料を支払いますが、その金額は州によって異なり、車種、年式、その価値などの条件をもとに計算されます。自動車保険の保険証や**自動車検査証**などが求められる場合もあります。多くの州では、車の登録をする前に安全性の検査に合格する必要があります。検査は通常、ブレーキ、ライト、タイヤ、**排気**などについて行われます。車検の頻度は州により様々で、年に一度の車検を義務付けている州もあれば、数年に一度で構わない州もあります。ただ、車の登

アメリカの車検は州ごとに規定が異なる。一部の州では義務付けられているが、そうでない州もある。頻度も年に1回から4年に1回など様々。新車で2年に1回、13年後以降は毎年義務づけられている日本よりかなり緩い。検査項目は日本より圧倒的に少ないため、アメリカの車検は概して、安くて時間もかからないとされる。

requiring annual inspections and others requiring inspections only once every few years. Either way, you need to update your car's registration every year, or else you will **get fined**.

When you buy a car in the US, you will need to pay **sales tax** on the purchase. The tax rate varies by state and can range from less than 1% to over 10% of the purchase price. In addition to sales tax, you may also need to pay an annual property tax on your car, which is based on the value of the vehicle.

In addition to the above requirements, there are other things to keep in mind when operating a car in the US. For example, you will need to have a **valid driver's license** (they expire after ten years) and follow the rules of the road, including speed limits, traffic signals, and **right-of-way laws**. You will also need to carry proof of insurance with you while driving, as it is required by law in most states.

### Gas Station (Basically Self-Service)

Almost all gas stations in America are self-service. The main exception is Pennsylvania, where a number of old laws make it illegal for customers to **pump their own gas**. Outside of Pennsylvania, you are expected to first pull up to and park at a **pump**. Some stations allow you to pay at the pump with a mobile or credit card, but others, often in lower-income areas, will require you to go into the gas station and pay in person before you start pumping.

After paying, you select which type of fuel you want and start filling up your car. Most gas pumps in the US shut off automatically when your tank is full, and you are not supposed to "top off" by trying to continue putting extra fuel in the tank. It is common for gas stations in America to offer a large selection of drinks, snacks, and even other household products depending on the size of the station. They also often have **car washes** attached, so you can clean your car if necessary.

録は毎年更新しなければならず、できなかった場合は**罰金が科せられます**。

　アメリカで車を購入する際は、**売上税**を支払う必要があります。税率は州によって異なり、購入価格の1%未満から10%以上までの幅があります。売上税に加えて、車両に対する固定資産税も毎年支払わなければなりませんが、その金額は車の価値によって決まります。

　上記以外にも、アメリカで車を運転する際に留意しておきたい事項がいくつかあります。**有効な運転免許証**を所持していることや（有効期限は10年間です）、制限速度、信号、**道路交通法**といった交通ルールを守ることなどです。また、多くの州法で義務付けられているように、運転中は自動車保険証を携帯しておかなければなりません。

## セルフサービスが基本のガソリンスタンド

　アメリカのガソリンスタンドのほとんどはセルフサービスです。ペンシルベニア州は例外で、いくつかの古い法律により顧客が**自分でガソリンを入れる**ことが違法とされています。ペンシルベニア州以外で給油する場合は、まず始めに**給油機**近くに車を停めます。スマートフォンやクレジットカードでそのまま支払いができるスタンドもありますが、特に低所得者層の多い地域などでは、給油の前に、店で直接支払いを済ませなければならないスタンドもあります。

　支払後は、ガソリンの種類を選び給油を始めます。アメリカのほとんどの給油機は、満タンになると自動的に給油が止まるため、余分にガソリンを「つぎ足す」必要はありません。スタンドの規模にもよりますが、ガソリンスタンドには様々な種類の飲み物やスナック、また日用品などが多数販売されています。**洗車サービス**が併設されていることも多いので、必要に応じて利用すると良いでしょう。

# 4 Health

## Health insurance

Health insurance in the United States is a complex and confusing topic due to the variety of programs and options available. Many businesses offer health insurance to their employees. This type of insurance is typically purchased by the employer and covers employees and their family members, but employees may need to pay for **a portion of the insurance**, usually as a monthly cost taken out of their paychecks.

The Affordable Care Act, also known as Obamacare, is a federal law passed in 2010 that aimed to improve **access to health insurance** for all Americans. It requires individuals to have health insurance or pay a penalty, and offers money to those who need help affording it.

Medicare is a federal health insurance program for people who are 65 or older, or **have certain disabilities**. Medicare is divided into several parts, each of which covers different services: Part A covers hospital stays, Part B covers doctor visits and outpatient services, Part C (also known as Medicare Advantage) is a private insurance option that includes Parts A and B and may offer additional benefits, and Part D covers prescription drugs.

---

# 4 健康

**キーワード** 保険、診断、専門医、予防注射、クリニック、救急車

## 健康保険

アメリカの健康保険は、様々な制度やオプションがあるため、複雑かつ難解です。多くの企業は社員に健康保険を提供しています。この種の保険は、社員やその家族を保障するため雇用主が加入するものですが、社員はその**保険料の一部を負担**しければならず、負担分は通常、毎月の給与から天引きされます。

オバマケアとして知られるアフォーダブルケア法は、全てのアメリカ人に**健康保険の加入**を広めることを目的とし、2010年に成立した連邦法です。健康保険の加入を個人に義務付けるもので、加入しない場合はペナルティーが課され、それでも加入が難しい人々には援助金が支払われます。

メディケアは65歳以上の高齢者、または**特定の障害を持つ人々**を対象とした連邦医療保険プログラムです。いくつかのプランがあり、それぞれ異なった内容をカバーしています。パートAは入院、パートBは医師の往診と外来、パートC（メディケア・アドバンテージとしても知られます）はパートAとBの内容を含む任意の民間医療保険で、追加のサービスが受けられるもの、そしてパートDは処方箋をカバーしています。

アフォーダブルケア法は正式には、The Patient Protection and Affordable Care Act。無保険者を減らしすべてのアメリカ人が医療サービスを受けられる国民皆保険を目指した法。

Medicaid is a **joint federal-state program** that provides health insurance to low-income individuals and families, as well as certain groups of people with disabilities. As usual, it varies by state, but generally, individuals must have **limited income** to qualify.

The health insurance system in the United States is difficult to make sense of, no matter your education or income level. However, medical care in the US is incredibly expensive without insurance, so if you will be staying there for an **extended period of time**, you should consult an expert to find out what kind of insurance coverage is right for you.

## Medical care system

Even with health insurance, the medical care system in America is complicated and confusing with many different types of healthcare providers and institutions.

**Primary care doctors** are usually the first point of contact for patients seeking medical care. These doctors provide **regular checkups** and treatment for common medical conditions. They are often the ones who refer patients to **specialized doctors** if needed.

Specialists are doctors who have completed additional training and certification in a specific area of medicine. Examples of specialists include cardiologists, dermatologists, and neurologists, who focus on heart, skin, and brain health.

If you're having a health problem that needs to be addressed quickly, your best course of action is to find an **"urgent care" clinic**. These places do not require appointments, and are much cheaper than visiting an emergency room in a hospital. The doctors at urgent care can make a diagnosis and treat you for your problem, and if necessary they can refer you to a specialist for follow-up care.

　メディケイドは低所得者の個人や家族、また特定の障害を持つ人々のグループを対象とした**連邦政府と州政府の共同プログラム**です。州によって違いはありますが、対象となるには**所得制限**があります。

　アメリカの健康保険制度は、学歴や所得水準に関係なく、分かりにくいものです。ただ、アメリカの医療費は保険の適用なしでは驚くほど高額になる場合があるため、もし**長期滞在**の予定があるなら、自身に適した保険を専門家に相談してみると良いでしょう。

## 医療制度

　アメリカの医療制度には様々な形態の医療提供者や医療機関があり、健康保険に加入していても複雑かつ難解です。

　通常、医療が必要な患者は、まず**プライマリ・ケア医**を訪れます。プライマリ・ケア医とは、**定期的な検診や一般的な症状に対して治療を行う医師**のことで、必要に応じて**専門医の紹介**をします。

　専門医とは、特定の分野において高度な訓練や認定を受けた医師のことを言います。心臓病専門医、皮膚科専門医、神経科専門医などは、それぞれ心臓、皮膚、脳などの治療を行います。

　もし、早急な対応が必要になった場合は、「**緊急医療**」**クリニック**を探すのがベストです。これらのクリニックは予約の必要がなく、病院の緊急処置室へ駆け込むよりもはるかに安く治療を受けることができます。緊急医療の医師たちは、それぞれの症状に対して診断と治療を行い、必要に応じて専門医の紹介やフォローアップを行います。

2024年2月時点で、緊急医療クリニックの数は全米で1万を超え、命を脅かさない様々な症状に対して、アクセスしやすい効率的な治療を提供し、医療システムの重要な一部となっている。

## Medical checkups and vaccinations

In the United States, medical **checkups and vaccinations** are an important part of staying healthy. The system of medical checkups and vaccinations is designed to help individuals detect and treat health problems before they become severe.

During a medical checkup, a healthcare provider will typically perform a physical exam, check vital signs (such as **blood pressure** and **heart rate**), and may order laboratory tests or imaging studies. Depending on the **individual's medical history** and any risky behaviors, the healthcare provider may also recommend specific tests, such as mammograms or colonoscopies, to detect certain diseases early. These tests are usually performed at a different location that has special equipment.

As we all learned during the Covid-19 pandemic, vaccinations are an important tool in preventing the **spread of infectious diseases**. In the United States, the Centers for Disease Control and Prevention (CDC) recommends a schedule of vaccinations for people of all ages, from infancy through adulthood.

These are typically given in **a series of doses**, starting in childhood and continuing into the adult years. Some vaccines, such as the flu vaccine, may need to be administered annually, while others, such as the human papillomavirus (HPV) vaccine, may be given in a series of doses over several months.

In the US, it is possible to get vaccines at either a doctor's office or a **chain pharmacy**. Although many people feel more comfortable getting a vaccine at a doctor's office, an appointment may need to be scheduled weeks in advance, while pharmacies are typically much more available. Beyond that, it does not really matter which option you choose, as both providers accept insurance.

## 健康診断と予防注射

アメリカでは、**健康診断と予防注射**は、健康維持のための重要な要素です。これらの制度は、健康上の問題が深刻化する前にそれを発見し、治療することを目的としています。

健康診断ではたいてい、医療従事者が検診やバイタルサイン（**血圧**や**心拍数**など）の測定を行い、臨床検査や画像診断を行うこともあります。また、**個人の病歴**や生活習慣によっては、特定の病気を早期に発見するためマンモグラフィーや大腸内視鏡検査など、特別な検査を勧めることもあります。これらの検査は通常、専用の設備を備えた別の施設で行われます。

コロナ禍で証明されたように、予防注射は**感染症の蔓延**を防ぐための重要な手段です。アメリカ疾病予防管理センター（CDC）は乳幼児期から成人期までのあらゆる年齢の人に対し、予防接種を計画的に受けるよう呼びかけています。

予防接種は通常、幼少期から成人期にかけて、**何回かに分けて**接種します。インフルエンザワクチンのように毎年の接種が推奨されるものもあれば、ヒトパピローマウイルス（HPV）ワクチンのように数カ月にわたり接種するものもあります。

アメリカでは、医師のいる診療所でも、**薬局のチェーン店**でも、どちらでも予防接種を受けることができます。医師の診察を受けてからワクチン接種をした方が安心という人も多くいますが、そのためには数週間前に予約を取らなければいけないため、薬局の方がずっと手軽です。また、どちらで接種をしても保険の対象になることから、どちらを選んでも大きな差はないでしょう。

アメリカでは薬剤師が予防接種を行う資格があるため、薬局での注射が可能になっている。Walgreens、CVS Health、Rite Aid、Walmart、Targetなど町のあちこちで見かけるチェーン店でも接種可能だ。

## Sicknesses Specific to the United States

As a diverse nation, there are not many **genetic-based diseases** that are specific to the United States. However, there are a handful of health problems that are generally associated with the fact that America is one of the most overweight countries in the world, with over 30% of adults classified as obese. **Obesity** is associated with a range of health problems, including diabetes, heart disease, and certain cancers. The US also has a high rate of type 2 diabetes, with around 10% of the US population suffering from this condition, which is a major cause of disability and death.

The US has been facing an opioid epidemic, with a high number of people becoming addicted to **prescription painkillers**. Sometimes these painkillers are given to a person after a surgery or major injury, but they can also be purchased illegally. Opioid addiction is associated with a range of health problems, including **fatal overdose** and infectious diseases like HIV and hepatitis.

Lastly, the US has a relatively high rate of Alzheimer's disease, which is a brain condition that affects memory and **cognitive function**. Around 5.8 million Americans are currently living with Alzheimer's, and the condition is a major cause of disability and death in older adults. It is not currently clear why the disease is so common in America, but it is possible that the increasing size of the elderly population in the country is the main factor.

## Emergency

No matter how careful you are, there is a chance of experiencing some kind of serious injury or sudden illness in the US. When that happens, it is best to have a friend or family member take you to the emergency room of the nearest hospital, also known as the ER. Unless the injuries are **life-threatening**, you should avoid calling 911 and taking an ambulance to the hospital because ambulance rides in America can cost thousands of dollars, and they might not

## アメリカ特有の病気について

多様な人々が暮らすアメリカでは、**遺伝性疾患**はあまり見られません。ですが、成人の30％以上が肥満に分類されるなど、アメリカは世界でも有数の体重過多が認められる国で、それに関連した健康上の問題も少なくありません。**肥満**は糖尿病、心臓病、特定の癌など、様々な健康問題を引き起こします。また、アメリカでは2型糖尿病の罹患率も高く、国民の約10％がこの疾患に悩まされており、障害や死亡の主な原因ともなっています。

アメリカはオピオイド危機にも直面しており、多くの人々が**処方鎮痛剤**の中毒となっています。こうした鎮痛剤は手術や大きなけがの後に処方されるものですが、違法に購入することも可能です。オピオイド鎮痛薬の中毒は**致死的な過剰摂取**やHIV、肝炎といった感染症を含む様々な健康問題とも関連しています。

最後に、アメリカは、記憶や**認知機能**に影響を及ぼす脳の病気であるアルツハイマー病の疾患率が比較的高い傾向にあります。現在、約580万人の人々がこの病気を患っており、高齢者の障害や死亡の主な原因となっています。この疾患がアメリカでこれほど一般的である理由は今のところ不明ですが、国内の高齢者人口の増加が主な原因ではないかと考えられています。

オピオイドによる麻薬性鎮痛薬の過剰摂取による死亡例は増加している。その死亡者数は交通事故による死亡者より多く、アメリカの公衆衛生上の喫緊の課題となっている。

## 緊急事態

どれほど注意をしていようと、アメリカで何らかの大けがや急病に見舞われる可能性はゼロではありません。そのような場合は、友達か家族の手を借りて最寄りの病院の緊急処置室（ER）へ連れて行ってもらいます。アメリカでは、救急車を手配すると何千ドルもかかったり、保険が適用されなかったりするため、**命に関わる事態**でない限りは、911に電話をし救急車で搬送されることは避け

be covered by insurance.

Not all hospitals will be part of your insurance plan, so it is a good idea to research the closest hospitals that you will be covered at. Furthermore, many hospitals have websites or apps that can show you the wait times at their ERs, so you can choose one with a shorter wait time

When you arrive at the ER, you will need to register at the front desk, providing your name, address, and insurance information. If you don't have insurance, you will still be treated, but you will almost certainly receive a very large bill for **the full cost of your treatment**. After you register, a nurse will check your condition to figure out how serious your condition is, because patients with the most severe symptoms are seen first.

Eventually, you will be seen by a doctor, who will examine you and order any **necessary tests**, such as **blood work** or x-rays. After that, you will receive treatment depending on your symptoms and condition. If you need to be admitted to the hospital for further care, you will be transferred to a hospital room. When your condition improves and you no longer need emergency care, you will be sent home from the ER with instructions on how to care for yourself and when to follow up with your regular doctor.

Afterwards, you will receive a bill for the services you received in the ER. If you have insurance, your insurance company will pay a portion of the bill, and you will be responsible for paying the remainder. If you do not have insurance, you will be responsible for paying the full bill. Remember, the cost of emergency care in the United States can be quite high, especially for those without insurance. If you have a non-life-threatening medical issue, it may be more cost-effective to see your regular doctor or the urgent care clinics mentioned earlier instead of going to the ER.

るべきです。

　あなたの保険が全ての病院で適用されるとは限らないので、対象となる最寄りの病院を調べておくと良いでしょう。また、ウェブサイトやアプリからERの待ち時間が確認できる病院も多数あるので、待ち時間の短い病院を選ぶことも可能です。

　ERに到着後は、受付で名前、住所、保険の情報を伝えます。保険に未加入でも、治療を受けることはできますが、ほぼ間違いなく**治療費の全額**が請求されるでしょう。受付の後は、症状が最も重い患者を優先的に治療するために、看護師があなたの症状の深刻度を確認します。

ER

　最終的な医師の診察では、**血液検査**やレントゲン検査など、**必要な検査**が行われます。その後、症状や状態に合った治療を受けることになります。さらに入院が必要な場合は、そのまま病室へと移されます。症状が改善し、緊急治療の必要がなくなれば、自身でケアをする方法や、かかりつけ医の経過観察のスケジュールなどの指示を受けて自宅へ帰ります。

　ERで受けたサービスの請求書は、後日受け取ることになります。保険に加入していた場合は、保険会社が請求額の一部を負担し、残りが自己負担となります。保険に加入していなかった場合は、全額が自己負担になります。アメリカの緊急医療費は、特に保険に加入していない場合は、かなり高額になることを覚えておきましょう。命に関わるような事態でない限り、ERへ駆け込むよりも、最寄りの医師や、前述の緊急医療クリニックを受診した方が、経済的でしょう。

# 5 Food

**Key Words** Diet, Carbohydrates ("carbs"), Organic, Vegan, Vegetarian, Fasting

## Breakfast

Cold cereal with milk is shown a lot in media as the classic breakfast choice for many Americans. In recent years, though, people have come to look at cereal as unhealthy, since it is often high in calories and sugars. It is still popular among some groups of Americans, particularly children, but young adults are eating it much less than in the past. Toast with butter and/or jam is a simple and classic breakfast option, but like cereal, it has become less popular as Americans who are **concerned about health** try to avoid unnecessary **carbohydrates**.

Scrambled, fried, or boiled eggs remain a popular choice for breakfast. Omelettes filled with cheese, vegetables, and/or meat are also common, as they are quick and easy to make while still being fairly healthy.

Pancakes and waffle are often served with butter and syrup or other toppings like berries, whipped cream, and chocolate chips. Of course, these dishes, while loved by Americans, are basically desserts, and most people do not eat them very often because they are not diet-friendly.

Breakfast sandwiches are popular in cities and among young adults. They typically consist of eggs, cheese, and meat (such

# 5 食事

**キーワード** 食事、炭水化物(「carbs」)、オーガニック、ヴィーガン、ベジタリアン、断食

---

## 朝食

　牛乳をかけたシリアルは、多くのアメリカ人の定番の朝食としてメディアにもよく登場します。ですが、最近では、糖分が多く高カロリーなシリアルは、不健康な食事と考えられるようになりました。一部のアメリカ人や、特に子供たちの間ではまだ人気があるものの、シリアルを食べる若者は、昔と比べはるかに少なくなっています。バターやジャムを塗ったトーストも、簡単で定番の朝食メニューですが、シリアルと同様に、**健康に気遣う人が不必要な炭水化物を避ける**ようになり、人気がなくなってきています。

　スクランブルエッグや目玉焼き、ゆで卵は依然人気の朝食メニューです。チーズや野菜、肉などの入ったオムレツも、ヘルシーでありながら素早く簡単に調理できることで人気があります。

　パンケーキやワッフルには、たいていバターやシロップ、ベリー類、ホイップクリーム、チョコレートチップなどが添えられます。もちろん、アメリカ人の大好きなメニューですが、基本的にはデザートで、ダイエットにもやさしくないことから頻繁に食べる人は少数です。

　都会の若者たちは、朝食によくサンドイッチを食べます。ベーグル、イングリッシュマフィン、ビスケットな

as bacon, sausage, or ham) served on a bagel, English muffin, or biscuit. You can eat them **while standing or walking**, which appeals to Americans who might be in a rush to get to work in the morning. Many **health-conscious Americans** choose yogurt for breakfast, either plain or flavored, and usually mixed with granola or fruit.

No matter what their cultural background or diet needs, most Americans start their day with a cup of coffee or tea. If you are unsure about what kind of breakfast to pick up for an American friend or coworker, they will almost certainly appreciate a cup of coffee.

## Lunch

Lunch is the most variable meal of the day for Americans, given that it comes in the middle of the school day for students and the work day for adults.

Many adults and students bring their lunch from home, which may include a sandwich, salad, fruit, yogurt, or **leftovers from dinner** the night before. They might also include a drink and a small snack such as a granola bar or piece of fruit.

Some adults may choose to grab a quick lunch from a nearby fast-food chain or restaurant. They might choose a burger, sandwich, or a salad **to go**, along with a drink and fries or chips. Although this option is not as healthy, it can provide relief for people who are feeling stressed at work or simply did not have time to prepare a lunch.

For adults who work in corporate settings or have meetings with clients, a business lunch is common. These lunches are typically held at more expensive restaurants or cafes and are often somewhat formal. They might include a starter, entree, dessert,

どに卵やチーズ、肉（ベーコンやソーセージ、ハムなど）を挟んだものが人気です。朝、急いで職場に向かう時でも、**立ったままや歩きながらでも食べられること**が理由です。**健康志向のアメリカ人**の朝食はヨーグルトで、プレーンや味付きのヨーグルトにグラノーラや果物を混ぜて食べるのが一般的です。

　文化的背景や食生活はどうであれ、ほとんどのアメリカ人は一杯のコーヒーか紅茶で一日をスタートさせます。アメリカ人の友人や同僚に、どんな朝食を買えばいいか迷った時は、まずコーヒーで間違いないでしょう。

## 昼食

　昼食は、学生にとっては学校での、大人にとっては職場での、一日の中間の時間にあたることから、最もバラエティーが豊富です。

　サンドイッチ、サラダ、果物、ヨーグルト、前日の**夕食の残り物**などを昼食として家から持参する学生や大人もいます。飲み物やグラノーラバー、果物などの簡単なスナックが付くこともあります。

　大人であれば、近くのファストフード店やレストランで、手早く昼食を済ませる人もいます。ハンバーガー、サンドイッチ、サラダなどに、飲み物、フライドポテト、またはポテトチップスなどを加えて**テイクアウト**をします。こうした昼食は健康的とは言えませんが、仕事でストレスを感じていたり、単に昼食の用意をする時間がない人にとっては有難いものです。

　会社勤めの人や取引先との打ち合わせがある人は、ビジネスランチをとることもよくあります。このような場合は、少し高めのレストランやカフェで前菜、メインディッシュ、デザート、ドリンクなどのフォーマルな食事

and drinks.

For young people, most schools have a cafeteria where students can purchase hot lunches. These lunches may include items such as pizza, hamburgers, chicken nuggets, and sandwiches. They often come with a side of fruit, vegetables, or chips, and a drink. There has been debate in recent years about how healthy the school lunch options are or should be, and whether or not students should be expected to pay for it. It is actually a political issue that Americans can become quite upset about, so be careful when discussing school lunch in the US.

Some students may choose a lighter lunch, such as a granola bar, apple, and a drink. These types of lunches are common for students who have **after-school activities** or sports practices and need something quick and easy to eat whenever they have some free time.

### What's in the Sandwich, What's in the Lunch Box

A typical American sandwich usually consists of two slices of bread (white, wheat, or rye) with various **fillings** in between. The fillings can include deli meat (such as turkey, ham, roast beef, or chicken), cheese (such as cheddar or Swiss), lettuce, tomato, onion, pickles, mayonnaise, mustard, and sometimes avocado or bacon.

Americans are quite **picky** about their sandwiches, and everyone prefers them a certain way. Some people like a lot of toppings, others are interested mainly in meat and cheese. Mayonnaise in particular is a source of arguments, as approximately half of Americans love it while the other half hates it. Regardless, a well-made sandwich is a combination of food and art for a lot of Americans.

In addition to a sandwich, a typical American lunch box may also

をすることが一般的です。

　若者は、たいてい学校に学生食堂があり、学生は温か
い昼食を買うことができます。食堂ではピザ、ハンバー
ガー、チキンナゲット、サンドイッチなどが販売されて
います。たいてい、果物や野菜、ポテトチップスなどの
サイドメニューと飲み物がついています。ここ数年学校
で提供される食事がどの程度健康的であるか、またはそ
うあるべきか、またその食事代を生徒に負担させるべき
かどうかについて議論が交わされています。実際これは、
アメリカ人にとって大変デリケートな政治的議論でもあ
るため、学生食堂を話題にする際は注意が必要です。

　グラノーラバー、リンゴ、飲み物などで、簡単に昼食
を済ませる生徒もいます。こうした昼食は、**放課後の課
外活動**やスポーツの練習の前に、空いた時間で手軽に食
べられるため生徒たちには人気です。

## サンドイッチの具、ランチボックスの中身

　典型的なアメリカのサンドイッチと言えば、パン（白パ
ン、全粒粉パン、ライ麦パン）に**具**を挟んだものでしょう。
具は、デリミート（七面鳥、ハム、ローストビーフ、チキン
など）、チーズ（チェダーチーズやスイスチーズなど）、レ
タス、トマト、玉葱、ピクルス、マヨネーズ、マスタード、
そしてアボカドやベーコンなどです。

　アメリカ人はサンドイッチには**こだわりがあり**、誰にも
自分の好きなサンドイッチがあります。たくさんの具材を
好む人もいれば、肉とチーズがメインという人もいます。
マヨネーズは特に意見が分かれるところで、マヨネーズを
好む人と嫌う人は、ほぼ半々に分かれます。いずれにせよ、
美味しいサンドイッチはアメリカ人にとっては食とアート
の融合体なのです。

　典型的なアメリカ人のランチボックスには、サンドイッ

include other items such as a piece of fruit (such as apple or banana), a bag of chips, a granola bar or cookie, and a drink (such as water, juice, or soda). Some people may also include other snacks or treats, like a pack of fruit candy or a small bag of trail mix. There is nothing even close to agreement on what Americans consider a reasonable snack, though, as some are incredibly health conscious while others are not.

## Dinner

It's difficult to describe a "typical" dinner in the US as there are so many different international cultures and regional cuisines throughout the country. However, there are some common dishes and practices that you may find at a "typical" American dinner.

The main dish typically consists of a protein, such as chicken, beef, pork, or fish, accompanied by a side dish such as potatoes, rice, or pasta. A vegetable dish such as green beans, broccoli, or carrots is often served as a side dish.

At more formal dinners, a small salad, usually consisting of lettuce, tomatoes, and cucumbers, is often served as a starter. And it depends on the culture, but dessert is often a sweet treat such as cake, pie, or ice cream. Other than water, soft drinks, beer, and wine are common beverages served with dinner, despite their health risks.

### Oven in Winter, Barbecue in Summer

American cooking preferences do tend to change based on the season. In the winter months, Americans crave warm and hearty meals that provide comfort from the cold weather. This often means using the oven to bake and cook dishes such as casseroles, pot pies, and roasts.

チの他に果物(りんごやバナナなど)、ポテトチップス、グ
ラノーラバー、クッキー、飲み物(水、ジュース、ソーダな
ど)などが入っています。フルーツキャンディーやトレイル
ミックスの小袋など、スナックやお菓子が入っていること
もあります。アメリカ人がどこまでをスナックと考えるか
については、なかなか相容れない部分もありますが、驚く
ほど健康志向の高い人もいれば、そうでない人もいます。

トレイルミックスとは、主に
ナッツやドライフルーツ、シ
リアル、チョコレートなどを
混ぜ合わせたスナックで、ハ
イキングの際に携行する食品
として開発された。

## 夕食

　アメリカには、実に様々な国の文化や地域に根付いた
料理があるため、「典型的な」アメリカの夕食について説
明することは困難です。とはいえ、「代表的な」アメリカ
の夕食と考えられるような料理や習慣はいくつかありま
す。

　メインディッシュは通常、鶏肉、牛肉、豚肉、魚など
のタンパク質が主で、ポテト、ライス、パスタなどのサ
イドディッシュが添えられます。インゲン豆、ブロッコ
リー、人参などの野菜料理が副菜として添えられること
もあります。

　もう少ししっかりとした夕食なら、レタスやトマト、キ
ュウリなどの簡単なサラダが前菜として出されることも
あります。また、文化にもよりますが、ケーキ、パイ、ア
イスクリームなどのデザートも一般的です。水以外の飲
み物では、健康に良くないものの、ソフトドリンク、ビ
ール、ワインなどが夕食と共に飲まれます。

アメリカには厳密には主食の
コンセプトがない。一般的に
食べられている穀物は、パン、
パスタ、米で、地域によっては
ビスケット、タコス、ブリトー
などもよく食べられている。
健康志向により、全粒粉パン、
玄米、キヌアなどの穀物も人
気がある。

### 冬はオーブン、夏はバーベキュー

　アメリカ人の好みの料理は季節によって変わります。冬
の間は、寒さを和らげる温かくてボリュームのある料理が
好まれます。キャセロール、ポットパイ、ローストビーフ
など、オーブンを使った料理です。

In the summer months, Americans tend to prefer lighter and fresher dishes that are cooked quickly and require minimal time in the kitchen. This often means using an outdoor barbecue grill to cook meats, vegetables, and even fruits.

In a sense, you can track the American food traditions by season.

**Winter:**  Slow-cooked stews and soups
Roasted meats, such as turkey, ham, and beef
Casseroles, such as lasagna and shepherd's pie
Baked goods, such as pies, cakes, and cookies

**Spring:**  Lighter soups and stews
Grilled meats, such as lamb and pork
Fresh vegetables, such as asparagus and peas
Lighter pasta dishes, such as pesto and primavera

**Summer:**  Grilled meats, such as burgers, hot dogs, and steaks
Fresh salads, such as Caesar and Greek
Seafood, such as shrimp and crab
Fruit-based desserts, such as pies and sorbets

**Fall:**  Comfort foods, such as macaroni and cheese and pot roast
Roasted vegetables, such as sweet potatoes and squash
Spiced desserts, such as pumpkin pie and apple crisp
Hearty soups, such as chili and tomato soup

Americans like to cook based on how available **seasonal ingredients** are, in addition to their desire for comfort or refreshment during different times of the year.

　夏場は、手早く調理ができ、キッチンに立つ時間を最短に抑えられる簡単で新鮮な料理が好まれます。野外のバーベキューグリルで肉、野菜、果物まで調理することがあります。

　ここでは、アメリカ料理の慣例を季節ごとに追っていきましょう。

冬：じっくり煮込んだシチューやスープ
　　七面鳥、ハム、牛肉などのロースト
　　ラザニアやシェパーズパイなどのキャセロール料理
　　パイ、ケーキ、クッキーなどの焼き菓子

春：薄味のスープやシチュー
　　ラムやポークなどのグリル肉
　　アスパラガスやエンドウ豆などの新鮮野菜
　　ペスト・ジェノヴェーゼやプリマベーラなどのあっさりとしたパスタ料理

夏：ハンバーガー、ホットドッグ、ステーキなどのグリル肉
　　シーザーサラダやギリシャ風サラダなどのフレッシュサラダ
　　エビやカニなどのシーフード
　　パイやシャーベットなどのフルーツ系デザート

秋：マカロニ・アンド・チーズやポット・ローストなどのコンフォート・フード
　　サツマイモやカボチャなどのロースト野菜
　　パンプキンパイやアップルクリスプなどのスパイス系デザート
　　唐辛子やトマトを使った具だくさんスープ

アメリカ人は、手に入りやすい**旬の食材**に加え、その時々の快適さや心地よさを料理に求めるようです。

## Health conscious eating

Despite America's problem with being overweight, younger generations are making more of an effort to eat healthy by avoiding foods that are high in calories, and **low in nutrients**. This approach to eating often includes options that are organic and vegetarian.

Organic foods are produced without the use of **synthetic fertilizers**, **pesticides**, or **genetically modified organisms** (GMOs). Many people choose organic foods because they believe they are healthier, safer, and more sustainable. Organic options can include fruits and vegetables, meat and poultry, **dairy products**, and packaged foods.

Vegetarianism is another health-conscious eating option that has gained popularity in the US. Vegetarianism involves avoiding meat, poultry, and fish, and instead relying on **plant-based foods** for protein and other nutrients. Some people choose vegetarianism for their health, while others do so for ethical or environmental reasons.

There are also different types of vegetarianism, such as lacto-ovo-vegetarianism (which includes dairy products and eggs) and veganism (which excludes all animal products, including dairy and eggs).

**Health-conscious eating** in the US emphasizes whole, unprocessed foods that are rich in nutrients and low in calories. This approach can include many different organic and vegetarian options, depending on individual preferences and beliefs.

### Changes in America's Fad Diets

Scientists have shown that long-term, sustainable healthy eating is the best way to lose weight and feel good. But many, many Americans want fast results without much effort, so trendy "fad" diets are always appearing, and social media has only increased their visibility.

## 健康重視の食事

　肥満に頭を抱えるアメリカ国民ですが、若い世代の人々は健康的な食事を心がけようと、高カロリーで**栄養価の低い**食事を避ける傾向にあります。そうした食の選択肢としてオーガニックとベジタリアンがあります。

　オーガニック食品とは、**合成肥料、農薬、遺伝子組み換え生物**（GMO）を使わず生産された食品のことを言います。多くの人に選ばれるのは、それらがより健康的で安全、サステナブルな食品だと考えられているからです。オーガニック食品には果物、野菜、肉類、**乳製品**、パッケージ食品などがあります。

　ベジタリアニズム（菜食主義）もまた、アメリカで人気のある健康重視の食事法です。ベジタリアニズムでは肉類や魚を避け、タンパク質やその他の栄養素を**植物性の食品**から摂取します。健康のためにベジタリアン（菜食主義者）になる人もいれば、倫理的、また環境的な理由からなる人もいます。

　また、ベジタリアニズムにはオボ・ラクト・ベジタリアニズム（乳製品と卵は食べる）やヴィーガニズム（乳製品と卵を含む全ての動物性食品を避ける）など、様々なタイプがあります。

　アメリカにおける**健康重視の食事**は、全体的に低カロリーで栄養価の高い非加工食品に重点が置かれています。個人の趣向や信念に応じて、様々なオーガニックやベジタリアンの選択肢があるのです。

有機農法で作られた材料を使用し工場などで作られた加工食品をパッケージ食品という。原材料、加工法のほか、パッケージもリサイクル可能な素材を使うなど環境に配慮している。USDAオーガニックの認証マークがあれば、正式に有機栽培認証機関が認めていることになる。

動物性の食品、乳製品をすべて避けている人たちをヴィーガン（完全菜食主義者）と呼ぶ。ベジタリアン（菜食主義者）は、卵、乳製品を食べるかどうかは本人が決めても良い。

### 変わりゆくアメリカのダイエットブーム

　長期間続けられる健康的な食事こそが、体重を減らし、心を健やかに保つための最善の方法である、と科学者たちは示してきました。ですが、アメリカでは多くの人々が、いかに少ない労力で早く結果を出すかということに注力

The ketogenic diet involves drastically reducing carbohydrate intake and replacing it with fat, which forces the body to enter a state of ketosis. Interestingly, it was actually developed as a way to treat certain medical conditions before catching on for its potential weight loss benefits. Like many fad diets, it can be perfectly healthy if followed correctly, but unhealthy or even dangerous if done wrong.

The Paleo diet encourages the consumption of foods that our ancient humans ate during the **Paleolithic era**, such as lean meats, fruits, and vegetables. This diet excludes **processed foods**, dairy, and grains. In effect, the Paleo diet encourages people to eat as if they were living only from what the Earth produces naturally, without farming or livestock.

**Intermittent fasting** involves limiting food intake to certain times of the day or week, alternating between periods of fasting and eating. This approach has been touted for its potential weight loss and health benefits. This **mimics** certain religious practices that forbid eating during the day time, and has been linked to a number of health benefits. However, it is easy to take intermittent fasting too far and damage your body by starving yourself, which unfortunately some people do.

Fad diets are attractive, and they can even help lose significant weight over a short period of time. For long-term weight loss and body health, though, it is best to find a balanced diet that you can stick to for years at a time.

するため、最先端の「ファド・ダイエット」が常に現れ、ソーシャルメディアによって広められてきました。

ケトジェニックダイエットは、炭水化物の摂取を極端に減らし、代わりに脂肪を摂取することで、体を強制的にケトーシス状態にする食事法です。興味深いことにケトジェニックダイエットは、その効果が注目される前は、ある特定の病気の治療方法として活用されていました。ほかの多くのファド・ダイエットと同様に、正しく実践すれば完全に健康的な方法であるものの、間違ったやり方をすれば不健康で危険な状態にさえなってしまう食事法です。

パレオダイエットは、**旧石器時代**に古代の人々が食べていた赤身の肉、果物、野菜などの摂取を奨励する食事法です。この食事法で**は加工食品**、乳製品、穀類の摂取は禁じられています。実際には、農耕や家畜が始まる前の、地球から自然に生み出されるものだけで生活していた頃と同じ食事を実践することを目指しています。

**断続的な断食**は、一日、あるいは一週間のうちの一定期間の食事量を制限し、断食と食事を交互に繰り返す食事法です。この方法は、減量や健康への効果が期待できるものとして注目されています。日中の食事を禁止する特定の宗教的慣習を**真似たもの**で、様々な健康効果があるとされています。ただ、過度な断食をすることで飢餓状態から体を壊すことがあり、残念ながら実際に体を壊してしまう人もいます。

ファド・ダイエットは魅力的で、短期間で大幅に減量できるものもあります。ですが、長期的に低い体重を保ち健康でいるためには、長い期間続けられるバランスのとれた食事法を見つけることが最善でしょう。

「fad＝一時的な流行、気まぐれな熱狂」という意味から、メディアなどで一気に盛り上がり、流行になるような話題のダイエットのこと。

ケトーシスとは、体内でケトン体（脂肪酸が肝臓で分解されたときに生じる物質でエネルギー源として利用される）が血中に増加した状態。この状態では、通常の糖質ではなく、脂肪がエネルギー源として利用されるため、体重減少やエネルギー効率の向上が期待できる。

# 6  Family

**Key Words**  Divorce, Blended Family, Spouse, In-law, Midwife, Daycare, Adoption, Settlement, Exotic, Genetic

## Diverse family structures

Traditionally, the typical American family has consisted of two parents and their children living in the same home. However, over the past few decades, there has been a significant increase in non-traditional family structures.

**Single parent families** are those where a parent lives with and takes care of their child(ren) without the presence of the other parent. These can exist for very different reasons, from the death of one parent, to a divorce or one parent simply not being present from the beginning. While these families have become more socially accepted than they were in the past, they generally put a great deal of financial and emotional stress on the one parent who must manage the entire family.

**A blended family** is a structure where two families are joined together, usually through remarriage, to form a new family unit. This can involve step-parents, step-siblings, and half-siblings. There can be some difficulty in forming new personal relationships, but there are also clear advantages to having the income and attention of 2 parents rather than 1.

**Multi-generation families**, in which grandparents, children, and grandchildren live in a household together, are less common in America than in most other countries. This is largely because

# 6 家族

**キーワード** 離婚、混合家族、配偶者、姻族、助産師、保育園、養子、和解、珍しい、遺伝的な

## 多様な家族構成

　従来、アメリカでは両親と子供が同じ屋根の下で暮らす家族構成が一般的でした。ですが、ここ数十年で、それとは異なる家族構成が増加してきています。

　**一人親家庭**とは、片親が、もう片方の親のいない状態で子供と生活をする家庭を言います。片方の親が死亡したり、離婚したり、また片方の親が最初から不在であるなどその理由は様々です。このような家族は以前に比べ社会的に受け入れられるようになってきたものの、家族全員を養わなければならない親には、経済的にも精神的にも大きなストレスがかかります。

　**混合家族**とは、一般的にふたつの家族が再婚により新しく家族になったことを言います。家族には義父母、義理の兄弟姉妹、異父母の兄弟姉妹が含まれることもあります。新しい人間関係に苦労することもありますが、片親だけでなく両方の親がいることで、収入や子供の世話などに明らかに利点もあります。

　祖父母や子供、孫が同じ屋根の下で同居する**多世代家族**は、アメリカでは他の国ほど一般的ではありません。アメリカでは、若者たちにできるだけ早く家を出るよう

混合家族とは、子連れ再婚同士によって構成された家族のこと。ステップファミリーと違い、夫婦それぞれに前の結婚からの子供がいる。

American culture encourages young adults to move out of their parents' home as soon as possible. With the US economy struggling to recover job and wage growth in the last decade, though, adults living at home with their parents has become more common, if not more socially accepted.

## Same-Sex Marriage as a Civil Right

**Same-sex marriage** in the United States has been a controversial and evolving issue over the past few decades. Prior to 2015, same-sex couples did not have the **legal right to marry** in the United States, but that changed when the Supreme Court ruled in favor of same-sex marriage in the landmark case of Obergefell v. Hodges.

Before the ruling, same-sex couples had to go through a **maze** of state laws, with some states recognizing same-sex marriage and others passing laws against it. In 2013, the Supreme Court struck down a key part of the Defense of Marriage Act (DOMA), which had defined marriage as between a man and a woman for federal purposes, but that did not make same-sex marriage legal in all states.

In 2015, the Supreme Court made a **historic decision** in the case of Obergefell v. Hodges, which declared that same-sex couples had the legal right to marry and that states could not ban same-sex marriage. This decision effectively legalized same-sex marriage throughout the United States, and same-sex couples could now marry and receive all the legal benefits that come with marriage, such as making important medical decisions, filing taxes together, and getting access to Social Security benefits.

Since the Supreme Court's ruling, some states have made efforts to limit same-sex marriage rights, particularly through laws that allow individuals or businesses to refuse services to same-sex couples on religious grounds. However, these efforts have been met with

勧める文化があることが原因でしょう。とはいえ、アメリカ経済が雇用と賃金の伸びの回復に苦戦し続けているこの10年で、大人になってからも実家で親と同居することが、社会的に受け入れられているとは言わないまでも、かなり一般的になりつつあります。

## 公民権としての同性婚

アメリカにおける**同性婚**の問題は、過去数十年にわたり激しく議論されながらも進展してきました。2015年以前のアメリカでは、同性カップルによる**合法的な結婚**は認められていませんでしたが、最高裁が「オーバーグフェル対ホッジス裁判」の画期的な事件でそれを認める判決を下したことで、事態が一変しました。

判決以前の州法は、同性カップルにとってはまるで**迷路**のようで、同性婚を認めている州もあれば、それに反対する法律を可決している州もありました。2013年、最高裁は、それまで結婚は1人の男性と1人の女性が結び付くことによって成立するとし、全ての州に同性婚を却下する権限を与えていた結婚防衛法（DOMA）の主要部分を破棄しました。

また、2015年、最高裁は「オーバーグフェル対ホッジス裁判」で**歴史的な判決**を下し、同性カップルには結婚する法的権利があり、各州はそれを禁止できないことを宣言しました。この宣言により、アメリカ全土で同性婚が事実上合法化され、同性カップルは結婚することで、重要な医療上の決定や税金の共同申告、社会保障給付の利用など、結婚に付随するあらゆる法的恩恵を受けられるようになりました。

最高裁の判決以降は、同性婚の権利を制限しようと躍起になる州もあり、特に個人や企業に対しては宗教を理由に同性カップルへのサービスの提供を拒否することを法律で認める州もありました。ですが、これらの奮闘もまた、**大**

**オーバーグフェル対ホッジス裁判**
ケンタッキー州で同性婚を禁止するのは憲法違反だとして4組のカップルが起こした裁判。2015年6月に、同性婚を憲法上の権利として保障する判決が降りた。オーバーグフェルは原告の一人で、ホッジスは被告でケンタッキー州保健局の長官。

**significant resistance** and legal challenges. And, in 2022, the Respect for Marriage Act made it even harder for state governments to attack same-sex marriage.

It is worth remembering that, while same-sex marriage is now legal and recognized throughout the United States, there are still continuing debates and legal battles surrounding issues related to LGBTQ+ rights and equality.

## Marriage

The **legal requirements** for marriage in America vary from state to state, but in general, both parties must be adults (18 years or older) and must not be closely related by blood.

In addition to legal requirements, marriage often involves a religious or cultural ceremony that may include the exchange of rings, promises, and other symbolic gestures.

Marriage in the US carries legal benefits and responsibilities, such as lower taxes, support for a husband or wife in the event of unexpected circumstances, and joint property ownership. However, it also involves legal responsibilities, such as the **division of property** in case of divorce or the responsibility to provide for a spouse and children in case of death or disability.

The US recognizes two main types of marriage: **civil marriage** and **common-law marriage**. Civil marriage is the most common type, and it requires a marriage license, a ceremony, and a certified person (called an officiant) to perform the marriage. Common-law marriage is recognized in some states and does not require a ceremony or a license. Instead, it is established through a couple's mutual agreement to be married, usually expressed by living together for ten years or more.

Extended family members gained through marriage are called "**in-laws**", and they are the subject of quite a lot of jokes in America. Given the variety of cultures in the United States,

**きな抵抗**や法的議論にさらされてきました。そして、2022
年に結婚尊重法が制定されてからは、州政府が同性婚を非
難することがますます困難になりました。

　現在、同性婚はアメリカ全土で合法的に認められていま
すが、LGBTQ＋の権利と平等に関する問題をめぐる議論
や法廷闘争は、今なお続いていることを忘れてはなりませ
ん。

## 結婚

　アメリカにおける結婚の**法的要件**は州によって異なり
ますが、一般的には当事者が成人（18歳以上）しており、
血縁関係がないことが求められます。

　結婚では法的要件に加え、指輪の交換、誓いの言葉、ま
たその他象徴的な行為を伴う宗教的、または文化的な儀
式が行われます。

　アメリカでは結婚すると、税金が安くなったり、予期せ
ぬ事態に陥った際に夫婦で助け合ったり、財産を共有し
たりと、法的な利点とともに責任も生じます。また、離
婚の際には**財産分与**や、死別や障害を負った際は配偶者
や子どもに対する扶養の義務を負うなど、法的責任も生
じます。

　アメリカには**民事婚**と**事実婚**のふたつの種類の結婚が
あります。民事婚は最も一般的で、結婚許可証、儀式、婚
姻を司る人物（司式者と呼ばれます）などを要します。事
実婚はそれを認めている州もありますが、儀式や結婚証
明書は必要とされません。というのも、事実婚は結婚す
るカップルの相互合意によって成立するもので、たいて
いは10年以上同居することなどで認められるものだから
です。

　婚姻によって増えた家族は「**姻族**」と呼ばれ、アメリカ
ではよくジョークのネタにされます。アメリカには様々
な文化があるため、姻族は家族同士の価値観の違いとい

司式者とは結婚式を司り、進
行する人のこと。キリスト教
カトリックの場合は神父、プ
ロテスタントだと牧師が務め
る。

in-laws are often divided not just by family values, but significant cultural differences. This can lead to conflict, but in recent years it has become more common to view the cultural mixing between in-laws as a positive thing and a source of growth.

## Online Encounters

As smart phones become a part of everyday life, online dating has become popular in the United States, particularly among **millennials**. Online dating provides individuals with access to a larger group of potential partners than traditional dating methods. This means that you can meet people from all over the country or even the world, which can be especially helpful if you live in a smaller town or city with limited dating options. It also allows you to connect with potential partners from the comfort of your own home, without having to worry about the time and expense associated with traditional dating methods. Even in big cities with plenty of people, going out on dates at restaurants and bars can get expensive quickly.

Many online dating platforms allow you to search for **potential partners** based on specific filters, such as age, location, interests, and more. This can help you to find someone who is more of a fit with your hobbies and lifestyle. And, with online dating, you have more control over the speed of the relationship and the information that you share with potential partners. This can be especially helpful for those who are shy or introverted.

While online dating profiles can provide a lot of information about a person, they may not always be completely accurate or truthful. It can be difficult to get a full understanding of someone's personality and character until you have met them in person. Some people may even use fake photos or pretend to be someone they're not. This can lead to disappointment and frustration when you finally meet them in person. Finally, meeting someone you don't know in person

うよりは文化面の大きな相違によって分断されてしまうことがよくあります。姻族同士の文化的な混ざり合いは衝突の原因になることもありますが、近年ではそれをポジティブなものとしてとらえ、成長の源とすることが一般的です。

## オンラインでの出会い

スマートフォンが日常生活の一部になるにつれ、アメリカではオンライン・デートが、特に**ミレニアル世代**の人々の間で人気となりました。オンライン・デートでは、人々は従来の出会いよりもはるかに多くのパートナー候補と出会う機会があります。国内だけでなく世界中の人々と出会えるということは、そうした機会の限られた小さな町や都市に住む人々にとっては、特に有難いものです。また、オンライン・デートでは従来のデートのように費用を気にすることなく、自宅でくつろぎながら将来のパートナーと繋がることができます。人の多い都会であっても、レストランやバーへ出かけると、すぐにお金がかかってしまいます。

オンライン・デートのプラットフォームでは、たいてい年齢や居住地、興味の対象など、特定のフィルターから**相手になりそうな人**を検索することができます。そうすることで、より自身の趣味やライフスタイルに合った相手を見つけることが可能です。また、交際スピードや相手と共有する情報を自由にコントロールすることもできます。これは、内気な人や内向的な人にとっては特に有難いことでしょう。

オンライン・デートのプロフィールは、その人物について多くの情報を提供していますが、それらは必ずしも正確かつ真実であるとは限りません。実際に会うまでは、その人の性格や人柄を完全に理解することは難しいでしょう。中には偽物の写真を使用したり、別人のふりをしたりする人もいます。そのため、実際に会うとがっかりしたり、フラストレーションを感じたりすることもあるでしょう。最

アメリカのミレニアル世代は、概ね1981年から1996年の間に生まれた人を指す。インターネットや携帯電話の普及初期を経験した1986年までに生まれたX世代後期、9.11やリーマンショックなどを経験した87年から92年の間に生まれたコア・ミレニアル世代、インターネットが普及したあとに生まれたZ世代前期（デジタルネイティブ）と呼ばれる世代に分けることができる。

can be risky, especially if you're not careful about sharing personal information or meeting in public places. It's important to take care to protect yourself when using online dating platforms.

## Raising Children

Pregnancy in the US can be discovered by kits bought at a pharmacy, but is typically confirmed by a healthcare provider through a blood or urine test. Once a pregnancy is confirmed, women are encouraged to receive regular medical care **throughout their pregnancy** to monitor the health of the mother and the baby. This care typically includes regular check-ups, blood tests, and ultrasounds. Women are also encouraged to take special vitamins to ensure they are receiving proper nutrients for the developing baby.

Childbirth in the US can take place in a variety of settings including hospitals and at home. Most women in the US give birth in hospitals with the assistance of specialized doctors or expert women known as **midwives**. During childbirth, women may receive medication to manage **labor pain**. Believing that any drugs in their system can negatively affect the baby, some women choose to have a natural birth without medication. After childbirth, women and their babies typically stay in the hospital for a few days to recover and receive medical care.

Once a baby is born, parents in the US have a variety of childcare options to choose from. Many parents choose to take parental leave from work to care for their newborns. In the US, there is no federal requirement for employers to offer paid parental leave, although some states have enacted their own laws. In the past, it was only socially and professionally acceptable for mother to take time off after having a child, but these days it has become common for father to take "**paternity leave**" as well.

後に、初対面の人との面会については、特に個人情報の共有や公の場での面会に注意を払わなければ、危険な場合もあります。オンライン・デートのプラットフォームを利用する際は、自分の身を守れるよう注意することも大切です。

## 子育て

アメリカでは、薬局で購入した検査キットで妊娠が判明することもありますが、医療機関での血液検査や尿検査で確認するのが一般的です。妊娠が確認されると、女性は母体と胎児の健康状態を観察するため、**妊娠期間を通じ**定期検診を受けることになります。検診では、たいてい診察、血液検査、超音波検査などが行われます。また、発育中の胎児に適切な栄養を送り届けるため、ビタミン摂取を勧められることもあります。

出産は病院や自宅など、様々な環境で行われます。ほとんどの女性は、病院で専門の医師や**助産師**と呼ばれる女性の補助を受けて出産します。出産中は**陣痛**を和らげるために薬が投与されることもあります。このような薬は、胎児に悪影響を及ぼす可能性があると考え、薬を使用しない自然分娩を選ぶ女性もいます。出産後は産まれた赤ん坊と数日間入院し、医療ケアを受けながら回復を待ちます。

アメリカで子供を授かった親には様々な選択肢が用意されています。多くの親は新生児の世話をするため、育児休暇を取得します。雇用主が社員に対し有給の育児休暇を提供することは、連邦政府によって義務付けられているわけではありませんが、独自の法律を制定している州もあります。以前は、出産した母親の休暇取得が社会的にも仕事上も容認されていただけでしたが、最近では父親も「**父親育児休暇**」を取得することが一般的になりつつあります。

As most families in America are just two generations of parents and children, getting help with childcare can be difficult. Grandparents often do not live close enough to help, and large extended families are not common in all cultures. Some parents choose to hire a nanny or send their child to daycare, although the cost of childcare in the US can be a **financial burden** for families.

## Adoption

Parents who are interested in adoption may choose to work with an **adoption agency** or **adoption attorney** to help them get through the process. They may also choose to work independently or pursue a **foster-to-adopt path**.

Adoptive parents typically need to complete an application that includes personal information, background checks, and references. Depending on the state and agency, there may also be training requirements.

A home study is a process in which a social worker visits the home of the **adoptive parents** to decide whether or not they would be good adoptive parents. This may involve interviews, home inspections, and background checks. If the adoptive parents are approved, they may be matched with a child. This may involve working with a birth mother or birth family, or it may involve adopting through the foster care system.

When a match is made, the adoptive parents and child may spend some time getting to know each other before the adoption is finalized. The finalization process involves a court hearing in which the adoption is made legal. This typically takes place several months after the child is placed with the adoptive parents. After the adoption is finalized, adoptive families may be required to have post-placement visits with a social worker to ensure that the child is adjusting well to their new home.

　アメリカではほとんどの家庭が両親と子供だけの二世代家族であるため、子育ての援助をしてもらうことは困難です。祖父母が近くに住んでいないことも多く、文化的にも大家族でない家庭がほとんどです。子供の世話をする人を雇ったり、子供を保育園へ通わせたりする親もいますが、アメリカでの保育料は家庭にとって大きな**経済的負担**となります。

## 養子縁組について

　養子縁組を検討する際は、**養子を斡旋する業者**や**養子専門の弁護士**などを通じて手続きをします。個人的に養子を探したり、**里親制度**から養子を迎えたりする人もいます。

　養子縁組の申し込みには通常、個人情報、身元確認、紹介状などの書類が必要です。州や斡旋業者によっては研修が必要な場合もあります。

　家庭調査とは、社会福祉士が**養親**の家を訪問し、養親として相応しいかどうかを判断する手続きのことです。これには面接や家庭訪問、身辺調査などが含まれます。相応と認められれば、養子との引き合わせが行われます。こうした一連の手続きは、実母や実家族と共に行われることもあれば、養子縁組制度を利用して行われることもあります。

　引き合わせが終われば、養子縁組の成立前に、養親と養子はお互いを知るためにしばらく生活を共にします。最終的な手続きでは、養子縁組を法的に成立させるため、裁判所での審問が行われます。この審問は通常、養子が養親のもとで暮らすようになってから数カ月後に行われます。養子縁組の成立後は、子供が新しい家庭に上手く適応しているかを確認するため、養親は社会福祉士との面会を求められることがあります。

最新の統計で、アメリカで養子縁組が成立した件数は約5万8,000件。2000年代は年間に12万以上の夫婦が養子縁組をしていたので、近年はかなり減少していると言える。

## Divorce

When a married couple has differences that they no longer want to work through, one of them may ask for a divorce. The process starts by one spouse filing an official **petition for divorce** in the state court where they reside. The petition must include the reason for the divorce, such as "irreconcilable differences (differences that cannot be solved)" or adultery, and may also include requests for property division, different types of financial support, and childcare responsibilities.

Once the petition is filed, the other spouse must be formally notified of the divorce proceedings. This is called "**service of process**" and typically involves delivering the divorce papers to the spouse in person or by mail. The spouse who received the divorce papers must file a response with the court within a specified period, usually 30 days. The response may agree or disagree with the terms of the divorce petition.

The spouses may negotiate and reach a settlement agreement on issues such as property division, **spousal support**, **child custody**, and support. This agreement must be submitted to the court for approval. Spouses who cannot agree on the terms of the divorce may be required to attend mediation and attempt to resolve their differences. If mediation fails, the case will go to trial, and a judge will make decisions on the contested issues. Once all issues are resolved, a final decree of divorce will be issued by the court. This decree includes the terms of the divorce, such as property division, spousal support, and child custody and support.

Paying for lawyers in the United States can become incredibly expensive. For this reason, most Americans will try to make the divorce process as fast as possible. However, hurt feelings and a desire to get the best possible deal out of the situation can lead to bitter court battles that drag on for months or even years.

## 離婚

　夫婦間において、修復し難い意見の相違などがあった場合、どちらか一方が離婚を切り出す場合があります。離婚の手続きは、一方の配偶者が居住する州の裁判所に正式な**離婚請願書**を提出することから始まります。請願書には「和解し難い相違（解決できない意見の相違）」や不貞行為など、離婚の理由を記載するとともに、財産分与や各種経済的支援、育児責任などについての希望を含めることも可能です。

　請願書が提出されると、もう一方の配偶者に離婚手続きにつ関する正式な通知が行われます。これは「送達」と呼ばれるもので、通常は手渡しか郵送で離婚届が届けられます。離婚届を受け取った配偶者は通常、指定された30日間の期間内に返答書を提出しなければなりません。請願書にある要件には同意することもできれば、同意しないこともできます。

　お互いの配偶者は財産分与、**慰謝料、子供の親権や養育費**といった事項について交渉し、和解に達します。和解内容については、裁判所へ提出し承認を得なければなりません。離婚条件の合意に達することのできなかった夫婦は、調停に出席し、互いの意見の相違について解決を試みます。調停でも解決ができなかった場合は、裁判となり、裁判官が争点について判決を下します。全てが解決した時点で、離婚の最終的な判決が裁判所より言い渡されます。この判決には、財産分与や慰謝料、子供の親権や養育費など離婚に関する条件が含まれます。

　アメリカの弁護士費用は、信じられないほど高額になることがあります。そのため、ほとんどのアメリカ人は離婚手続きを出来る限り早く済ませようとします。ただ、心に傷を負っていたり、少しでもいい条件で手続きを進める場合は、数カ月、あるいは数年に及ぶ苦しい法廷闘争が繰り広げられることもあります。

最新の統計で、アメリカ人夫婦の離婚率は約40~50%となっているが計算方法が一定でないとも言われている。傾向としては若いカップルの離婚率の低下がある。結婚する年齢が高くなり、結婚生活がより安定していることも要因の一つと言われている。

261

## Remarriage and Step-families

Remarriage is the act of getting married again after a previous marriage has ended. In the United States, remarriage is relatively common, and many people go on to establish step-families after their remarriage.

A step-family is a family unit that consists of a couple and one or more children from a previous marriage or relationship. In some cases, both partners in the new marriage may have children from previous relationships, creating a **blended family**. Step-families can take many different forms, and the dynamics between family members can vary widely.

Around 40% of adults in the United States have at least one step-relative, either a stepparent, step-sibling, or step-child. The majority of step-families in the US are formed through divorce and remarriage, although some are created through the death of a spouse.

Step-families can face unique challenges as they navigate the process of blending two separate families into one unit. Issues such as **discipline**, parenting styles, and emotional commitments can arise, and it may take time and effort for family members to adjust to their new roles and relationships.

However, with patience, communication, and a willingness to work through challenges, many step-families are able to form strong, loving bonds and create a happy and fulfilling home life together.

## 再婚とステップファミリー

　再婚とは、前の結婚が終わった後に再び結婚すること
を言います。アメリカでは、再婚は一般的で、再婚を機に
ステップファミリーを持つようになる人も多くいます。

　ステップファミリーとは、夫婦と、そのどちらかの以
前の結婚相手または交際相手との間にできたひとり以上
の子供とで構成される家族単位のことです。場合によっ
ては、新たに結婚する双方の男女に以前の相手との子供
がいることもあり、その場合は**混合家族**となります。ス
テップファミリーの形態は様々で、家族間の力関係も多
種多様です。

　アメリカでは成人の約40％の人に少なくともひとりの
義父母や義兄弟姉妹、義理の子供といったステップファ
ミリーがいます。多くは離婚と再婚によって形成された
家族ですが、配偶者の死別によって形成される場合もあ
ります。

　別々のふたつの家族からひとつの家族を形成するステ
ップファミリーには、その過程で独特の問題に直面するこ
とがあります。**しつけ**や育児スタイル、心の問題などの課
題が生じることもあり、それぞれの家族が新しい役割や
関係に適応するには時間と労力がいることもあります。

　ですが、忍耐とコミュニケーション、そして困難を乗
り越えようとする強い意志から、多くのステップファミ
リーは深い愛情で結ばれた、幸せで充実した家族生活を
送っています。

## Why are de facto Marriages on the Rise?

There are several reasons why **de facto (or common law) marriages** are on the rise in the United States.

First, social attitudes toward marriage are changing. Many young adults believe that marriage is no longer a necessary part of being in a **long-term committed relationship**.

Secondly, the legal rights of unmarried couples have expanded in recent years, making it more easier for couples to live in common-law marraiges. For example, many states now recognize common-law marriages and grant legal rights to unmarried couples who have lived together **for a certain amount of time**.

Thirdly, common-law marriages can provide financial benefits, particularly for couples who may not be able to afford a traditional wedding or who want to avoid the expenses associated with a possible divorce.

Finally, common-law marriages may be seen as a more flexible and less formal alternative to traditional marriage, particularly for couples who value their **independence and freedom**.

Despite their popularity, common law marriages do not have the same legal protections as traditional marriages, and couples who choose this route should be aware of the potential problems in the future.

## Pets

Pet ownership is very popular in the United States, with many households owning at least one pet. According to the American Pet Products Association, as of 2020, approximately 67% of US households (about 84.9 million households) own a pet. Among that 2/3 of Americans, it is normal to consider the pet a small member of the family.

Dogs are the most popular pet in the US, with around 63.4

## 事実婚が増えているのはなぜ？

　アメリカで**事実婚**が増えている理由はいくつかあります。

　ひとつには、結婚に対する社会的見方が変化しつつあるということがあります。多くの若者たちは、**時間をかけて関係を築く**上で、結婚はもはや必要ないと考えています。

　また近年、未婚のカップルの法的権利が拡大し、事実婚のカップルがより住みやすくなったということがあります。例えば、最近は結婚をしていないカップルでも、**一定期間**同居をしていれば法的な権利が得られるなど、多くの州で事実婚が認められています。

　また事実婚は、特に伝統的な結婚式を挙げる余裕のないカップルや、離婚に伴う出費を避けたいカップルにとって、経済的な利点もあります。

　最後に、事実婚は、**自立や自由**を好むカップルにとって、従来の結婚より柔軟で堅苦しくないということがあります。

　ただ、このように人気のある事実婚ですが、従来の結婚と同様の法的保護があるわけではないため、この選択をするカップルは、将来に起こりうる問題に目を向けておく必要もあります。

事実婚は定義が明確でないため、統計を取るのが難しいと言われるが、様々な調査をみると特にミレニアル世代の事実婚の割合が高いようだ。

## ペット

　アメリカでは多くの人々がペットを飼っており、一家に少なくとも一匹のペットがいると言っても過言ではありません。アメリカペット製品協会によると、2020年時点でペットを飼っているアメリカの家庭は、全体の約67％（約8,490万世帯）を占めていました。また、そのうち3分の2の人々が、ペットを小さな家族であると考えています。

　中でも人気のあるペットは犬で、約6,340万世帯で少な

million households owning at least one dog. Cats are the second most popular pet, with around 42.7 million households owning at least one cat. Other popular pets include fish, birds, and small mammals such as hamsters and guinea pigs.

Pet ownership in the US is not limited to just dogs and cats. Many households own **exotic pets** such as reptiles and amphibians, as well as horses and other large animals. If you want to get an exotic pet, you need to carefully check your state laws. Some states, most notably California, are strict about what types of pets are allowed.

Pet ownership in the US comes with a financial responsibility. Pet owners are responsible for providing their pets with food, shelter, and medical care. According to the American Pet Products Association, Americans spent approximately $99 billion on their pets in 2020. This includes expenses such as food, health care, grooming, and other pet-related services.

## Breeder or Shelter

Deciding whether to adopt a pet from a breeder or a shelter is a personal choice that every pet owner must make.

Adopting from a shelter helps reduce the number of animals that are killed each year in the United States. Many shelters are crowded, and adopting from a shelter can help free up space for other animals in need. Additionally, adopting from a breeder can contribute to the mistreatment of animals in "puppy mills."

Breeder pets don't have perfect health, but successful breeders will typically screen their animals for **genetic issues**. Interestingly, **pure breed dogs** often have genetic problems, and mixed breed mutts tend

くとも一匹の犬が飼われています。次に人気のあるペットは猫で、約4,270世帯で少なくとも一匹の猫が飼われています。その他には、魚や鳥、ハムスターやモルモットなどの小型哺乳類なども人気です。

アメリカで飼われているペットは犬や猫だけではありません。爬虫類や両生類などの**珍しい動物**を飼っている人もいれば、馬やその他の大型動物を飼っている人もいます。珍しい動物を飼う場合は、州法を確認する必要があります。カルフォルニア州などでは、飼えるペットの種類が厳しく規制されています。

アメリカでペットを飼うことは、経済的な責任も伴います。飼い主は、ペットに食べ物や住む場所を用意し、医療も提供しなければなりません。アメリカペット製品協会によると、2020年にアメリカ人がペットのために支払った金額は約990億円にもなりました。この金額には食事や健康管理、グルーミング、その他ペット関連のサービスなどへの支払いが含まれます。

## ブリーダーかシェルターか

ペットをブリーダーから迎えるか、シェルターから迎えるかは、ペットを飼う人なら誰もが考えなくてはならない選択です。

ペットをシェルターから迎え入れることは、毎年アメリカで殺処分される動物の数を減らすことにつながります。多くのシェルターは混雑しており、そうすることで居場所を必要とする他の動物たちを助けることができます。また、ブリーダーからペットを引き取ることは、「パピーミル(子犬工場)」での動物虐待を助長することにもなりかねないでしょう。

ブリーダーが扱うペットの健康状態は万全とは言えませんが、成功しているブリーダーは通常、動物の**遺伝的な問題**がないかを選別しています。興味深いことに、**純血種**

アメリカの動物シェルターには公立と民間運営のものがあり、アメリカ全土に4~6,000カ所あると言われている。動物愛護意識の高まりもあり、シェルターの数は増加している。

ブリーダーは営利目的で大量に犬を生産する。概して劣悪な環境で、粗末な食事、限られた運動など、悪質なブリーダーも少なくない。

to have healthy DNA. Getting a dog from shelter doesn't guarantee that the animal will be free of health issues, but many shelters provide medical care and testing before adopting out animals.

If you have a specific breed or temperament in mind, a breeder might be a better choice. Breeders specialize in certain types of dogs and can provide information about their personalities and possible health issues. Shelters, on the other hand, often have mixed-breed animals, making it harder to predict their behavior and future medical needs.

Regardless of where you choose to adopt from, make sure to do your research, ask questions, and choose a responsible source to ensure the health and well-being of your new furry friend.

**の犬**は遺伝的な問題を抱えていることが多く、雑種犬の方が健康なDNAを持っている傾向があります。シェルターから迎え入れる犬に健康上の問題がないという保証はありませんが、多くのシェルターでは、動物を受け渡す前に医療的なケアや検査を行っています。

　心に決めている特定の犬種や気質がある場合は、ブリーダーから迎え入れると良いでしょう。ブリーダーは特定の犬種を専門に扱っており、そうした犬の性格やかかりやすい病気などについて情報を提供してくれます。その反面、シェルターには雑種犬が多く、それぞれの行動や将来必要となる医療について予測することは困難です。

　どこからペットを引き取るにせよ、ふわふわの新しい仲間が健康で快適に暮らせるよう、調査や質問を十分にし、信頼できる引き取り先を選びましょう。

# 7 Education

**Key Words** Nanny, Preschool, Kindergarten, Elementary, Tuition, Endowment, Rigorous, Certification, Marginalized

## Early childhood education

Early childhood education in America used to start at 5 years old, with kindergarten. These days, children get started in preschool, or pre-kindergarten, as early as 3 years old. As this kind of **earlier schooling** becomes common, many parents feel like it is important to send their children to preschool programs early in order to keep them from falling behind the other kids. Some states offer free or low-cost pre-kindergarten programs for 3- and 4-year-olds, but most of these early childhood education services are private and expensive.

In general, there is no **public child care** in the US, which puts a serious burden on middle or lower income families who must make difficult choices between working and paying for child care. While there are federally funded programs that provide education, health, and nutrition services to low-income families with children ages 1 to 5, the majority of working-class Americans do not qualify for them. For middle class Americans working at "white collar" jobs, employers may also offer childcare benefits as part of their employee benefits package. Unfortunately, "blue collar" Americans working lower-paying jobs are less likely to be offered childcare benefits, despite being less able to afford such

# 教育

**キーワード** ナニー、プレスクール、幼稚園、初等、授業料、基金、厳格な、資格、疎外された

## 幼児教育

　アメリカの幼児教育は、以前は5歳から幼稚園へ通うことが主流でした。ただ、近年では子供たちは早ければ3歳からプレスクールやプレ・キンダーガーテンに通い始めます。このような**早期就学**が一般化するにつれ、多くの親は自分の子供が他の子供たちに遅れをとらないよう、なるべく早くこうしたプログラムに通わせるべきだと考えるようになりました。3、4歳児を対象に無料、または低料金のプレスクール・プログラムを提供している州もありますが、こうした幼児教育のサービスは高額な私立により提供されている場合がほとんどです。

　アメリカには通常、**公的保育**がなく、中低所得層の家庭は仕事をするか保育料を支払うかの厳しい選択を迫られ、重い負担を強いられています。出生から5歳までの幼児を持つ低所得世帯を対象に、教育や保健、栄養に関するサービスを提供する連邦政府の資金補助プログラムもありますが、ほとんどの労働者階級の人々は、対象にはなりません。「ホワイトカラー」の仕事に就いている中流階級の人々には、雇用主が福利厚生の一環として育児手当を支給する場合もあります。ですが、残念なことに、低賃金労働者である「ブルーカラー」の人々は、実費でこうしたサービスを利用する余裕がないにもかかわらず、育

プレスクールは2歳半から4歳までの子供を対象にして、主に遊び、ダンスを通して社会性や運動能力を育むことが目的。それに対してプレ・キンダーガーテン（Pre-Kとも呼ばれる）は、4〜5歳が対象で、読み書きなどもカリキュラムに含まれる。

271

services on their own.

For those who can afford it, there are a few **paid childcare** options in the US. Large childcare centers are **licensed facilities** that look after children on a regular basis. They may offer full-time or part-time care and may be open year-round or only during the school year. On the other hand, family childcare homes are small, **licensed childcare facilities** that operate out of a provider's residence. They may provide care for a small group of children, and are seen as offering a more personal touch than larger facilities.

At the other end of the spectrum, there are professional **nannies** who provide **in-home care** for children of any ages. Such one-on-one care is expensive, and highly qualified nannies cost even more money. Some even provide tutoring and educational services with their childcare duties, filling the role of preschool education in a more controlled environment.

All childcare centers and family childcare homes in the US are required to be licensed and regulated by the state. Licensing requirements vary by state, but typically include health and safety standards, minimum staff-to-child ratios, and background checks for providers. Even so, it is a good idea to research any place before dropping off a child there. Many states have quality rating systems in place to help parents choose the best possible childcare providers and ensure that their children will be in a safe and caring environment.

## Required education

In the US, formal education typically begins with elementary school, which starts at age 5 or 6 and lasts for 6 years. After

児手当を支給されることもありません。

　金銭的に余裕のある人々には、**有料の保育を受ける**という選択肢があります。日常的に子供の世話をする**認可施設**としては、大規模なチャイルドケア・センターがあります。一日、または短時間子供を預かり、年中無休でサービスを行っている施設もあれば、学期中のみ開園している施設もあります。一方、ファミリー・チャイルドケア・ホーム（託児所）は子供を預かる人が自宅でサービスを運営している小規模な**認可保育施設**です。大規模な施設に比べ、少人数の子供を預かるため、より個人的な触れ合いを大切にしていると考えられています。

　その他のサービスとしては、子供の年齢に関係なく、**家庭内で保育を行うプロのナニー（子供の世話役）**がいます。ナニーによる一対一のサービスは高額で、高度な資格を持つナニーの場合はさらに料金が高くなります。中には子供の世話をしながら、勉強を教えるなど、教育的なサービスを行うことで、より目の行き届いた就学前準備の機会を提供するナニーもいます。

　アメリカの全てのチャイルドケア・センターとファミリー・チャイルドケア・ホームは、州の認可を受け、規則を守ることが義務付けられています。認可の要件は州により異なり、一般的には健康と安全性の基準、職員数と子供の数の最低比率、職員の身元調査などが含まれます。とはいえ、子供を預ける前には施設についてよく調べることが大切です。多くの州は、保護者が最良の保育先を選び、子供たちが安全で思いやりのある環境で過ごせるよう、クオリティ評価のシステムを設けています。

### 義務教育

　アメリカでは通常、義務教育は小学校から始まり、5歳または6歳から6年間を小学校で過ごします。小学校卒業

completing elementary school, students move on to middle school or junior high school, which usually spans grades 6-8. High school follows, typically spanning grades 9-12. Despite what many people think, it is usually not legally required for students to stay in school until they are technically adults.

In most states, students are required to attend school until they are at least 16 years old or have completed 10th grade. During this time, students study a **range of subjects**, including math, science, English, language, arts, social studies, and physical education. High school students typically have some ability to choose their courses and may have the opportunity to take advanced classes, such as Advanced Placement (AP) courses, which can earn them **college credit**. Upon completing high school, students may choose to pursue higher education or enter the workforce.

The main division in education is between **public and private schools**. Public schools are operated and funded by the government using taxes, and are free to attend for all students who live within their school district. They are subject to government regulations and are required to follow specific educational standards set by the state. Public schools are intended to provide a basic education to all students, regardless of their background or ability to pay.

Private schools, on the other hand, are funded by private sources, such as **tuition fees**, donations, and **endowments** (money given by past graduates). They are owned and operated by private individuals, organizations, or religious groups, and are not subject to the same government regulations as public schools. Private schools often have more flexibility in their curriculum and teaching methods and may offer specialized programs or a more rigorous academic environment. However, they can be expensive and are thus not accessible to all students.

後は、ミドル・スクール、またはジュニア・ハイスクール（どちらも中学校）へと進み、6年生から8年生まで過ごします。続く高校では、たいてい9年生から12年生までを過ごします。多くの人々の考えに反し、実際には成人するまで学校に通うことが法律で求められているわけではありません。

　たいていの州では、少なくとも16歳になるか10年生を修了するまでが義務教育とされています。義務教育では、生徒たちは数学、理科、英語、国語、美術、社会、体育など、**様々な教科**を学びます。高校生になると、通常はある程度のコース選択が可能で、アドバンス・プレースメント（AP）プログラムなどの上級クラスを受講し、**大学の単位**を取得することも可能です。高校卒業後は、さらなる高等教育を受けるか、社会人になるかを選択します。

　教育の主な区分には、**公立学校**と**私立学校**があります。税金をもとに政府が運営している公立学校へは、校区内の生徒であれば無料で通うことができます。学校は政府の規制を受けており、州が定めた特定の教育基準に従わなければなりません。公立学校は生い立ちや支払い能力に関係なく、全ての生徒に基本的な教育を提供することを目的としています。

　一方、私立学校は**授業料**や寄付金、**基金**（過去の卒業生による）といった私的な資金源によって運営されています。民間の個人や団体、または宗教団体などによって所有、運営される私立学校は、公立学校のように政府の規制を受けることはありません。カリキュラムや教授法に柔軟性がある場合が多く、専門的なプログラムや厳格な教育環境が整っている場合もあります。ただ、費用が高額なため、どんな生徒でも通えるわけではありません。

**アメリカの教育システム**

| キンダーガーテン | |
|---|---|
| 1年生 | |
| 2年生 | 小学校（6年） |
| 3年生 | |
| 4年生 | |
| 5年生 | |
| 6年生 | 中学校（3年） |
| 7年生 | |
| 8年生 | |
| 9年生 | 高校（4年） |
| 10年生 | |
| 11年生 | |
| 12年生 | |

※地域によって異なる場合もある。

## Extracurricular Activities in the US

**Extracurricular activities** in the US education system refer to activities that take place outside of regular classroom instruction and are intended to enhance a student's personal or academic development. These activities vary widely from school to school, but there are a handful of common ones.

Schools offer a variety of sports programs, including football, basketball, baseball, soccer, and track and field. Students can try out for the team and compete against other schools in their district or state.

Schools also offer a wide range of clubs that focus on various interests such as academic, arts, music, language, or hobbies. Examples of clubs include debate team, chess club, drama club, robotics club, and photography club. Students can also participate in **student government** by running for office or joining committees. They can represent their classmates in making decisions about school policies and organizing school events. Many schools require or encourage students to participate in community service projects, such as volunteering at a local soup kitchen or helping to clean up a park.

Schools organize various **academic competitions**, such as spelling bees, math contests, and science fairs, where students can display their skills and knowledge. Finally, there are performing arts programs, such as band, choir, and theater, where students can showcase their artistic talents and develop their skills.

Participation in extracurricular activities can provide many benefits for students. They can help students develop leadership skills, build social connections, and develop a sense of responsibility and commitment. Additionally, extracurricular activities can be an important factor in **college admissions decisions**, as they demonstrate a student's involvement and dedication to their interests.

## アメリカの課外活動

　アメリカの教育制度における**課外活動**とは、通常の授業以外で行う活動を言い、生徒の人間性や学問的知識を高めることを目的としています。これらの活動は学校によって様々ですが、いくつか一般的なものもあります。

　アメリカン・フットボール、バスケットボール、野球、サッカー、陸上競技など、学校では様々なスポーツ・プログラムが用意されています。生徒はチームを代表し、地区や州の他校と戦います。

　また、学問や芸術、音楽、語学、趣味など、様々な関心に焦点を当てた幅広いクラブ活動も用意されています。これらのクラブにはディベートチームやチェスクラブ、演劇クラブ、ロボットクラブ、写真クラブなどもあります。立候補や委員会の運営を通じて、**生徒会**に参加することもできます。生徒会ではクラスメイトを代表し、学校の方針を決定したり、学校行事を企画したりします。地域の炊き出しや公園清掃のボランティアなど、社会奉仕活動への参加を生徒たちに義務付けたり、奨励したりしている学校も多くあります。

　生徒たちが自身の技術や知識を披露するスペリング・コンテストや数学コンテスト、科学フェアなど、様々な**学業上のコンテスト**も開催されています。音楽バンドや合唱、演劇などの舞台芸術プログラムを通じて、自身の芸術的才能を磨き技術を伸ばすことも可能です。

　課外活動の参加は、生徒にも良い影響があります。課外活動を通じてリーダーシップ能力を養い、社会とのつながりを構築し、責任感や達成感を育むことができるためです。また、課外活動は自身が興味のあることに没頭し、献身的に取り組んだ成果として、**大学入学判定**の重要な要素にもなります。

## Universities

The university system in the United States is complex and diverse, with many different types of institutions and programs available to students. There are three main types of institutions: state universities, private universities, and community colleges.

**State universities**, like the public schools mentioned above, are funded by the state government and are typically larger than private universities. They offer a wide range of undergraduate and graduate programs, and the most well-known ones have advanced research facilities and popular sports teams. State universities tend to be more affordable than private universities for in-state residents, but can be more expensive for out-of-state students.

**Private universities**, on the other hand, are funded by **private donors**, tuition, and endowments, just like a private high school. They tend to be smaller than state universities and often have more focused academic programs. Private universities are typically more expensive than state universities, but they may offer more **financial aid** opportunities to students from different backgrounds. They are widely seen as offering a more personalized form of education than state schools, but that really depends more on the school itself and the types of classes taken.

Community colleges are two-year institutions that offer **associate degrees**, certification programs, and job training. They are typically much more affordable than four-year universities and can be a good option for students who want to save money or are unsure about their academic goals. Community colleges also offer transfer programs for students who want to complete their bachelor's degree at a four-year university. In the past there was a negative view of community colleges, particularly among middle and upper-class Americans, but spending 2 years at one is

## 大学

　アメリカの大学制度は複雑で多岐にわたっており、様々な種類の機関やプログラムがあります。それらは、3種類の機関——州立大学、私立大学、そしてコミュニティカレッジに大別されます。

　**州立大学**は前述の公立学校（p. 275）と同様に、州政府の資金によって運営され、私立大学よりも大規模であることが一般的です。幅広い学士課程や修士・博士課程のプログラムを提供し、高度な研究施設や人気のスポーツチームを擁する有名大学もあります。州立大学は、その州に住む学生にとっては私立大学よりも学費が安くなる傾向がありますが、州外の学生にとっては割高になる場合があります。

　一方、**私立大学**は私立高校と同様に、**個人の寄付**や授業料、基金によって運営されています。州立大学と比べ規模が小さく、より専門的な学術プログラムを提供する傾向があります。私立大学はたいてい州立大学よりも学費が高いですが、学生の状況によっては、手厚い**学費援助**を行っている場合もあります。州立大学と比べ、より個性を重視した教育を行っているような印象がありますが、実際には通う学校や履修する教科によって大きな違いがあります。

　コミュニティカレッジは、**準学士号**の取得や資格取得、職業訓練などを提供している二年制の教育機関です。一般的に四年制大学よりもはるかに手頃な学費で通うことができるため、学費を節約したい学生や、将来の進学目標が定まっていない学生にとっては良い選択肢と言えます。コミュニティカレッジはまた、四年制大学での学士号取得を目指す学生向けに編入プログラムも提供しています。以前は、特にアメリカの中流階級や上流階級の人々から、コミュニティカレッジに対する否定的な見方もあ

アメリカの高等教育で重要な役割を果たす有名州立大学
1. カリフォルニア大学バークレー校
2. ミシガン大学アナーバー校
3. バージニア大学
4. テキサス大学オースティン校
5. ウィスコンシン大学マディソン校
　など。

アイビーリーグはアメリカ北東部にある8つの私立大学
1. ブラウン大学
2. コロンビア大学
3. コーネル大学
4. ダートマス大学
5. ペンシルベニア大学
6. プリンストン大学
7. イェール大学

高い選抜水準と厳格な入学過程があり、世界中から優秀な学生を引き寄せている。

increasingly viewed as a wise way to save money while figuring out potential career paths.

## Affirmative Action

Affirmative action is a policy in the United States that seeks to promote **equal opportunities** for historically disadvantaged groups in education, employment, and other areas. The policy has been extremely controversial since its creation and continues to generate debate today.

Supporters of affirmative action argue that it is necessary to address historical and ongoing discrimination against certain groups, including people of color, women, and people with disabilities. They argue that without affirmative action, these groups would continue to face barriers to taking part in education and employment opportunities.

Opponents of affirmative action argue that it amounts to just a **new form of discrimination**, as it involves giving preferred treatment to members of certain groups over others. They argue that this policy can result in less qualified individuals being admitted to universities or hired for jobs over more qualified individuals from groups that aren't seen as needing help.

Critics of affirmative action also argue that it promotes stereotypes and can lead to unhappiness among groups who feel that they are being unfairly disadvantaged. Some critics also believe that affirmative action creates a **sense of entitlement** among some members of marginalized groups, leading to a lack of effort or a sense of deserving opportunities regardless of qualifications.

The debate over affirmative action has been shaped by a series of court cases over the years, including the Supreme Court case of Bakke v. University of California, which upheld the use of affirmative

りましたが、現在では、コミュニティカレッジで二年間を過ごすことは、自身の進路を模索しながら資金を節約する賢明な方法として見直されています。

## アファーマティブ・アクションについて

アファーマティブ・アクションとは教育や雇用、その他の分野において、歴史的に不利な立場に立たされてきた人に**平等な機会**を与えようとするアメリカの政策です。この政策は、制定以来、激しい物議を醸しており、その是非については今なお議論が続いています。

アファーマティブ・アクションを支持する人々は、有色人種、女性、障害者などを含む特定のグループの人々が歴史的、また継続的に受けてきた差別に対し、何らかの処置が必要であると主張しています。こうした政策がなければ、これらのグループの人々は教育や雇用の場で障壁に直面し続けるだろうと考えています。

一方、アファーマティブ・アクションを批判する人々は、こうした政策は特定のグループの人々を他のグループよりも優遇することであり、**新しい形の差別**を形成するに過ぎないと主張します。この政策の結果、支援に頼る必要のない有能な人材ではなく、不適格な人材が大学に入学したり、会社に採用されたりしかねないと考えています。

彼らはまた、アファーマティブ・アクションはステレオタイプを助長し、不当に不利な立場に置かれたと考える不幸な人々を生み出すとも主張しています。さらに、社会から疎外されている一部のグループの人々に**権利意識**を芽生えさせ、資質がないにもかかわらず、努力なしに機会が与えられるという感覚を植え付けかねない、と主張する批評家もいます。

アファーマティブ・アクションをめぐる議論は、長年にわたる一連の判例によっても具体化されており、「カリフォルニア大学対バッキー裁判」（人種による入学者数の下

**カリフォルニア大学対バッキー裁判**
アラン・バッキーという若者が、合格点をとっていたにもかかわらず、大学のアファーマティブ政策に基づきマイノリティの学生に優先され入学を拒否された時に起こした裁判。1978年、最高裁判所は人種のみを基準とした入学枠の割り当ては無効と判決を下した。

action in university admissions but struck down the use of racial quotas (minimum and maximum numbers of students admitted based on race). More recently, the Supreme Court has continued to weigh in on the issue, with decisions such as Fisher v. University of Texas, which upheld the use of affirmative action in university admissions but required that it be carefully focused to achieve specific diversity goals.

The controversy over affirmative action in the United States reflects deeper debates about the role of government in promoting equal opportunities, the meaning of fairness, and the existence of discrimination and inequality in modern American society.

限と上限の設定）では、大学入試での政策の適用は支持されたものの、人種ごとの定員の割り当てについては却下されました。最近でも、最高裁はこの問題について継続的に意見を表明しており、「テキサス大学対フィッシャー裁判」の判決では、大学入試におけるアファーマティブ・アクションの適用は支持しつつも、その政策は多様性に関する特定目標を達成すべく、慎重に焦点を絞らなければならないとしています。

　アメリカでのアファーマティブ・アクションをめぐる論争は、機会均等を勧める上での政府の役割や公正の意味、またアメリカの現代社会における差別と不平等に関する根深い意見の食い違いを反映しています。

**テキサス大学対フィッシャー裁判**
アビゲイル・フィッシャーという学生は、合格点を取っていたにもかかわらず、マイノリティの学生が優先され入学を拒否されたことで、テキサス大学を訴えた。

# 8 Weddings and Funerals

Key Words Engaged, Proposal, Secular, Reception, Wake, Casket, Coming-of-Age

## Weddings

Many couples in the US get engaged before getting married. This often involves a proposal, usually with an engagement ring. Depending on the two people getting married, there might be an engagement party with friends and family to celebrate before beginning to plan the wedding itself.

That planning process can take several months or even a year. The couple will often choose a guest list and location for the wedding, hire vendors for food and drink services, a photographer, a DJ, and perhaps someone to decorate the wedding with flowers. Hiring these services for a wedding often costs double or even triple what they normally would. There are many possible reasons given for this, but the simple truth is that all businesses charge more for wedding services because they know it is possible and socially accepted to do so.

The wedding ceremony is typically held in a church or other **religious institution**, although **secular ceremonies** are more common every year, since younger generations of Americans tend to be less religious. The couple will exchange vows, rings, and have a ceremony that reflects their values and beliefs. The bride will typically wear a white wedding dress, and the groom will wear a suit or tuxedo. The wedding "party", made up of the

# 冠婚葬祭

**キーワード** 婚約、プロポーズ、非宗教、披露宴、通夜、棺、成人

---

## 結婚

アメリカでは、結婚の前に婚約をします。婚約指輪を渡し、プロポーズをすることが一般的です。カップルによっては、結婚式の準備を始める前に友人や家族を招いて婚約披露パーティーを開くこともあります。

結婚式の準備には数カ月から一年かかることもあります。招待客のリストを用意し、場所を決め、食べ物や飲み物を手配し、カメラマン、DJ、そして式場を花で飾るフラワーデザイナーを雇うこともあります。これらのサービスを結婚式のために手配すると、通常の2倍から3倍の費用が掛かることが一般的です。これには様々な理由が考えられますが、単純にどの企業も、結婚式のためなら高額な費用を請求することができ、それが社会的にも認められると考えているからです。

結婚式は通常、教会などの**宗教的な施設**で行われますが、若い世代の間では宗教色の薄い、**無宗教の施設**で行うことが年々一般化しつつあります。結婚式では誓いの言葉を交わし、指輪を交換し、自分たちの価値観や信念に沿った式を行います。花嫁は白のウエディングドレスを、花婿はスーツかタキシードを着るのが一般的です。親しい友人や家族を招いて行われる結婚パーティーでは、新

couple's closest friends and family, will often wear matching outfits or colors. Guests are expected to bring gifts for the couple, either to the bridal shower or the wedding reception. Depending on the culture, it is also acceptable to give the married couple cash, since a young couple typically has a lot of expenses to deal with.

After the ceremony, the couple and their guests will often have what is called a **reception**. This usually involves dinner, dancing, and other festivities. There may also be speeches and other traditions, such as the couple's first official dance together. After the wedding, the couple will often go on a honeymoon, a luxury vacation to celebrate their marriage.

## Bridal and Baby Showers

Bridal and baby showers are popular events in the United States that are typically hosted by family members, friends, or co-workers to celebrate upcoming weddings or the arrival of a new baby.

A bridal shower is typically held a few weeks before the wedding and is a celebration of the **bride-to-be**. The event is usually organized by **the maid of honor**, bridesmaids, or close family members. Guests typically bring gifts for the bride-to-be, such as household items or vacation clothing, and there are usually games and activities to keep everyone entertained. Common games include trivia about the bride and groom, guessing games, or silly activities such as making a wedding dress out of toilet paper.

A baby shower is held to celebrate the expected arrival of a new baby. It is typically organized by a close friend or family member of the **soon-to-be mother** and is usually held a few weeks before the due date. Guests bring gifts for the new baby, such as clothing, diapers, or baby gear. Activities at a baby shower may include guessing games, advice for the new parents, or even diaper-changing contests.

郎新婦がお揃いの衣装や色を合わせた衣装を着て登場します。招待客はブライダルシャワーか披露宴のどちらかに、結婚祝いのプレゼントを持参します。文化にもよりますが、たいてい何かと物入りな若いカップルには、現金を贈ることも許されています。

　結婚式が終われば、新郎新婦と招待客は**披露宴**を開きます。そこでは夕食、ダンス、その他の催しを楽しみます。スピーチをしたり、新郎新婦が初めて公の場でダンスを披露したり、伝統的な余興が行われることもあります。その後、カップルはハネムーンに出かけ、豪華な休暇で結婚を祝福します。

結婚するカップルが実際に欲しいものをリストして招待客に事前に渡す習慣があり、そのリストをwedding registryと呼ぶ。ゲストはその中からプレゼントを選ぶことができる。

## ブライダルシャワーとベイビーシャワー

　ブライダルシャワーやベイビーシャワーは、アメリカでは一般的なイベントで、間近にせまった結婚式や、赤ちゃんの誕生を祝うために、家族や友人、同僚などの主催で行われます。

　ブライダルシャワーはたいてい、**花嫁となる女性**を祝福するために結婚式の数週間前に行われます。**花嫁の付添人**、ブライズメイド、または親しい家族が企画することが一般的です。日用品や休暇用の洋服などが贈り物としてゲストから手渡され、皆でゲームや催しなどを楽しみます。新郎新婦に関するたわいもないクイズやゲーム、トイレットペーパーでウエディングドレスを作るといったような羽目を外した余興なども行われます。

　ベイビーシャワーは、間近にせまった赤ちゃんの誕生をお祝いするために行われます。**母親となる女性**の親しい友人や家族が企画することが一般的で、出産予定日の数週間前に行われます。衣類やおむつ、ベビー用品など、赤ちゃんへの贈り物がゲストから手渡されます。モノ当てクイズや、初めて子供を持つ夫婦へのアドバイス、おむつ替えコンテストが行われることもあります。

Both bridal and baby showers are typically attended by women, although **co-ed** events are becoming more popular. The events are usually held at someone's home or at a location such as a restaurant. In recent years, there has been a trend toward more personalized and unique showers, with themes such as brunch, garden party, or even a spa day. Overall, bridal and baby showers are a fun way to celebrate important steps forward in a person's life and are a beloved social and **family tradition** in the United States.

## Funeral

Funerals in the United States are normally viewed as serious and respectful occasions to honor and remember the life of the person who has died. One common aspect of American funerals is that they typically involve a visiting period or "wake", where family and friends gather to pay their respects to the deceased and offer emotional support to the family. The visitation often takes place at a funeral home or church and usually lasts for a few hours. During the visitation, guests may view the body in an open casket, sign a guestbook, and share memories of the deceased with others in attendance.

The funeral service itself usually takes place the next day, with the deceased's body present in a casket at the front of the room. The service may be led by a **religious leader**, family member, or friend, and often includes readings, prayers, and speeches remembering the deceased. Following the service, **mourners** usually proceed to a cemetery for a service or to a reception to share food and memories.

Funerals are also sometimes seen as an opportunity to offer financial support to the family of the deceased. In place of flowers, it is common to **make a donation** to a charity or to provide monetary support to the family to help cover funeral expenses.

　ブライダルシャワーやベイビーシャワーは、たいていは女性が参加しますが、最近では**男女共**に参加することも増えてきています。どちらのイベントも、誰かの自宅やレストランで行われることが一般的です。近年ではブランチを楽しんだり、庭でパーティーをしたり、スパへ行くなど、より個性的でユニークなイベントに変化しつつあります。概して、ブライダルシャワーやベイビーシャワーは、人生の大切な一歩を祝福する楽しいイベントであり、アメリカでは社会的な**家族の伝統行事**なのです。

## 葬儀

　アメリカでは通常、葬儀は亡くなった人の人生を敬い偲ぶための、敬意に満ちた場であると考えられています。葬儀において共通することは、家族や友人が集まることで故人を偲び、遺族を精神的に支える「通夜」と呼ばれる面会期間があることです。この面会はたいてい、葬儀会場や教会で数時間にわたり行われます。参列者は棺に横たわる故人と面会し、芳名帳に署名をしたり、他の参列者たちと故人の思い出を語り合ったりします。

　告別式は通常、その翌日に行われ、故人の遺体が棺に横たわる状態で会場の前方に安置されます。**宗教指導者**や家族、友人による朗読や祈り、スピーチなどが故人を偲んで行われます。告別式が終わると、**弔問者**たちは引き続き礼拝のために墓地へ向かうこともあれば、思い出を語り合うために会食の場へと向かうこともあります。

　葬儀の場はまた、しばしば故人の遺族に対して経済的な支援をほどこす場でもあります。花を供える代わりに慈善団体に**寄付をしたり**、葬儀費用をまかなうために遺族に金銭的な援助をしたりすることが一般的です。

## Cremation and Burial

In the United States, families have the choice between **cremation** (burning the body) or **burial** for their loved ones. Cost is often a significant factor for families when deciding between cremation and burial. Generally, cremation tends to be less expensive than burial, since preparing a body and **purchasing a plot of land** both cost a good deal of money. Cremation can also offer greater flexibility in terms of timing and location of services, as well as what is done with the remains. For example, families can choose to scatter ashes in a meaningful location, keep them in an urn, or even turn them into jewelry or artwork.

Religious and cultural beliefs may also play a role in the decision between cremation and burial. Some religions, such as Judaism and Islam, **ban cremation**, while others, such as Hinduism, traditionally practice it. Similarly, some cultural beliefs may place greater emphasis on burial as a way of honoring and remembering the deceased.

Personal beliefs and preferences can also influence the decision. Some individuals may have a strong preference for one method over the other, while others may be open to either option. For some, the environmental impact of burial versus cremation may be a consideration. Burial can take up significant land and resources, while cremation can release carbon emissions and other forms of pollution.

As usual in America, younger generations have a tendency toward less traditional practices, and therefore favor cremation. These services have expanded so much that they are even more expensive than traditional burial in areas with enough demand among younger customers.

## Birthdays

Birthdays are an important event in the US, and they are typically celebrated with friends and family members. Birthday parties can

## 火葬と埋葬

アメリカでは、愛する家族の埋葬方法として**火葬**（遺体を焼く）か**埋葬**かのどちらかを選択することができます。その選択にあたっては、多くの場合、費用が重要な要素になります。一般的に、埋葬は遺体の準備や**土地の購入**にそれなりの費用がかかることから、火葬のほうが安価になる傾向があります。火葬はまた、時期や場所、遺骨の取り扱いについても、より柔軟性があります。例えば、家族は遺骨を思い入れのある場所に散骨したり、骨壺に入れて保管したり、またアクセサリーや美術品に創り変えることもできます。

火葬と埋葬の選択は、宗教的、また文化的な信条によるところもあります。ユダヤ教やイスラム教のように**火葬を禁止**している宗教もあれば、ヒンドゥー教のように伝統として火葬を行う宗教もあります。同様に、故人を敬い偲ぶための方法として埋葬を特に重視するような文化的信条もあります。

個人的な信条や趣向も選択に影響します。どちらかの方法に強くこだわる人もいれば、どちらの方法でも構わないという人もいます。また、中には埋葬と火葬の環境への影響を考慮する人もいます。埋葬は土や資材が大量に必要となる一方で、火葬は炭素の排出やその他の汚染が生じる可能性があります。

ここでもまた、アメリカの若い世代の人々は伝統的な習慣を重んじず、火葬を選択する傾向があります。こうした人々の急増により、若い世代からの十分な需要のある地域では、火葬の費用が伝統的な埋葬のそれよりも高額になっている地域もあります。

## 誕生日

誕生日はアメリカでは大切なイベントであり、友達や家族と祝うことが一般的です。誕生日パーティーは親し

range from small gatherings of close friends and family to larger celebrations with many guests. At children's birthday parties, there may be games, decorations, and a birthday cake. At adult's birthdays, there may be a dinner party, **a night out**, or maybe just a trip to the movie theater.

A birthday cake is the key part of most birthday celebrations in the US. The cake is typically decorated with candles, which the birthday boy or girl blows out **after making a wish**. In some cases, the birthday person may also be expected to take the first bite of the cake, as it is considered good luck.

Friends and family members almost always give the birthday person presents, such as books, clothes, tools, or other items that the person would enjoy. The gifts are usually presented at the birthday party, or they may be ordered and delivered some other time. Loved ones may also send a card with either a funny or emotional birthday greeting. Some people also send electronic cards or messages through social media.

Birthdays in the US are a time for celebration and appreciation of the person who is having a birthday. Whether it's a big party or a small gathering, the focus is on making the birthday person feel loved and appreciated as an individual.

### Bar Mitzvah and Sweet Sixteen

Bar mitzvahs and sweet sixteen celebrations are both **significant milestones** in the lives of young people in the United States. While there are some similarities between the two events, there are also some key differences.

Bar mitzvahs are Jewish **coming-of-age ceremonies** that typically take place when a boy turns 13. The ceremony marks the transition from childhood to adulthood, and the boy is expected to take on

い友人や家族だけで集まる小規模なものから、たくさんのゲストを招いて行う盛大なものまで様々です。子供の誕生日パーティーでは、ゲームや飾り付け、バースデーケーキなどが用意されます。大人の誕生日では、夕食会を開いたり、**夜に出かけたり**、あるいはただ単に映画館へ行くこともあります。

バースデーケーキは、誕生日を祝う際には特に大切です。ケーキに立てられたロウソクは、誕生日を迎えた男の子や女の子が、**願い事をした後**に吹き消します。誕生日の人がケーキの最初の一口を食べると縁起が良い、とされることもあります。

友人や家族は、たいてい本や洋服、グッズなど、誕生日を迎えた本人が喜びそうなプレゼントを用意します。それらはたいてい、パーティーの場で渡されますが、別の時に注文をして届けられる場合もあります。親しい間柄では笑いを誘うような、または感動的なメッセージカードを贈ることもあります。ソーシャルメディアを活用して、電子カードやメッセージを送る人もいます。

アメリカにおける誕生日とは、誕生日を迎える人に祝福と感謝を伝える日です。盛大なパーティーであれ、小さな集まりであれ、その人が個人として愛され感謝されていることを伝える特別な日なのです。

## バル・ミツバーと、スウィート・シックスティーン

バル・ミツバーと、スウィート・シックスティーンは、どちらもアメリカの若者たちの人生にとって**大切な節目**にあたる儀式です。これらには共通点もありますが、大きな相違点もあります。

バル・ミツバーはユダヤ教の**成人式**で、通常13歳になった少年を祝福します。この儀式は、子供から大人への節目を祝い、少年はユダヤ人社会の中で新たな責任を担うこ

new responsibilities within the Jewish community. Bar mitzvah celebrations often include a religious service, a party, and gifts for the boy turning 13.

Sweet sixteen celebrations, on the other hand, are **non-religious celebrations** across cultures that mark a girl's 16th birthday. In the United States, turning 16 is seen as an important step in life because it represents a child's transition into young adulthood. With cars and driving being such an important part of American culture, turning 16 (the legal driving age in most places) represents independence. Sweet sixteen celebrations often include a party with friends and family, as well as gifts. Some families may choose to spend thousands of dollars hosting an incredible celebration that is almost on the level of a wedding.

One major difference between bar mitzvahs and sweet sixteen celebrations is their religious significance. While bar mitzvahs are deeply rooted in Jewish tradition, sweet sixteen celebrations are not tied to any particular religious or cultural tradition. Another difference is the gender-specific nature of these events, with mitzvahs traditionally being for boys and sweet sixteen celebrations for girls.

Despite these differences, both bar mitzvahs and sweet sixteen celebrations are important moments in the lives of young people in the United States. They are both opportunities for young people to celebrate their growth, **maturity**, and accomplishments, and to mark the transition into a new phase of life.

とになります。宗教に則った祈りをし、パーティーを行い、13歳になる少年にプレゼントを贈ることが一般的です。

　一方、スウィート・シックスティーンは、どの文化とも関係のない**非宗教的な儀式**で、16歳になった少女を祝福するものです。アメリカでは、16歳になることは人生の重要なステップと考えられており、成人期への移行を意味します。また、車の運転はアメリカ文化の重要な側面であるため、16歳（多くの地域では法定運転年齢）になることは子供が自立したことを意味します。スウィート・シックスティーンでは、友達や家族とパーティーをしたり、プレゼントを贈ったりすることが一般的です。何千ドルもの資金をかけて、結婚式に匹敵するような豪華なお祝いをする家族もあります。

　バル・ミツバーと、スウィート・シックスティーンの大きな違いは、その宗教的な意義にあります。バル・ミツバーはユダヤ教の伝統に深く根差した儀式である一方、スウィート・シックスティーンはどの宗教や文化的伝統にも関りがない儀式です。もうひとつの違いは、バル・ミツバーが伝統的に少年のためのものであるのに対し、スイート・シックスティーンが少女のためであるという、男女の違いです。

　こうした相違点はあるものの、バル・ミツバーと、スウィート・シックスティーンは、どちらもアメリカの若者たちの人生にとって大切な瞬間です。自分たちの成長や**成熟**、達成を祝福する機会であり、人生の新しいフェーズを祝う門出なのです。

**English Conversational Ability Test**
国際英語会話能力検定

● E-CATとは…
英語が話せるようになるための
テストです。インターネット
ベースで、30分であなたの発
話力をチェックします。

www.ecatexam.com

● iTEP®とは…
世界各国の企業、政府機関、アメリカの大学
300校以上が、英語能力判定テストとして採用。
オンラインによる90分のテストで文法、リー
ディング、リスニング、ライティング、スピーキ
ングの5技能をスコア化。iTEP®は、留学、就職、
海外赴任などに必要な、世界に通用する英語力
を総合的に評価する画期的なテストです。

www.itepexamjapan.com

日英対訳
# アメリカ暮らし完全ガイド

2024年6月2日　第1刷発行

著　者　ダニエル・ヴァン・ノストランド

翻　訳　八町晶子

発行者　賀川　洋

発行所　IBCパブリッシング株式会社
　　　　〒162-0804 東京都新宿区中里町29番3号 菱秀神楽坂ビル
　　　　Tel. 03-3513-4511　Fax. 03-3513-4512
　　　　www.ibcpub.co.jp

印刷所　株式会社シナノパブリッシングプレス

ISBN978-4-7946-0814-7